ARCHITECTURE IN WOOD

How Maximilian I as a young man learned the technique of building in wood.
A woodcut of *c.* 1515 by Hans Burgkmair from the *Weisskunig*, an illustrated chronicle of the Emperor's life compiled at his command.

Contents

Introduction

Important buildings in wood have from the first existed side by side with the famous stone-built monuments of western architecture, the pyramids, temples, cathedrals and palaces. But the durability of stone buildings has made them more accessible to historical enquiry. That may explain why so little attention has been paid to wooden buildings in general histories of art and architecture.

The technique of building in wood is probably older than that of building in stone, for the nomads of the Old Stone Age, when they could not find shelter in caves, must surely have preferred to erect tent-like huts of branches and twigs covered with animal hides to building heavy stone walls. And throughout recorded history there has been building in wood as well as in stone. Thus until the beginning of the nineteenth century wood was by far the most widely used building material in most of Central and Northern Europe and in North America. Cities like Strasbourg, Rouen, London, and even New York contained almost as many wooden or timber-framed buildings as solid stone ones. The craftsmen whose standing was highest in the building trade in these cities at that time were not the bricklayers or the masons but the carpenters. The Renaissance building of the old Hamburg Exchange was made of wood, as was the building of the British East India Company which, with a vast painting of sailing ships on its gable and a large carved dolphin crowning its ridge, was from 1648 until 1726 one of the main focal points of the City bank of the Thames in London. During Venice's heyday the wooden Rialto bridge enjoyed no less renown than does the marble structure erected in 1587–91 after the wooden bridge had collapsed. And we read in the *Weisskunig* of c. 1515, the Emperor Maximilian I's chronicle of his life, that together with the art of erecting buildings in 'stonework' the carpenter's craft was one of the most important skills he had learnt in his youth.

The purpose of the present book is to show the development of architecture in wood – a subject which few scholars have treated at any length – and to discuss its surviving monuments. It will therefore form the first general history of the carpenter's art and will supplement those comprehensive histories of architecture which have presented in detail the works of bricklayers and masons. There have always been wooden buildings serving the same purposes as buildings in stone. This applies to everything from the simple dwelling-house to the hall, the temple, the Romanesque stave-church, and the richly carved timber-framed façades of the multistoreyed houses of the middle classes, and to castles, bridges, towers and defence-works. The many prehistoric strongholds in England and northern and central Europe, for example, the Roman camps in the same areas, the Russian forts in Siberia and the American ones in the uncolonised West were built entirely of wood, usually defended by earthworks reinforced by palisades. There is, however, another field where the technique of building

Excavations near Ahrensburg in Holstein have uncovered circles of stones which may have served to weight the tent walls of Stone Age reindeer hunters. They date from the twelfth millennium B.C. These tents would have been man's first 'wooden buildings'. They were constructed with posts that were presumably covered with animal hides. Out of these shelters, at first extremely simple and designed only to give protection against wind and rain, the first true huts developed. In the cave of La Mouthe in the Dordogne, there is an engraving of a framed structure that appears to be of the Magdalenian period and to represent a large tent-like hut made of posts and branches.

Circular or oval clay pits above which tent-like structures were probably raised, existed in Neolithic Egypt. Traces of buildings consisting of wooden posts between which rush walls were secured have been found in round dwelling-pits in predynastic Merimde. In Ma'adi, too, walls of straw or rushes have been found that were held by wooden posts. Yet these modest round buildings made of rushes with wooden supports were a scarcely less primitive form of hut than those in African villages today; and they are structures whose tent-like character suggests that they originated at a nomadic period. For it is not until a people becomes settled in one place that the tent is replaced by the permanent house, and that the framework of poles, easily erected and taken down and covered with mats or skins, becomes a permanent skeleton of posts and beams whose interstices are finally filled with wattle and daub, or bricks, to form lasting habitations.

The more permanent structures with their heavy, horizontal systems of beams for walls and roofs may perhaps have favoured a rectangular ground-plan, and it is possible that the new rectangular, cubic house became the prototype for the first temples. It must, however, be said that the earliest temple building so far known, that of the sanctuary of Eridu (with a rectangular ground-plan), dating from the fifth millennium B.C., was in Mesopotamia where, unlike in the Nile valley, we know of practically no wooden buildings which might have preceded the earliest architectural work.

The temple of Eridu already had walls made of stamped clay. Clay, often mixed with chaff, and made into bricks dried in the open air, or, later, fired and glazed, remained the traditional building material of Mesopotamia. The Egyptians, however, were the first to build with stone quarried out of the natural rock and hewn into shape. But, wherever suitable trees have grown in sufficient numbers, men throughout the world have built with wood for choice since prehistoric times. Even so, the Mesopotamian tradition of brick-building and the Egyptian art of stonemasonry have long existed side by side with wood building.

That applies to the whole of western central Europe, France and England, among

Left: Stave-church at Hopperstad, Sogn, c. 1130.

11

other areas. Even if since Roman times much of the building in the area has been of stone and brick, wood was the dominant material for both peasant and middle-class houses throughout the whole of the Middle Ages and to some extent into the nineteenth century.

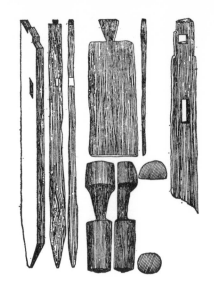

It can, moreover, be shown that building in wood and in solid materials did occur together in the earliest period, too (with, indeed, some measure of interdependence). As Ricke has demonstrated, the earliest deducible works of Egyptian architecture may be divided into two groups: buildings in wood and buildings in brick, or, in other words, buildings which consisted of a supporting wooden frame hung with mats (skeleton construction), and buildings which were built of bricks made of Nile mud and dried in the open air, or their earlier forms (solid construction). Ricke does not consider that these two basically different Egyptian methods of building were successive, the wood and matting method of an originally nomadic tent-dwelling people gradually giving way to brick building, with the final addition of the use of dressed stone after political power had been consolidated. He shows, rather, that the different methods co-existed in a process of hybridisation. It was, he says, the meeting of nomad and farmer in the formation of the state which had such extraordinarily important consequences for the art of Egypt. For 'in every area in which culturally developed population groups with different customs meet during the formative period of a state, whether in warlike encounter or in peaceful penetration, a social stratum is generated in which the dominant role falls to the nomad who is in process of becoming settled.' The situation in Egypt was in general no different from that when the Achaeans and Dorians later penetrated into Greece or that of the late Roman Empire at the time of the barbarian invasions when the Teutonic tribes were settling. Ricke thinks that when the nomad settled he tried to maintain the social exclusiveness and dominance of his old way of life by clinging to its traditions. 'This may, for example, take the form of wearing special dress that in the case of the king would include the marks of his kingship: fan, crook and bull's tail, which have often been conjectured to have originated in a culture of cowherds.

'And in the field of architecture, tent-building, originally purely practical, was perhaps raised to the monumental level by being given architectural form, so that the light skeleton construction of the chieftain's tent became transformed into the wood and matting palace of the king. Portability has now become superfluous and the tent has acquired instead an inner significance: the demonstration of a legitimate title to sovereignty through an architectural form.

'Shortly before the formation of the state in Upper Egypt nomads in tents and farmers in brick houses were living side by side. The nomads were dominant in the formation of the state and their cultural development had progressed so far that the types and forms of building required to satisfy the monumental demands of the state could be drawn from the sphere of their customs and ideas. Thus it was that tent construction gave rise to monumental skeleton construction (wood and matting). In Lower Egypt, as the state slowly became consolidated, monumental architecture evolved from the customs and ideas of the farmers; so that permanent dwelling houses gave rise to monumental solid constructions (brick). When these two states merged to

12

become the united kingdom of Egypt, two evolved monumental forms of fundamentally different type and artistic character came face to face; this hybridisation gave rise to Egyptian architecture of the historical period.'

It is of interest to the historian of architecture in wood that one of these two types was a wooden construction. And at least one monumental type – the royal palace made of matting in Upper Egypt – was erected entirely by the system of skeleton building. 'A monumental building of this kind can arise only in an area in which nomads who have lived in tents have developed their nomadic culture to the point at which they begin to demand such buildings. A palace of matting would never have been erected for the king of Upper Egypt after the foundation of the state of Upper Egypt if the prince of the population group dominant during the formation of the state had previously lived in a brick-built house. The small amounts of wood required for the skeletons of nomadic tents were obtainable in Egypt itself. For the chieftain's tent, heightened to monumental form in the matting palace of Upper Egypt, the timber had to be imported from abroad; for although trees probably used to grow in Egypt in considerably greater numbers than they do today, they never included kinds which would have afforded timber that was particularly suitable for building. Brick-building, however, whose methods had long been known to the settled population at the time of the foundation of the state of Upper Egypt, could rise to whatever heights of monumentality were desired, and without the expense of procuring material from abroad. Thus the cause of the emergence of monumental tent building can only have lain in the traditions of thought of evolved nomads. There must be an intellectual reason for the fact that a monumental skeleton construction continued to form the dwelling of the king of Upper Egypt long after he had become settled, and that it can be shown that official buildings continued to be constructed in this way into the third dynasty. This intellectual reason is precisely the title to sovereignty of the nomadic people who triumphed at the formation of the state, and of their kings, earthly and divine.

'It is true that no remains have been found of the tent-palaces of the kings of Upper Egypt, but they are recorded in impressions from cylinder seals of the first dynasty. These suggest that they were skeleton constructions with vertical walls and a curved roof and that the laths which secured the roof-covering were arranged in a diamond pattern. The walls of the royal tent are vertical or only slightly inclined; the cylinder seals show them to be timber-framed walls, the characteristic construction. We must think of this framework as covered with matting, although of course the door at the right end remained uncovered, or was closed with a special piece of matting. The roof was curved, not in a simple barrel-shape, but like the line of a ridged back, and was clearly copied from the back of an animal; and in an entirely naturalistic touch an animal's tail hung down at the rear end of the building. The narrow, left-hand end of the building in the impressions from the cylinder seals is the main front and we must imagine the door which is shown at the side, or probably a second one, to be here. This front is again constructed as a wooden skeleton. It finishes at the top in an arch-shape in the cross-section of the roof. Horns are attached to the vertical posts of the front truss and jut out sideways in the drawing. Three horns are usually depicted,

Left and above: Shaped building timbers from houses of the Feddersen Wierde near Bremerhaven, about the beginning of the Christian era.

13

though this number probably simply represents plurality since four are sometimes shown.' Ricke states credibly that these horns symbolise rhinoceros horns which were thought to ward off evil, arouse fear and thus make the building, the king's 'tent' itself, a 'monster'.

Ricke has plausibly demonstrated that the Maison du Sud of King Zoser goes back to the technique of building in wood and matting and exemplifies the monumental building in wood that evolved from the original nomadic tradition. His interpretation of the section of cornices on buildings of the Old Kingdom which he traces back to earlier courses of logs, beams and boards is also convincing.

Here in Egypt, at the beginning of historical time, is a method of construction which we shall meet repeatedly, right up to the present day: timber-framing and a skeleton construction made of laths covered in this case with matting, but elsewhere filled in with wattle and daub, rushes, mortar made of clay and rushes, mortar made of rubble (as at Herculaneum) or bricks.

The material used by the early builders of the Mediterranean countries was largely determined by the geological nature of the various areas and by the lack, or scarcity, of timber. Stone, clay and wood were used at all periods and in all areas. And the art of forming clay into sun-dried bricks for use in conjunction with timber framing is doubtless older in the Mediterranean than it has yet been possible to show from dateable evidence. Bühlmann maintains that timber-framed constructions with bricks dried in the open were already used at Troy. However, fired clay, although known to potters at an early date, was seldom used in architecture before the seventh century B.C. except for pipes and sometimes floors; and fired bricks for the façades of walls or for columns were probably not used by the Greeks until after the time of Alexander the Great. But Minoan and Mycenaean walls contain fillings of rubble and even regularly laid masonry, often combined with wooden beams – sometimes forming complete timber framing. The Cretans used rectangular stone columns for the most part, but not exclusively, on the ground-floor and frequently as props or supports for wooden columns of the less important rooms on upper floors. Wooden columns or pillars on stone footings were the typical Minoan and Mycenaean form, and wooden columns were still in use in the early days of Doric architecture. When stone columns were introduced in the seventh century B.C., those responsible were presumably following a practice which was then nearly two thousand years old. In Italy, particularly in Etruria and Latium, the use of wood in conjunction with elaborate terracotta decoration lasted far longer than it did east of the Adriatic and, as we shall see, it evolved completely original forms there.

Classical Greek architecture was thus in the main a direct development of local traditions, and the powerful influence of Egypt at this period was largely limited to inspiring the Greeks to use natural stone instead of wood and sun-baked bricks. Pausanias in the second century A.D. was in time to see at the Heraion at Olympia, then about seven hundred years old, a single wooden column, the last of the forty original wooden columns of the outer building. The others had been replaced by stone columns. Not all at once, but in the course of centuries, each being made according to the rules of the period – the earlier ones with sharply tapering shafts and widely projecting

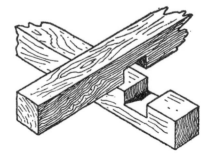

14

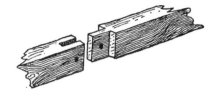

Ancient Greek wood joints: halving (left) and mortise and tenon (above), after Orlandos.

cushion capitals, the most recent ones slenderer, their capitals tighter; so that the main course of development of the Doric column from the moment of its transposition into wood could be read from the columns of the Heraion. That the architrave was originally made of wood is confirmed by the finds not only at the Heraion but also at several other ancient buildings, where walls, capitals and columns have been found with not one single stone of an entablature.

The earliest form of Greek temple was undoubtedly that with a portico *in antis* and was made up of a closed hall and an open portico bounded by posts which supported the roof and, as Bühlmann has insisted, originally represented no more than 'a dwelling-house for the godhead built with more than usual care.' In ground-plan it is similar to the Greek dwelling-house of the type current from the third millennium B.C. The walls of these earliest houses consisted, as they still do in the east, of clay or sun-dried bricks laid in the spaces between horizontal wooden frames; only the base was made of stone. Vertical timbers were used for the ends of the walls and the jambs of the doors. The ceiling and roof were also made of wood, as were their supports. We should think of these wooden supports primarily as simple uprights which were tenoned into the horizontals, the architrave, in the manner still in use among carpenters. The uprights were either round or rectangular; both forms still occur in the porches of Greek and Turkish rural dwelling-houses. A tenon, however, will only hold when the upright and horizontal are of the same breadth at the joint and are rectangular. Lower down the upright may be rounded and may taper as it nears the ground. It was the finishing of a round wooden column with a rectangular bearing at the top in order to avoid weakening the tenon joint with the architrave that resulted, according to Knapfuss, in the emergence of the abacus.

'In the tapering of the round shaft towards the foot there may indeed be a reminiscence of an earlier period when support for the ceiling was provided by a post set in the ground. Compare the round holes in which the downward-tapering wooden columns in the light-well of the palace at Knossos stood: they surely hark back to the post-holes into which the downward-tapering wooden posts had to be rammed. There must be some such reminiscence, for technically this construction does not make sense since holes made in the floor for the wooden columns would only favour the rise of damp from the ground through the cross-cut surface at their bases. The hole for a column of a grave at Assos derives from the same notion, but it at least has a base-like moulding round it which was intended to prevent water seeping in; the lack of bases to the Mycenaean and Doric columns in general can be regarded as a survival of the form of post that was rammed into the ground.

'Placing the shaft with the tapered end downwards not only offers a practical method of ramming the still pointed post into the ground, but also means that the naturally broader end of the tree-trunk is uppermost to act as a bearing. The support can thus accommodate a broader horizontal timber than if the narrow end of the shaft were at the top. The transition from the round stem to the rectangular bearing, the abacus, gave rise to an aesthetic solution of the problem, the capital proper, paralleled by that found for feet of furniture for the same reasons and at widely separated periods. When the wooden columns of the Mycenaean period were transposed into stone, the shaft continued to be tapered as it neared the ground, the round column continued to pass into the rectangle (abacus) of the earlier wooden post and the graining of the wood was retained.' This last, Bühlmann thinks, was the inspiration of the rhythmic zigzag ornament of Mycenaean stone columns. 'By this time, the capital with the rectangular bearing and the round shaft of the column could be made in stone in two separate pieces. The principal advantage was that the heads (capitals) could be given a much more elaborate profile than before, when it had been limited by the thickness of the tree trunk. Thus, once transposed into stone, the profile of the head of the downward-tapering wooden support that had been driven into the ground like a pole, gradually evolved into the Mycenaean stone capital with its greater breadth of projection. The Mycenaean capital is in its turn very closely related to the Doric capital of the earliest period. As in the Cretan-Mycenaean capital, the abacus and echinus project considerably; the transition from the broad projection of the capital to the vertical beginning of the shaft of the column is effected by a leafy collar-like circlet.'

Bühlmann believes that the wooden construction that preceded the stone entablature can have been evolved only in a house with portico *in antis* which was raised in status to become the dwelling-place of the deity. As regards the origin of the classical frieze of triglyphs and metopes, he assumes that we should seek the holes *(okai)* for the heads of the joists behind the triglyphs, and that the triple triglyphs represent a carpenter's contrivance designed to protect the cross-cut surfaces of the joists from the weather, like the barge boards of alpine farm houses. Nailing three separate small boards grooved on both sides to the cross-cut surface had, he thinks, the advantage over covering them with a single board that they could expand and contract under the influence of weather without splitting. By the seventh century, the surface of the walls between the holes *(okai)* for the heads of the beams was already being faced with fired and painted clay plaques – metopes – which may have been preceded by painted or carved wooden boards.

Kähler in his study of the images on Greek metopes says that nothing has remained of the entablature of various temples except many clay, or sometimes stone, metopes and the clay plaques and fired bricks which covered and faced the roof, and concludes that in these buildings the triglyphs too were made of wood, as well as the roof frame which, in his opinion, rested on them. Thus, unlike Bühlmann, he (probably rightly) does not regard the triglyphs as 'barge boards'. But this is a detail of constructional technique and does not affect the basic validity of his conclusions: 'We now know all the phases of the transition from building in wood to building in stone; thus in the temple at Thermon only the bases of the columns and of the temple building are of stone, everything else was made of brick and wood. At the Heraion at Olympia the whole entablature was made of wood. At the treasury at the sanctuary of Hera at Foce Sele not far from Paestum the architrave and corona were made of wood but the triglyphs and sculpted metopes were of stone. The wooden elements have, of course, not survived. Yet when a large number of architectural elements made of stone – such as capitals – have survived from a building but no single fragment of a shaft, we may conclude with fair certainty that the shaft was composed of a perishable material.

16

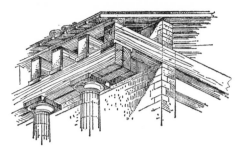

Doric entablature in wood (after Durm).

The multiplicity of forms of the early stone buildings has nothing to do with the fact that they were conceived in stone; it shows that there was still no confidence in the new material. Many a bitter experience must surely stand behind the natural weight of the earliest stone buildings and inexplicable feeling for monumentality which must be considered one of the basic impulses towards building in stone at all. If we wish to trace the forms of wooden buildings in Doric stone buildings, we shall naturally seek the earliest surviving monuments. But in so doing we must be clear that precisely in these earliest stone buildings proportions will differ greatly from those in wooden buildings because the tensions of wood are entirely different from those of limestone and tufa poros. This is also one of the reasons why the temples and fountains in the paintings on black-figure vases appear so much more graceful and airy than the architecture of the time, of which only those monuments that were built of stone have survived. Even when they were depicting stone buildings, the imagination of the vase painters was often still moving in the world of wooden architecture. What then do we discover from the Doric frieze in stone buildings and what may we infer from what is discoverable about the original wooden forms of wood building? A triglyph occurs above the column and at the corners of the building. There is also a triglyph in the centre of the frieze. The triglyph is divided vertically and thus obviously has a vertical alignment like the column; as the column is surmounted by a capital so is the triglyph surmounted by a flat slab. Vitruvius calls it a *capitulum* or little capital. The metope recedes slightly in relation to the triglyph. Clearly the metope was originally of secondary importance, and this also emerges from the fact that it was not the metope but the triglyph which gave the name triglyphon to the Doric frieze in the terminology of the architects of antiquity.

'The metopes are infilling surfaces within a timber-frame – like fabric consisting of vertical supports, the triglyphs, and horizontal beams, the architrave and corona. The spaces between the triglyphs may at first have been filled by plain boards. They may have been painted, or motifs made of metal or terracotta may have been nailed to them – motifs like the four large gorgons' masks made at Gela at the turn of the seventh and sixth centuries B.C. The extensive remains found show that they were nailed to a wooden base, just as a vast gorgon's mask of clay was later nailed to the tympanum of the pediment of the middle acropolis temple at Selinunte. The panels themselves were later made of fired clay.' So says Kähler.

Kähler's theory supports the hypothesis – now no longer verifiable – that the images in metopes and the sculptures of the tympana were originally woodcarvings (painted in colours?), and that in pre-classical Greece there were probably wooden temples with carved decoration.

The early Etruscan temples of the Campagna, Latium and Etruria, which made their appearance in about the second quarter of the sixth century B.C. and form a homogeneous group, though with local variations, were built largely of wood and sun-dried bricks. Stone was used mostly for walls and columns but never for the panelling, which was always of wood, though frequently faced with painted terracotta. Many of these temples stood on a high podium, with steps at one end only; this particular feature, rare in Greece itself, may derive from Asia and was later adopted in

Rome. There are a few sources which enable us to infer something of the appearance of these timber-framed buildings. The clearest impression comes from certain small models made in antiquity and found in Italy. More may perhaps be learnt from some of Vitruvius's statements which probably relate to earlier temples still standing in his day, particularly the great Temple of Ceres near the Circus Maximus, which he seems to have seen before it was destroyed by fire in the year 31 B.C. Wiegand made reconstructed drawings from this information. The wooden columns of the portico were widely separated and the architrave consisted of two beams placed side by side with a gap left between them for ventilation. Above the architraves, which joined the corner columns to the antae, lay a second course of beams, called *mutuli*, which ran along the top of the walls of the cella and jutted forwards to a length equal to about a quarter of the height of the columns. The wall of the tympanum rested on the architrave of the front; it was made either of wood or of some more solid material, although the details of its construction remain doubtful. The ridge *(columen)* rested on the tympanum and projected as far as the *mutuli*. The brick roof rested on a system of laths *(cantherii)* and rafters *(templa)* and reached to the end of the *mutuli* and *columen*, which meant that a large overhang was possible. The terracotta decorations in these early timber-framed temples on Roman soil, like those in the classical Greek temples, and their sculptured figural decorations – especially those of the tympanum – derive in all probability from carved wood decoration.

Amoretti sawing planks, from a wall-painting at Pompeii, about the beginning of the Christian era.

Later Roman monumental buildings were seldom made of wood. But we can tell from Pompeii, Herculaneum and Stabiae that timber-framing was quite a common method of constructing dwelling-houses and the more modest secular buildings.

The *Casa a Graticco,* a modest house at Herculaneum, is a well-preserved example of an ancient building technique which Vitruvius called *opus craticiom* (timber-framing) and which entailed filling the spaces between rectangular timber frame irregularly with brickwork and mortar. There are many examples of this technique in Pompeii, but the house at Herculaneum is the only one so far discovered that consists entirely of timber-framing. Roof-frames constructed of rafters and laths have also survived at Pompeii, including those of various *atria*, of which Vitruvius named five different types. The simplest was the Tuscan: it was a square court and its roof, which sloped inwards, was, as Overbeck has stated, 'supported by two principal beams and two secondary beams tied into the former. The ends of the principal beams lay in the walls, and in Pompeii most of the holes for the beams have been preserved.'

Mazoi has made a reconstructed drawing of a roof of this type which we reproduce: *a* represents the walls, *b* the principal beams *(trabes)*, *c* the secondary beams *(tigilli* or *trabeculae)* fitted into the principal beams so that a square inner opening is formed, *d* the mid-beams *(interpensivae)*, which ensure that the whole system of beams is of uniform height, *e* the sloping rafters, and *f* the laths, on which the tiles lay.

This account of the structure of a Tuscan roof ends our study of the wooden buildings of antiquity, and it is a truly representative example because, in all areas where, as in ancient Rome, most building was in stone or brick, at least the roofs and ceilings – including their often splendid decoration – were constructed in wood by carpenters. But wood, unlike stone and brick, does not last for thousands of years and

Right: Interior of the stave-church at Torpo, Hallingdal, second half of the 12th century.

18

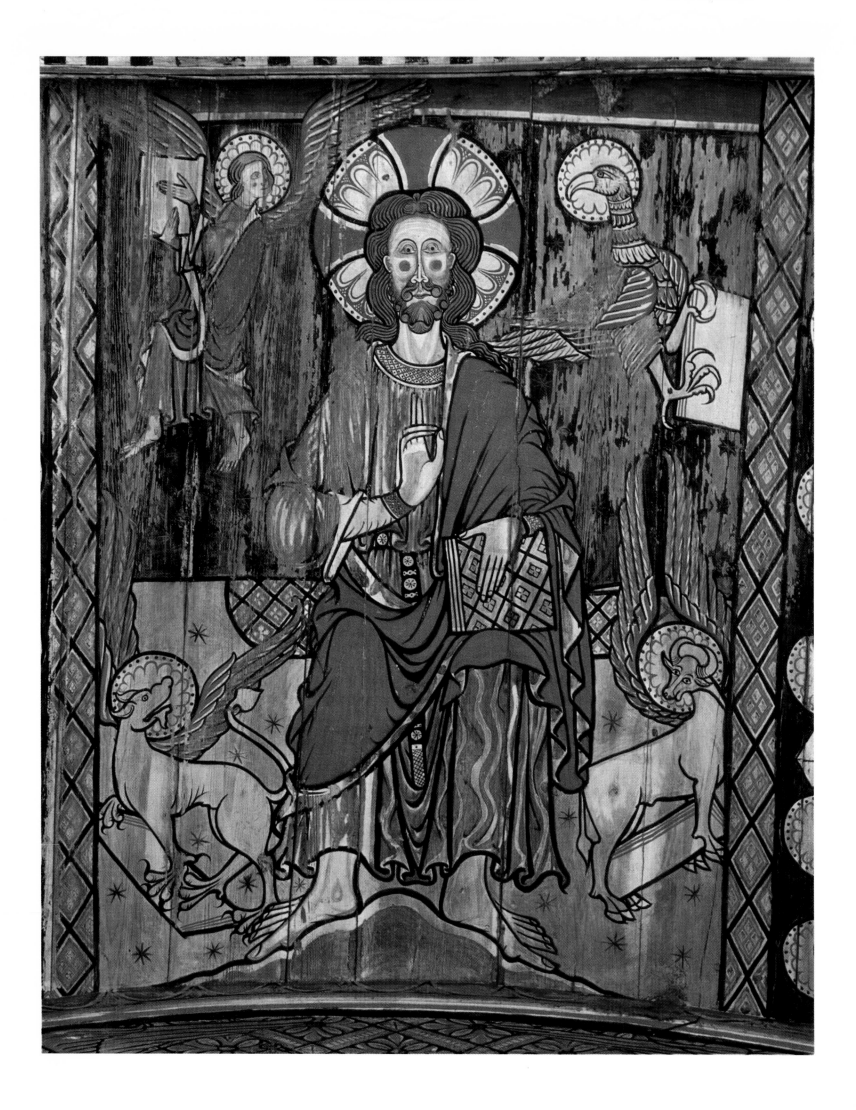

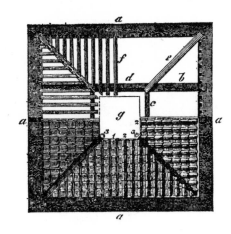

Structure of the roof of a Tuscan house with atrium (after Vitruvius).

22

12; 13; 22

Left: Christ enthroned with evangelists' symbols. Detail of painted ceiling in the church at Torpo (cf. 19), mid-13th century.

21

our knowledge of the art of wood building in antiquity must therefore remain incomplete. The Teutonic tribes which attacked the Empire came from densely wooded areas; their language included no vocabulary for the materials, tools or techniques of building in stone or brick. They did, however, have specific words for all the concepts of the carpenter's craft. In areas like Italy and Spain where they abandoned their language and their independence (and found no forests) they soon learnt the Roman methods of solid construction; but in those, like Germany, where they continued to live in a heavily wooded habitat and preserved their language and traditions, it was not until the Carolingian renaissance that they began to erect larger buildings that were not made of wood. In northern Europe this did not happen until even later. However, it will be virtually impossible to establish how much the earliest surviving wooden buildings of the High Middle Ages in these areas draw upon their own craft traditions and how much upon the Roman carpenter's highly developed art. Many features of the timber-framed buildings of medieval towns certainly suggest Roman traditions. Nevertheless, excavations in Celtic, Teutonic and Slav areas have shown that a noteworthy technique of building in wood, clearly independent of ancient traditions, existed in these areas at a relatively early date. In about 700 B.C. there existed at Biskupin in Poland a town surrounded by massive wooden bastions, with parallel log roads and more than a hundred dwelling-houses of a type constructed on a basis of vertical posts regularly jointed with tongue and groove and horizontal boards. Haarnagel has uncovered on the Feddersen Wierde near Bremerhaven well-preserved outlines of houses in wood measuring up to twenty by a hundred feet and dating from about the beginning of the Christian era. They show that the houses were all constructed as three-aisled hall buildings, such as were widely distributed in north-west Europe from the La Tène period onwards. Finds of tools and especially of semi-manufactured articles show that, in addition to many other craft activities, fairly advanced procedures of wood-working, such as carving, turning on a lathe and plaiting willowtwigs to fill the divisions of the walls of houses, had been employed – but there was nothing to suggest that stone had been worked or masonry constructed. The building timbers which have been found testify to considerable skill in the carpentering of the frame. Pegs and wedges were used and widely varying methods of jointing wood were known. Thus the tenon was known: parts of interior posts had rectangular cavities to receive tie-beams and a tenon at the head, to which a plate (a longitudinal timber resting on the posts and supporting the rafters) may have been attached. There were round cavities in the heads of the exterior posts in which exterior head beams lay, to which the rafters were either birdsmouthed or tailed in. Other finds included thick logs cut away near the end, which was rounded; these were presumably anchor-beams (a form of tie-beam) which were slotted into the posts. Boards might also be secured by rectangular or dovetailed grooves. These details represent techniques most of which are still employed by carpenters. On one of the posts a strictly geometrical carving of an eight-pointed rosette, obviously drawn with a compass, has survived in exactly the same form as that in which it occurs more than fifteen hundred years later as decoration on timber-framed buildings in central Europe.

Head of a post with carved rosette from the Feddersen Wierde, now in the Morgenstern Museum, Bremerhaven, about the beginning of the Christian era.

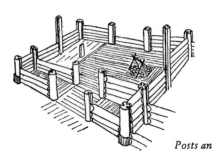

Posts and walls of house at Biskupin, Poland, c. 700 B.C. (after Kostrzewski).

22

Wood has remained the favourite building material in the northern countries right up to the present day. This is true of both Scandinavia and Finland; and even in Iceland, where practically no trees grow, wood from the thickly afforested parent country of Norway and driftwood have always been used for building. The wooden buildings of Finland, especially eastern Finland, show affinities with those in the bordering Russian and Siberian territories; while Danish houses – most of which are timber-framed structures, above all in the towns – are closely related to those of northern Germany. The most impressive monuments of typically Scandinavian wooden architecture have, however, been preserved in Norway, where the many medieval stave-churches are undoubtedly among the earliest and most important of all buildings in wood.

9; 10; 19; 20; 25

Much of Norway is covered with natural forest, with the result that wood has been used for building since earliest times. In the eastern part of the country and in Tröndelag the forests are mostly of tall coniferous trees, whereas in the coastal regions of the west, and north of them, there are more deciduous trees, although further inland there are some conifers too. In many of the coastal regions, however, especially in northern Norway, building timber has to be brought from a long way away.

Traces of posts in the ground have been found in the earliest dwelling-places to have been excavated, but there are no clues about the structures which carried the roof. Nor do we know what the elongated Norwegian houses of the Iron Age between 500 B.C. and 500 A.D. looked like. They were between sixteen and twenty-six feet wide and between a hundred and two hundred feet long. The holes for the posts are usually in two rows a short distance inside the longitudinal wall which was made of stone, turf or some other material. Clay or something similar may have served as the

filling. The later Scandinavian wooden houses are built on two main principles: as vertical structures with upright posts, and by the log-building method of horizontal timbers known in Norway as the *lafte* technique. The prehistoric dwelling-places mentioned above must have been built by some version of the vertical method.

The *lafte* technique appears to have reached Scandinavia before the year 1000 A.D., presumably from eastern Europe. By this method the walls were built of round timbers laid closely on top of one another and notched together at the corners with ingenious indentations. The natural material for this is conifer wood; deciduous wood is also suitable but has been little used. Log-building is employed in the burial chamber of the tenth century at Gokstad in Norway, though that tells us nothing about how generally it was known at the time. At all events, its introduction must have brought with it a radical change in building customs. In place of the elongated buildings in which human beings and cattle lived under one roof, shorter houses were now being built, their length usually depending upon the natural length of the logs. Separate buildings were constructed for different purposes: a small dwelling-house for the men and women, a building with a hearth for cooking, a store-house, stalls for cows and horses, and barns for corn and hay.

In districts where timber was scarce the vertical method of construction persisted, particularly if the houses did not need much in the way of heat insulation. After the introduction of the *lafte* technique both main methods of building were practised side by side, and especially in secular houses. Here the vertical system of

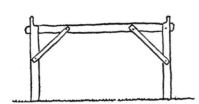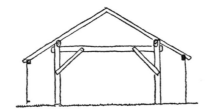

construction underwent a modification in the so-called *grindbygginga*, meaning literally 'grid building'. A 'grid' (or truss) is constructed from two posts with a horizontal beam resting on them. These three elements are stiffened by diagonal braces. The structure was assembled on the ground and then erected, the number of 'grids' deciding the length of the house. There are still examples of this method, which has continued up to the present, and everything suggests that it goes back to the distant past. The walls may be clad with boards, fixed either directly on to the logs or on a special outside wall, but sometimes they are made of a different material.

These two main building methods applied also to wooden churches. Most were stave-churches. We know that over seven hundred such buildings existed at one time, but it is not known how many there were altogether. In contrast, only two medieval log-built places of worship – chapels – are known, although obviously there may have been more. There are about twenty-five stave-churches still standing in Norway. The *stav* of *stavkirke* means 'staff' in the sense of a post, pole or prop, and they are built of posts in a way which plainly differs from the method used in secular building. Even from the outside the difference is great: roof rises upon roof in architectonic exuberance; and great artistic richness is seen in details such as dragons' heads on the roofs, peepholes in the surrounding arcades, and carvings on the portals. But first we must see how they were built.

The visitor entering a fully developed stave-church – the exterior of which may produce a highly complex effect – will discover that it is a well ordered building with free-standing roof-bearing columns within; the columns are arranged in a rectangle, with the chancel adjoining the short side. The chancel always occupies the east end, the main entrance the west. Beneath the whole building lie four strong ground sills,

239a, b; 267a, d

Right: Posts and braces in the stave-church at Lom, Böverdal, 13th century. Page 26: (a) Barrel vault in the church at Oosthuizen, North Holland, 1510; (b) Roof timbers in the church of S. Croce in Florence, 14th century.

a

b

crossing at the corners, so that altogether eight arms project from the points of intersection. The vertical posts, which have given their name to this type of church, stand upon the ground sills. They are tall, strong posts supporting the main roof. The sills for the walls are laid at the extreme end of the ground sills. They have grooves for

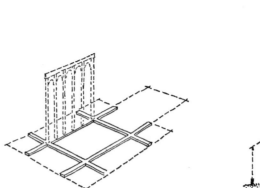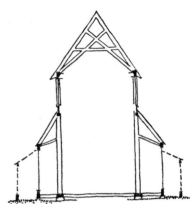

the floor planks . The wall reaches no higher than the middle of the posts. This means that there are narrower roof surfaces, lean-to roofs, which are rather lower than the main roof and thus make room for a lower wall between the upper and lower roofs. There are small peepholes in this wall, through which light enters the church. The characteristic three-aisled cross-section reminds one of the Early Christian basilicas with their tall central nave and two low side-aisles. This has led many scholars to conclude that the stave-churches are a direct transposition from stone into wood, an idea to which we will return. On the outside walls an arcade surrounds the nave and chancel, its roof lower than the side roof and forming a yet lower tier in the roof surface. The roofs on the turrets above the nave also create a tiered effect. There are usually two or three roofs. When yet more roofs over west, south and north portals interlock with those already mentioned, the total number may be sizeable – and we have so far said nothing about the chancel. In the largest churches the chancel is a square space closed by a small semicircular apse. The chancel too may have side roofs, which, taken together with the roof of the surrounding arcade, create a many-tiered roof-surface. The same tiers continue through to the roof over the apse. All this helps to produce an effect of vertical monumentality, so that even quite small churches dominate the landscape.

We may now try to account for the surprising stability of this type of building. The weight of the roof is transmitted downwards by the posts. There are usually between four and eight posts on the long sides and four posts on the short sides, standing, as explained, on a strong framework of ground sills. These split up the weight on the ground so that it is equalised and divided among a number of posts if the ground subsides irregularly or cracks during a thaw. The beams of the side roofs help to support the main posts horizontally. The posts are also held together by horizontal clamping and by St. Andrew's crosses; thus the space is fully braced both longitudinally and laterally. The clamping beams consist of two flat planks for each post, each with a semicircular piece cut out. They are laid edge to edge and pressed together so that they clamp the whole range of posts. In the roofs and under the clamping beams curved knee-braces are inserted which further increase the strength of the bracing. All joints

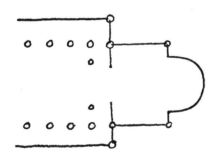

Page 27: Interior of the Guildhall of the Lord Leycester Hospital, Warwick, c. 1390.
Left: Interior of the church of Ste.-Catherine, Honfleur, 15th century.

29

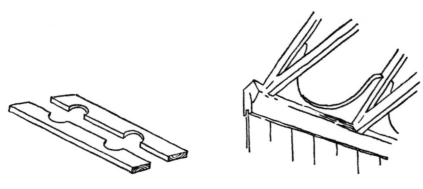 

are of the tenon and mortise type and no material other than wood is used. We may assume that most of the jointing was done while the structure was still on the ground as described in the passage on 'grid' building. But, instead of the posts being erected in pairs, each of the four main walls was probably set up separately and then fitted together with the corner posts.

Besides these highly developed stave-churches there are also simpler types, churches with elongated naves and no aisles, in which the posts are let into the plank walls instead of being free-standing. Naves of this type usually do not have central

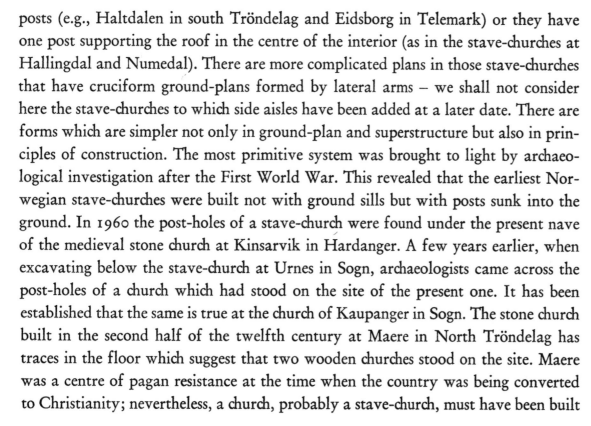

posts (e.g., Haltdalen in south Tröndelag and Eidsborg in Telemark) or they have one post supporting the roof in the centre of the interior (as in the stave-churches at Hallingdal and Numedal). There are more complicated plans in those stave-churches that have cruciform ground-plans formed by lateral arms — we shall not consider here the stave-churches to which side aisles have been added at a later date. There are forms which are simpler not only in ground-plan and superstructure but also in principles of construction. The most primitive system was brought to light by archaeological investigation after the First World War. This revealed that the earliest Norwegian stave-churches were built not with ground sills but with posts sunk into the ground. In 1960 the post-holes of a stave-church were found under the present nave of the medieval stone church at Kinsarvik in Hardanger. A few years earlier, when excavating below the stave-church at Urnes in Sogn, archaeologists came across the post-holes of a church which had stood on the site of the present one. It has been established that the same is true at the church of Kaupanger in Sogn. The stone church built in the second half of the twelfth century at Maere in North Tröndelag has traces in the floor which suggest that two wooden churches stood on the site. Maere was a centre of pagan resistance at the time when the country was being converted to Christianity; nevertheless, a church, probably a stave-church, must have been built

30

here at an early date. We may certainly expect to find further traces of stave-churches under wooden and stone churches that have not yet been excavated. Some similar finds have been made under churches in Denmark and all such discoveries have provided new material for discussion of the origin of the Norwegian stave-churches.

The traces under the stave-church in Urnes may be those of a church which, to judge from coins that were found, was built in *c.* 1050, although this dating is not entirely secure. The nave is fifteen or twenty feet square and the chancel about ten feet square. The marks in the ground show that not only the posts but also the planks of the walls were sunk, so that the wall of planks is reminiscent of a palisade. There are also traces of four interior posts, although it is not known whether they supported a higher roof over a central nave as in other stave-churches. The present church in Urnes has a richly decorated corner post and some decorated wall planks, which belonged to an earlier church. We cannot say for certain whether they belonged to the church of which the traces remain in the ground or whether there were other churches between the first and the present one. If the former was the case, the surviving finely decorated elements must also have been sunk in the ground, a method of construction which may sound unusual but is nevertheless reconcilable with the dating of the planks proposed on stylistic grounds by a number of scholars. If the second alternative is correct and these pieces belong to a possible second church, the first two churches cannot have stood unchanged for long before the present one – usually dated to the first half of the twelfth century – was built.

The contention that the stave-churches are a transposition into wood of the Christian stone basilicas rests upon architectonic details existing at Urnes and in many *267a* other churches. Like stone columns, the posts have bases and capitals. The naturalistic knees, too, which have been let into the spaces between the posts for bracing purposes are exactly the same shape as Romanesque stone arches. It has now turned out that the posts at Urnes probably come from an earlier church and that the bases were added later. Other similarities of detail between the earliest churches and those in stone may very well have been common. Yet on closer examination the basic form of the stave-church is not entirely similar to that of the three-aisled basilica. In the stave-churches the 'aisle' space runs parallel not only with the long walls – as in the basilica – but also with the two short sides, so that there is space between nave and chancel too. Some of the stave-churches have the same number of inner posts on both the long and the transverse walls (Borgund, Heddal, Ringebu). In this way the character of the interior becomes much more centralised than it is in the elongated basilica. Nevertheless, the similarity between the stave-church and the basilica cannot be disputed. Yet the question arises whether the influence of the basilica did not work gradually and whether it was still active into the twelfth century. At all events, the basilica was not the sole source of inspiration for the stave-church. As we shall see, the stave-church later freed itself of this influence, as the system acquired new features.

It has been said that the stave-churches were once pagan places of worship. We are dealing here with unconfirmed assumptions, for we possess no account and no remains of any pagan place of worship which could support these contentions. On the contrary, the sagas say that the Christian missionaries had pagan places of worship torn down and churches built. Nor have we documentary evidence of any place of worship being purged of its pagan and dedicated to Christian usage.

Christianity was introduced into Norway in *c.* 1000. This means that all the stave-churches must have been built within a period of three hundred years, and most of them within a much shorter period. This circumstance is difficult to reconcile with the fact that the technique of stave-building is highly evolved. It reveals an understanding of statics, construction is carefully thought out and a convincing union of technique and form has often been achieved. It is difficult to understand how the builders were capable of such elaborate work and such a logical system when they had no existing tradition of wood building to start from. We know, certainly, that in the period under discussion the system was subject to fresh influences; yet it seems highly improbable that builders in the eleventh century would have been able to find such convincing solutions to the problems posed by the nature of wood if the point of departure had been simply a piece of architecture in stone. The Norwegian stone basilicas are probably contemporary with the earliest stave-churches, so there would hardly have been time for stone building to be transposed into wood. A more credible theory might be that foreign models were followed, but here too it is unlikely that such results could have been achieved in so short a time. There is also the fact, already mentioned, that the west gable and the addition of the chancel would have been different had the basilica been the immediate model. It is possible that there was a European tradition of building churches (or places of worship in general) in wood, on which the builders of the Norwegian stave-churches based their work. Although our knowledge on this point is insufficient, a few scattered facts are known. For instance, in the Carolingian period in Saxony, when it was newly converted and still closely linked with north European culture, even the episcopal churches continued to be made of wood at first (e.g. in Hamburg). The Bayeux Tapestry of the eleventh century depicts towers and temples made of wood. There must have been a tradition on which the high level of architectonic development of stave construction was based, and it is to be hoped that evidence of it will yet emerge in Norway and other countries.

Many structural details show, however, that important and probably purely Norwegian contributions were made in the development of the stave-church. Thus the introduction of ground sills in the twelfth century was a considerable improvement. Posts and planks driven into the ground could not have lasted very long without needing to be renewed. Learning by experience, the church builders laid the ground sills on a foundation, which we have already mentioned. The ground sills had a hole into which the planks of the wall were fixed. When a downpour beat against the wall rainwater would collect in the holes and the sills would rot. The builders guarded against this by extending the holes slightly downwards at an angle to a small outlet for the water. These holes sometimes form a decorative row on the outsides of the ground sills. Early wooden churches in Sweden and England have no ground sills, although they were probably more usual than surviving examples in Norway lead one to suppose. We also find drainage holes in ground sills which today lie within the exterior wall, showing that the exterior wall is a later addition, and that most of

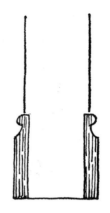

Right: Wooden vault in the church at La Croix-du-Perche near Chartres, 15th century.
Page 34: (a) Chancel vault in the church at Kapelle, Zeeland, c. 1325; (b) wooden vault in the Oude Kerk, Amsterdam, 14th and 15th centuries; (c) interior of the church at Petäjävesi, central Finland, Jaakko Leppänen, 1764; (d) interior of the cruciform church at Lemi, eastern Finland, Juhana Salonen, 1786.
Page 35: Interior of the Touro Synagogue, Newport, Rhode Island, Peter Harrison, 1759–63.
Page 36: The onion towers and roof of the Church of the Transfiguration, Kizhi, Karelia, 1714.

32

a

b

c

d

a

b

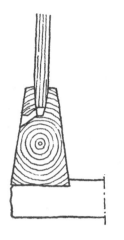

the arcades were secondary to the nave of the church. Examination of the chancels in certain of the earliest churches also reveals traces of rebuilding. Thus at Hopperstad, Urnes and Borgund (all in Sogn) the semicircular apse was built on later, probably in the Gothic period. Churches with rectangular chancels show the same features as the Anglo-Saxon church, although they were not necessarily directly influenced by it. The apse, however, is undoubtedly a borrowing from stone churches.

The bracing of the posts was a problem on which much work was done. Many solutions were found. In the churches of Urnes, Kaupanger, Hafslo (demolished), Fortun (now Fantoft) and others the posts are only tied together at the top by plates and braced to these by curved knees (braces). Thus each wall is braced longitudinally only by firm and accurate jointing. This method of construction has been vindicated by the fact that churches so built have survived for over eight hundred years. The attempt was nevertheless made to solve the problem with other constructions. Clamping beams, which we have discussed in our account of the fully developed system of the stave-church, were added – either a single clamping beam with a St. Andrew's cross above it (as at Hopperstad in Sogn) or, more usually, two such beams with a St. Andrew's cross between them. This innovation was probably introduced during the thirteenth century or soon afterwards, and it is regarded as a specifically Norwegian contribution to building which has no counterpart elsewhere. It obviously owes nothing to stone architecture.

Once the idea of the clamping beam had gained acceptance, it was found that the weight of the roof could be supported on fewer posts. To begin with, every other post was carried down only as far as the lower clamping beam, and this left a double space between the posts and gave a freer opening between the entrance and the nave. Even before the clamping beam had been introduced as a means of bracing, the central post between nave and chancel had been removed, thus providing a wider opening to the chancel. On the long walls, too, posts below the bracing were abandoned. The church builders became increasingly bold and soon did away with the intermediate posts on the transverse walls, while on the long walls they took away the middle ones (as at Gol and Hegge), or even all of them except the corner-posts (Höre or Hurum in Valdres). In this way the interior of the church became less compartmented. The posts stood as before from the clamping beam to the roof and only below were they omitted. The curved braces became larger than before and helped to transmit the weight of the roof in a bolder manner. We do not find a corresponding reduction in the weight-carrying elements in stone building and this great simplification of the static system appears to have been a discovery made by the builders of the Norwegian stave-churches based on their own experience of wood building as they moved from one assignment to another. It is, in fact, extremely likely that the church builders were specialised craftsmen who worked on commission. It is impossible to say for certain whether a master-builder travelled round and was presented with his craftsmen at the building site or whether they formed a mobile team, a kind of itinerant builders' lodge.

Below the bracing the posts continue to show details similar to those of stone architecture: the base and the capital. Above the bracing the details are different, no matter whether the posts are all in one piece or jointed. The posts are in most cases flattened towards the joints with the cross-beams and carry at the top grotesque masks with gaping mouths and enormous eyes. The powerful way in which they are carved makes them clearly visible in the weak side-light, despite the fact that they are so far above the observer's head. The carvings round the portals are even more striking. Some ninety portals with their decoration have been preserved, the earliest dating from the time of the Vikings. They contain elements which vary from simple geometric patterns to complicated compositions involving animal and plant motifs. There are also examples of motifs with literary themes, for example the Völsunga Saga.

Almost all the stave-churches were built before 1349. In this year the Black Death raged in Norway, as in all Europe. It ravaged half, if not two thirds, of the population, with serious consequences for every activity in the country. Revenue from taxes was reduced by more than half and the economic resources of the churches were much reduced. Also, since the population had been halved, new building would have been pointless; there were enough churches and houses for those who had survived. The problem was rather to find the resources and manpower to keep the buildings in repair. It took about three hundred years for the population to regain its previous size. It is therefore probable that very little was built during this period and that church building too was almost at a standstill. When churches began to be built again the tradition of the stave-church had been lost. There was nobody to carry on the tradition of the old master-builders and the new craftsmen worked upon quite different assumptions. The technique of stave-building, which had formerly been regarded as the only means of putting up monumental buildings in wood, now survived only in inferior secular buildings and in a completely changed form. The wooden churches which were erected were log buildings.

There are churches built of logs with a simple ground-plan, a rectangular nave and a narrower, rectangular chancel. When the nave reached a certain length, lateral bracing became a problem. This was solved by building on projections from the walls at right angles. These lateral reinforcements projected even further when the church had a cruciform body. Experiments made with interiors of stone churches now left

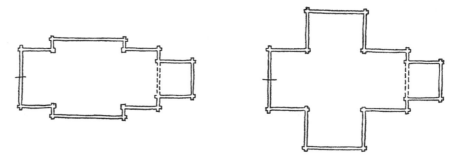

their mark on wooden churches. Thus there are log-built churches with Y-shaped or L-shaped ground-plans, and they were designed to have clad walls rather than ones in which the round logs remained exposed. The same applies to the other wooden churches. The Hospital Church in Trondheim was built in 1705. It is an octagonal clad log building and during the eighteenth and nineteenth centuries became the model for many similar churches in other parts of Norway. Many nave churches with cruciform and other ground-plans were built at the same time. In many areas most of the churches are neo-Gothic wooden buildings dating from the end of the nineteenth century. Modern church-builders prefer non-inflammable material; but some wooden buildings are still put up and most of them are traditional in form.

As we have already said, the technique of log-building which made its appearance at the time of the Vikings and remained for centuries the commonest method of building over wide areas of Scandinavia, must have brought fundamental changes with it. A farmstead which had previously consisted of one or two large hall-like buildings now formed a whole group of ten or twelve or more houses and, since a farmstead was sometimes divided between several farmers, the number of buildings could run to many times that figure. Nearly all of them had roofs made of sods of earth on which grass grew. The old house known as a *skaale* was left standing until it gradually fell to pieces and finally vanished altogether. The word *skaale* later became debased and came to mean inferior quarters or sheds for wood, tools and other stores.

It would be beyond the scope of the present chapter to enumerate every category of new house which was put up in place of the old *skaale*. In areas where there were coniferous forests all the houses were log-buildings; elsewhere, as we have said, some were built by other techniques. Log-building *(lafte)* is an art which makes great demands on the craftsman, because the long logs have to be very accurately fitted on top of one another and jointed at the corners. There were various methods of executing the corners and in some cases buildings can be dated from them. Not all, perhaps a small minority, fulfil the most rigorous demands of art and craftsmanship. We may assume that the fifty or so *lofte* or balconied granaries and the ten or twelve little houses known as *stove* and other carpentered buildings that have survived from the Middle Ages are good examples of wood building in Norway at the time, and that the average quality was probably below this level.

The most important free-standing building of the farmstead was the small dwelling-house *(stova)*. The ground-plan was simple: a principal room with one or two secondary rooms. The fireplace was in the middle of the room with a smoke-hole immediately above it; this let out the smoke and let in a uniform top light. The open-

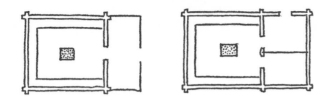

ing could be closed with a transparent animal hide. There was no window-glass. The room had space for sleeping and cooking. Another form of fireplace appeared in the Middle Ages; it was the stove with smoke flue which was set up in a corner near the door; a chimney on the roof, though not unknown in the Middle Ages, was unusual. The hearth was in a separate building resembling the dwelling-house and was used for rougher cooking, brewing beer, baking and suchlike. The earliest two-storeyed building was the balconied granary or *loft*. The commonest type had one room on the ground-floor and one on the first floor. Most of the *lofte were* log-built from ground to roof. A more lightly constructed wooden balcony ran round the house, forming open galleries on one or more sides. A staircase to the upper floor rose outside the carpentered inner structure to the balcony. The practice grew up in some areas during the eighteenth century of enclosing the staircase in a gallery on the ground-floor too. Stores were kept in the ground-floor room; on the upper floor was a bedroom which was also used to keep clothing. It was usually the best room in the farmstead, where guests slept. It seldom had a fireplace. Other types of medieval balconied granaries had two rooms on each floor – seldom more. It is evident not only from the elaborate carpentry – usually carved logs and decorated quoins – but also from the wealth of detail in the decoration of the door-frames that the *loft* was a superior building. There are portal-shaped entrances which are Romanesque or Gothic in style: the *183c* ornament may include animal, vegetable and geometric motifs. Even the small medieval dwelling-houses have the same beautifully decorated doors.

The *stabbur* were storehouses which originally consisted of ground-floor only *77a; 97c* but later copied the *lofte* in having an upper floor. All these houses are dwelling-houses. According to the size of the estate there were probably also a varying number of other dwelling-houses, as well as a series of subsidiary buildings, such as stables, cow-sheds, sheep-pens and barns. Only in very few exceptional cases have medieval buildings of this type survived, though there is documentary evidence to tell us what they looked like. Outside the farmstead too there were buildings such as field-barns, *seter* (huts in the mountain pastures), fish stores and sheds for fishing tackle.

Methods of building in towns were often the same as those in the country, and our sources tell us that towns also had the same free-standing houses. Since, however, building space in the towns was limited, the buildings took on other forms; in addition, special buildings were needed to meet the requirements of trade and the crafts. Most of the town houses about which we have information were built in two parallel ranges with a narrow lane or *Veit* between them. These lanes had a gate at both ends. The neighbouring houses lay in a parallel lane, so that the rows, separated only by a drip, were very close together. These groupings were sometimes varied by courtyards and double courtyards. Fires in towns spread fast at this period, and in the interests of rebuilding as quickly as possible after a fire, the sites were levelled and

Right: Detail of the roof of the Church of the Transfiguration, Kizhi, Karelia, 1714.
Page 46: (a) Church tower at Hampton Bishop, Herefordshire, 19th century; (b) shingle roofs at Bad Dreikirchen, South Tirol.

190; 231b

44

a

b

a

b

a

b

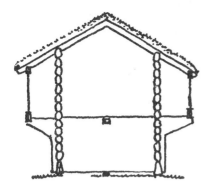

184d

86a

houses erected within the same ground-plan. The earliest surviving buildings – like, for example, the houses on Bryggen (the former German Bridge) in Bergen, which were rebuilt after the fire of 1702, are thus witnesses of a remote past. For aesthetic and military reasons the streets of Trondheim were widened after the fire of 1681. The only narrow lanes, relics of the old street network, remaining in the city are those in the quarters between the main streets. Wooden buildings were put up in Norwegian cities until late in the nineteenth century, although the regulations required stone. Regulations could be evaded, however, by giving timber framing a cladding of brick. This technique came from central Europe via Denmark but was little used in Norway, except briefly in the large towns. From the eighteenth century onwards the outside walls of town houses were mostly panelled, that is, clad with boards. One of the most important examples of Norwegian panelled architecture is the Monastery Court in Trondheim, built c. 1770. The façade, neo-classical in its over-all effect, is striking for its balanced proportions and the charming way in which alternate window surrounds show rococo or neo-classical elements. In the country too it became increasingly common to cover buildings with boards; the dwelling-houses were the first to be so treated and subsidiary buildings followed. The technical prerequisite for cladding was the existence of saw-mills in which boards could be cut cheaply. The first water-driven saw-mills in Norway date from towards the end of the sixteenth century and mark the beginning of an industry which grew in importance both for home use and for export. After the Black Death in 1349, little was built either in the towns or in the country until about 1600 or perhaps a little earlier, as we have seen. New influences now made their impact. The open fireplace with a stone or brick chimney was the technical innovation which made it possible to build small heatable dwelling-houses with an upper floor, like the balconied granaries. Small windows were now put into the houses and granaries and later into other buildings also. Thanks to the technique of cladding, the houses were adaptable to European styles. We can trace the course of artistic influence from the continent particularly in such details of the façade as cornices and door and window surrounds. During the eighteenth and nineteenth centuries, roofs of earth and shingle began to disappear in the towns and on the manor farms. They were replaced by tiles, or, in districts where it was obtainable, by slate. Panelling became increasingly common, as did the construction of built-in furniture in the inner rooms.

In the country there were local differences in custom, though there was a tendency to bring together under one roof buildings which had previously been separate; the division of space remained the same in the new buildings as it had been in the old. In certain districts the new long buildings embraced both the the old dwelling-house and the old granary under one roof. In other regions the old dwelling-house and the old detached kitchen were combined, as were in some places the kitchen and the stalls for the cattle. Out-buildings too were run together: cattle stalls and barn, and stables and barn, were combined as early as the early nineteenth century. And during the nineteenth century, particularly in eastern Norway, concentration went so far that all the out-buildings were once more united under one roof, as in the Viking period long ago. So, after some thousand years, the wheel had come full circle in the layout

Page 47: (a) Double cruciform church at Lappee, eastern Finland, Juhana Salonen, 1792–94; (b) town-hall (now school house), Kokkola, Finland, 1696; Left: (a) Church at Kopparbarg, Sweden, 1635; (b) mosque with wooden porch and minaret, Plav, Montenegro.

of the Norwegian farmstead.

Norwegian wooden architecture, in country and town and in church-building, is closely paralleled in neighbouring Sweden, a country equally rich in forests; indeed, the stave-churches, so early and so entirely singular, are the only exceptions worth mentioning. The method of log-building known in Norway as the *lafte* technique can be traced back in Sweden also to the time of the Vikings and the log house has predominated, at least in the country, from the regions of the coniferous forests in the north to far into central Sweden, until very recently. Here too, in the tradition which can be traced right up to the High Middle Ages, the farmsteads consisted of a number of separate buildings each serving a different purpose. There was also in central Sweden a method of building like the Norwegian 'grid' technique which involved cladding with horizontal boards between vertical posts. In Scania to the south, once part of Denmark, the dominant type is the long low reed-thatched house with timber frame infilled with clay and later with brick, typical of all parts of Denmark.

85a

The open-air museum at Skansen, near Stockholm, created in 1891 and the model for many similar establishments throughout the world, provides a vivid impression of the main types of Swedish wooden house, the earliest of which date from the sixteenth century. We can see, for example, a farmstead from Mora in Dalarne with the typical two-storeyed, log-built balconied granary dating from the year 1574, which has a staircase made of triangular pieces of timber leading to the gallery; and a granary on posts, dated 1595, with its substructure of tall posts designed to protect the stored grain from rats and damp – a type which is also found in other parts of Sweden, and in Norway and Finland, as well as in the Pyrenees and the Alps. There are farmsteads from east and west Gotland with log-built dwelling-houses, stalls for cattle and barns, built in a technique involving studs and rails with an infilling of stones without mortar. The kitchen from Älvdalen built in 1659, and its dairy and its stalls and barns, is a simple log-building. The Älvros farmstead dates from the seventeenth century, comes from Härjedalen and consists of fifteen log buildings in pinewood. One of these, a splendid two-storeyed granary with first-floor balcony, is dated 1666. The ground-floors of these granaries were usually used to store provisions, while the upper floors provided accommodation for labourers during the summer and were used in winter to store linen and clothing. A characteristic Swedish wooden church has also been set up at Skansen; it dates from 1730, comes from Seglora and is an aisled log building with weatherboard cladding; its square tower has a roof with three slopes and dates from some fifty years later; there is also a bell-tower from Hällestad in the northern part of east Gotland. This delightful monument to the northern carpenter's art dates from the year 1742; it is constructed of pinewood beams and boards clad externally with oak weather-boarding and represents a type which is still found in a number of variants all over Sweden and Finland. The wooden houses in the Swedish towns resemble in general those of Norway; but only very few early ones – built, that is, before 1700 – have survived, one example being that at Ornäs near Falun where Gustavus Vasa hid in 1520.

266a
75b; 245d

68a, b, d
265a

In Finland, where most of the buildings are still wooden, log-building predominates. Here too, however, with the rise of the saw-mill industry in the nineteenth century, much building began with posts and a cladding of boards, although logs without cladding were still used. Wood remains to this day the favourite material in Finland for the separate buildings of the farmsteads and for single-family houses and summer houses. The most modern types of Finnish buildings have recently had a stimulating effect on the style, method and distribution of wooden building throughout Europe, and particularly on interior decoration, for which walls and ceilings lined with wood have recently become very popular. In the past also there was a typical Finnish style of architecture in wood, although in the coastal districts Swedish and, in the east, Russian influences were always of some consequence.

The best preserved of the surviving Finnish wooden churches of the seventeenth and eighteenth centuries are architectural monuments of original character, unique even from an international point of view. It was characteristic of the period and its works that the master-builders were men of the people; names of master-builders have been known since the seventeenth century. The earliest surviving Finnish wooden churches of the early seventeenth century belong to the type known as nave churches, and have either no tower or a west tower. In style and technique they go back to vanished medieval forerunners. In northern Finland the naves were strengthened by a curious form of timber buttress, square in plan and hollow, partly inside and partly outside the building, to take the weight of the walls and roof; Strzygowski called them 'block pillars'. This system is thought to be a Finnish invention of the fifteenth century. Of the dozens of examples of this type of church that once existed thirteen have survived in northern Finland.

The so-called cruciform church appeared in Finnish church architecture after 1660. Originally found only in the towns, it later spread in a slightly different form to the country. Stylistically it goes back to the centralised churches of the Italian Renaissance, the type passing to Finland through the church of St. Catharine in Stockholm, a stone church begun in 1656 that was not without influence on the wooden churches of Sweden. When this type of church was transposed into wood in Finland forms were simplified and a number of conservative features were added. Then in the mid-eighteenth century there arose in east Finland a type of cruciform church in which the transepts taper at the ends. A particularly monumental type occurs in east Finland in the form of the so-called double cruciform church, where not only are there transepts but also separate projections at the angles. Of sixty old wooden cruciform churches built in Finland up to 1763 about a quarter still exist, of which the purest stylistically is that of Petäjävesi in central Finland with its handsome cross vaults modelled upon stone prototypes; it was built in 1763–1764 by the master-builder Jaakko Leppänen the Elder. In the north of Finland the cruciform church acquired other individual features at the hands of well-known church-builders. Worth mentioning in this connection is the church of Kiiminki dating from the year 1760, a modest but harmonious weatherboarded building. With its typical Finnish bell-tower, it forms a unit which is among the most beautiful of surviving groups of church buildings in Finland. Together with the cruciform church, a new type of bell-tower, the three-storeyed Renaissance tower, came into use in Sweden and Finland. It occurs in Finland in three main forms: the east Bothnian type, the south-western

Finnish type and the eastern Finnish type, which has an octagonal bottom storey.

At the beginning of the nineteenth century the master-craftsmen, who had been men of the people, were replaced by trained architects, a trend which had an effect upon church design. A new official type of wooden cruciform church was designed in the Finnish department of building; it had an immense central dome. A unique and monstrous specimen of this is the huge church of Kerimäki erected in 1847 on the western shore of Lake Puruvesi. The considerable resources demanded by the project were raised by a community effort involving contributions of money, materials, and the active co-operation of craftsmen as well as gifts from the local timber industry. E. Lohrmann, a German architect who had succeeded Engel as the director of the Finnish department of building, designed the church. The plan was originally based on much smaller proportions, but the elders of the community wanted a more imposing building and an assistant subsequently enlarged the measurements of Lohrmann's plan. The result was that this large country parish acquired a church which is capable of holding over five thousand people and is the largest wooden church in the world.

Neo-classicism was followed in Finland by Empire and later by the Gothic Revival as the international style of church building deriving from the continent of Europe; thus over eighty Gothic Revival churches were built in Finland of wood, most of their motifs deriving from Germany.

The Finnish farmhouse reflects very ancient features. Log-building goes back to the prehistoric period (before 1150), as does the low-pitch saddleback roof and entrance to the living-rooms from the gable, but the basically asymmetrical medieval manner of building has left few traces. Renaissance principles of architecture were applied and resulted in the building of rectangular courtyards, two-roomed houses and long 'residential ranges'. And particularly in the rich, fertile west, it was the Renaissance tradition which left its mark upon the Finnish landscape in the form of the Finnish farmhouse.

By the end of the eighteenth century in the western part of southern Finland the main building put up on the farms sometimes rose to two storeys. Symmetry gained yet more emphasis later in the Empire style. Larger windows, at first of six lights with double transoms, then, towards the end of the nineteenth century, of three lights formed by a mullion and transom, with weather-boarding, assimilated well to the existing tradition. Guest houses on the prosperous farms in southern Häme and in Satakunta are sometimes built in an impressive Empire style and are the work of skilled carpenters.

Until the last century the outsides of farmhouses in Finland usually remained unpainted; the custom of painting began in western Finland. Red ochre was normally used and during the seventeenth and eighteenth centuries it was the typical colour for manor houses, although in the nineteenth century the houses of the nobility were painted in light colours in accordance with Empire taste. Painting of the outsides of log-built houses has still not penetrated to the remote villages of eastern and north-eastern Finland and in some parts of these regions villages and houses are the same dull grey they have been for centuries. The tradition of the large two-roomed house

65; 229a

Right: Spire of Christ Church, Philadelphia, Pennsylvania, Robert Smith, 1754.
Page 54: (a) Crossing-tower, Church of St. Bavo, Haarlem, 1518; (b) tower of the Mint, Amsterdam, beginning of the 17th century; (c) crossing-tower, Church of St. Cosmas, Stade, 1682 (cf. 178); (d) bell-tower of the Church of St. Mariana, Plovdiv, Bulgaria.
Page 55: Roof timbers of the Grande Salle of the Palais de Justice, Poitiers, 15th century; barrel-vault of the Hospital, Tonnerre, 15 th century.
Page 56: (a), (b) Roof timbers of the Round Shaker Barn, Hancock, Massachusetts, beginning of the 19th century (cf. 88a).

86f

a

b

c

d

a

b

a

b

a

b

a

b

c

d

a

b

persisted longest in the wooded districts of eastern Finland. Large, undecorated timbered rooms, often measuring thirty feet square, are not infrequent in these buildings.

A completely different type from those already mentioned has migrated in modern times from the north of Russia to the Greek-Catholic parishes of the Finnish border with Karelia, east of Lake Ladoga. This is a two- or three-storeyed house, known as the northern Great Russian house, in which living rooms and domestic offices, cattle stalls and barns are all under one roof. Beyond the present Finnish frontier its forms, passing into the Russian boyar house and types of building of Byzantine derivation, became extremely decorative, often with richly carved ornamentation.

75d

74a

114a

To sum up, wooden dwelling-houses dating from before 1700 are extremely rare. A few examples, however, of that jewel of the farmstead, the fine two-storeyed balconied granary, have survived from the seventeenth century. As in the related Swedish types, the rooms served to accommodate labourers and to store clothes, provisions and grain. Windmills, often most imposing examples of rural architecture in wood, came from the west to Finland towards the end of the Middle Ages. A number of them are still in existence.

Wood was the principal building material for the farmhouses too on the manorial estates of Finland. The so-called closed farmstead with two rectangular yards round which stood several dwelling-houses and domestic offices, made its appearance towards the end of the Middle Ages and was gradually abandoned in the farms of the seventeenth century. The two-roomed dwelling-house also came in time to be used only by peasants. Towards the end of the seventeenth century and during the eighteenth century in the dwelling-house of the nobility space was apportioned in the so-called Caroline manner, with six rooms grouped symmetrically round a large

218a

central hall. During the eighteenth century in Finnish farmsteads and parsonages, as in Sweden, rococo architecture and the mansard roof became popular; and in

204b

47b

response to French influences, native architects evolved the Swedish-Finnish rococo farmstead style with its characteristic appearance of general well-being. Neo-classicism made no impact until after 1790, as, for example, in the wood-built mansion of Mustio. The influence of the celebrated architect C. L. Engel was felt at the beginning of the nineteenth century. In 1824 he became the head of the Finnish department of building and his many balanced creations – country mansions in the Empire style and town-houses in wood and stone – are celebrated for their fine proportions and simple decorative motifs. The practice of cladding with horizontal boards was borrowed from the Russian Empire.

Page 57: (a) Roof timbers of a timber-framed house, Niederaula, Hesse, 17th century; (b) timber-framed wall with wattle and daub infilling, Gramschatz, near Würzburg, 18th century.
Page 58: (a) Church of the Assumption, Warsugi, near Murmansk, 1674; (b) Uspensky Church, Kondopoga, Karelia, 1774; (c) Church of SS. Peter and Paul, Hamburg-Bergedorf, 16th century, spire by Ernst Georg Sonnin, 1759; (d) church at Dedham, Massachusetts, c. 1790.
Page 59: Church at Hingham, Massachusetts, 1742 (cf. 191a).
Left: (a) Shakers' assembly house, Mount Lebanon, New York, beginning of the 19th century; (b) the 'Saal', The Cloister, Ephrata, Pennsylvania, 1740.

The earliest surviving wooden town building in Finland is an example of Caroline Baroque. It is the former schoolhouse in the coastal town of Kokkola in eastern Bothnia; it has a saddleback roof and dates from the year 1696. The end of the eighteenth century saw intensive building activity in the Finnish towns and at that time building was still mainly in wood. The houses of the well-to-do became larger, often extending to two storeys, window-panes were larger, outsides of houses were painted and mansard roofs made their appearance. In the artisans' districts and the poorer quarters, where, for example, the seamen lived, the houses remained small and remote from general changes of style and fashion. In about 1820 the Empire style gained ground in the towns too and streets and sites became broader and larger. It was no longer master-craftsmen but architects who now designed town-houses. Squares and streets flanked by wooden houses in the Empire style have survived in certain towns to this day. Those roomy summer-houses which prosperous city-dwellers of the last decades of the nineteenth century built on the shores of the Finnish lakes are late examples of building in wood. Characteristic of these, as of the town villas, which were often built in the same national romantic style, were a free ground-plan, verandahs, balconies, towers, hipped roofs and boldly-projecting eaves similar to those which were fashionable at this time in many pensions and hotels in the seaside and mountain resorts of central Europe.

218b
219b

Recent excavations have brought to light new facts about the four fine Viking citadels on Danish soil. They consist of large ramparts of up to 750 feet in diameter which still conspicuously dominate the landscape. All four – Trelleborg on Zealand, Nonnebakken on Fünen, Fyrkat and Aggersborg in Jutland – date from about the year 1000. They are of interest to the student of early Teutonic architecture in wood because within the circular fortified area stood groups of four elongated houses (twelve at Aggesborg) arranged in strictly regular squares. It is true that no part of any of them remains, but their ground-plans can be ascertained with the greatest accuracy from the post-holes which have been found. Reconstructions have been attempted on this basis, including one by C. G. Shulz, from whose information a Trelleborg house with curved longitudinal walls and bent roof-ridge has been erected. The double rows of post-holes were at first thought to indicate that the houses had galleries, but recent studies by Holger Schmidt show that at Fyrkat, and at Trelleborg too, the holes are not vertical but slope inwards at an angle of seventy degrees. Schmidt's hypothesis that the outer holes were for rafters extending from the ridge to the ground seems therefore more logical than the earlier hypothesis of galleries similar to those of the Norwegian stave-churches.

75a
63

The earliest surviving Danish farmhouses are of the low timber-framed type with a reed roof which already predominated in the southernmost part of the Scandinavian peninsula, the former Danish province of Scania. Timber-framed town-buildings, however, of which examples survive from the sixteenth century onwards, clearly reflect the then predominant cultural influence of north Germany. Façades, including their carved decoration, at Helsingör, Köge or Naestved could equally well be at Stade or Brunswick. Half-timbered houses continued to be built far into the nineteenth century and many can still be found in the streets today; a whole series of them has been preserved in the Gamle By at Aarhus and grouped in a clear and historically meaningful way.

85a; 87e
265b
232c; 248a
229b

Iceland grows no wood apart from low birch forests. Nevertheless roof-bearing members have always been made of wood since the country was settled from Norway in about the year 1000. Except for these post-constructions – similar ones may have occurred in the earliest excavated Norwegian dwelling-places mentioned at the beginning – the walls up to roof-level were made of sods of earth or turf, or of stones. Icelandic farmhouses were later given wooden gable-ends, which were

86b

often decorated with carving. Rows of several such gable-ends looking as though they had grown up out of the ground and also frequently decorated with carving became a characteristic feature.

As regards the interior furnishing of Scandinavian wooden buildings, certain pieces of furniture or fittings, such as shelves, seats and later cupboards and alcove-like bedsteads, have clearly been built-in from the beginning and are thus literally parts of the building. In rustic log-buildings the unclad walls with their horizontal timbers gain a special charm from the primitive quality of the exposed raw wood. But other, simple, interiors, clad with boards or sometimes more luxuriously panelled, have an air of comfort which explains why builders and architects today readily respond to the example of such rooms, and can once more appreciate wood and welcome it as a building material.

129a; 132a–d; 270b

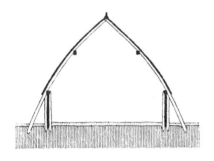

Section of a house in the Viking Fyr-kat, Denmark, c. 1000 (after Schmidt).

Jesus helps Joseph in the carpenter's shop, woodcut from Petrus de Natalibus: Catalogus Sanctorum, beginning of the 16th century.

Right: Interior of the church at Keri-mäki, eastern Finland, E. Lohrmann, 1847 (cf. 229a).
Page 66: Timber-framed farmhouse with wattle and daub infilling from Beuningen, Twente, now in the Netherlands Open-air Museum, Arnhem, 17th century.

a

b

c

d

In prehistoric and early medieval times wood was used for buildings almost everywhere in the British Isles, their traces or remains having been found by archaeological excavation over the past thirty years. Surviving timber buildings have a much more limited distribution, being confined mainly to lowland England and parts of Wales; they are now unknown in Scotland and Ireland, and in those countries even such old wooden roofs as remain are of relatively late date. The reasons for this situation lie in the differing course of social, economic and technological history in the four countries.

In Britain, as indeed all over northern Europe, wood was the usual material throughout the High Middle Ages for all buildings except those of the greatest consequence, excluding thereby most churches and the many palaces and castles built of stone. The contemporary wooden structures which far outnumbered them have, with only a single exception, disappeared, and the reason for this is to be found less in any inherent weakness of the material than in the methods of construction used. In order to give stability, that is, the strength to resist wind pressure, the posts were first set upright in pits prepared for them, often about two to three feet deep, and then the earth was rammed tight against them. Consequently the damp to which the wood was subject limited the useful life of buildings to the time it took the principal posts to rot; when that had happened to a few it was not worth replacing them because the rest of the structure was not sufficiently well built to justify replacement of its largest and most expensive members. That these early timber buildings were not normally well built can be inferred from the irregular spacings of the principal posts and the lack of any clear relation between them and the posts of the side and end walls; irregularity of this sort precludes prefabrication and the possibility of precise jointing together of the timbers. All old wooden buildings which remain at the present time owe their survival to a far-reaching change made sometime during the twelfth century whereby posts were set upon footings of stone, with or without the interposition of a sill-beam. To make up for the resulting loss of stability the horizontal and vertical components of a building had to be braced together far more effectively than before in order to create a rigid, self-supporting structure. Simple though the change sounds, it was a technical revolution.

Any change in building practice demanding a higher standard of craftsmanship is expensive. It follows that an improvement which extended the life of a building from the term set by natural agencies to that for which some use could be found for it, was first applied at the highest social levels where most resources were available; the extent and speed at which it was applied lower down the social scale were dictated by the distribution of wealth within society. Hence it is social structure rather than agricultural potential which has determined the forms and extent of wooden

Page 67: Front of a farmhouse, Reichenbach im Kandertal, Bernese Oberland, 1752.
Left: Bell-towers: (a) Frösö near Östersund, Sweden, 18th century; (b) Jukkasjärvi near Kiruna, Sweden, 18th century; (c) Egestorf, Lüneburg Heath, 17th century; (d) Ruokolahti, eastern Finland, 1752.

architecture in the past, and within geographically comparable areas, human rather than natural factors are the prime determinants. Viewed in this way the secular wooden architecture of England and Wales shows the successive applications of techniques of permanent building to the requirements of particular classes, with a gradual descent down the social scale and modifications to meet new needs.

Building in wood in Great Britain has been limited by geology as well as history. In the limestone uplands which form a broad belt from south-west to north-east, from Dorset to Lincolnshire, some timber-framing survives in the towns and there is more in the countryside, particularly in Northamptonshire; but none of it is important. In the south-western peninsula wooden buildings, which hardly exist in rural areas, were sometimes of considerable size and architectural quality in towns, but this region is principally important for some fine wooden roofs.

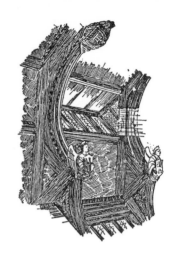

Hammer-beam roof at Adlington Hall, Cheshire, early 16th century; windows 19th century.

Another factor in the evolution of wooden architecture is the existence of regional traditions of carpentry. England was divided, from at least as early as the thirteenth century up to the eighteenth century, into three regions, each with distinct carpentry traditions, which changed and interacted but never lost their identity; though this can be demonstrated by distribution maps it has yet to be explained. Wales is also divided into two distinct regions, both of which are ultimately dependent on adjoining English regions. Tradition and social structure on the one hand, the source of income and its amount on the other, these are the four variables to juggle with in seeking to account for the widely differing form and pace of development which is apparent in secular timber building from one district to another.

With one striking exception wooden churches add little to the information obtainable from houses. For the immediate purpose the main interest of ecclesiastical architecture is in the large stone churches of the thirteenth century, where the problem of roofing wide spans produced solutions which were subsequently adapted to the less ambitious scale of domestic work, and in the astonishing visual effects of the later East Anglian parish church roofs. The exception noted above, the stave-built nave of Greenstead church (Essex) of *c.* 1013, is the oldest wooden structure in the British Isles as well as the sole survivor of what may have been a fairly common form of timberwork, yet stave-construction has had no discernible effect on later work. Originally the upright split logs (staves) were set in the earth, and doubtless decay had gone quite far before the interposition of a timber sill standing on brick footings halted it in the sixteenth century.

97*b*

It was probably sometime during the twelfth century that the great change from setting posts in the earth to standing them on stone bases began. We do not know if Westminster Hall, built with massive outer walls of masonry at the very end of the eleventh century and the largest of all the great aisled halls of the Middle Ages, embodied this improvement in its two timber arcades; the contemporary hall in the royal palace at Cheddar (Somerset) certainly did not. Nevertheless by the second half of the twelfth century the representational halls of magnates incorporated stone bases for the arcades, so that at Leicester Castle hall the main posts contemporary with the stone outer walls remain, albeit mutilated by the destruction of their scalloped capitals. At Hereford, where rather more of the hall of the episcopal palace

70

survives, the cushion capitals on the posts and the bold dog-tooth ornament on the round arches follow very closely contemporary forms in masonry, and the filling of the spandrels of the arches with plastered wattle-and-daub implies deliberate copying of a stone structure. Such imitation was probably common in buildings put up by feudal magnates and in those of the richer manorial lords, such as the early fourteenth century stone-walled Kentish manor house called Nurstead Court, where, besides elaborately moulded arches, capitals and bases, like those in contemporary church work, the arcade spandrels were boarded in to give the effect of solid arches.

From the middle of the thirteenth century the new technique of timberwork becomes commoner in several parts of England, and with it appear regional variations of both structure and ornament. Since these are common to all kinds of wooden structures they will be described first and the specific buildings in which they appear later. The fundamental division is between areas where the thirteenth and fourteenth century buildings, together with a few late outliers of the fifteenth century, are commonly aisled, and those areas where virtually all medieval buildings are of a single span. The distinction is not confined to wooden buildings; and the two areas overlap. There is a concentration of aisled buildings in south-east England, a thin scatter over much of the lowland zone, and a few outliers in the highland zone on the fringes of Wales and on the east of the Pennines. In the midlands and west country, including the whole area where the thin scatter is found, buildings of comparable size and date are almost invariably roofed in a single span. This is the simplest way to discriminate the two regions; roof construction presents a broadly similar picture (which is more complicated in detail).

Where aisled buildings are concentrated they and their aisleless contemporaries and successors have three types of roof structure. The simplest, from which the others stem, is the collar-rafter roof, comprising uniform pairs of rafters (couples), each joined by a collar-beam; to remedy its instability the two succeeding types were developed. They are the passing-brace roof, in which, to provide lateral stability, long timbers, sloping in the vertical plane and called passing-braces, are engaged by means of halved joints to all the horizontal or vertical members they pass – hence the name; and the collar-purlin roof, in which both the lateral and longitudinal stability of the couples are assured by a collar-purlin – an axial beam on which the collar-beams rest – which is supported by crown-posts standing on the tie-beams, the crown-posts being strutted in four directions to prevent movement.

The aisleless, single-span buildings of western England also have three types of roof, all founded on the quite different principle of transmitting the weight of the common rafters to the ground through a few trusses (inner frameworks) rather than uniformly along the side walls. The simplest type is the cruck, in which two curved timbers standing on flat stones rise to the apex of the roof and are joined by purlins and a ridge-piece which support the common rafters. Closely related to it is the base-cruck, in which the curved timbers rise to a collar-beam well below the apex, upon which stands what is virtually an independent upper roof. A third and more distantly allied type is the roof with principal rafters (sometimes called blades) which carry the purlins supporting the common rafters and which are joined together either at their feet by a tie-beam or half way up by a collar-beam.

In all types the main points at which support is provided, by whatever means, divide the roof into structural units called bays.

But the two major categories of aisled and aisleless buildings and their associated roofs are not completely independent of each other; an interaction between them is evident, and to explain it the concept of hybridisation – the union of structural or decorative elements drawn from two distinct traditions – has been introduced. It explains, for instance, the very varied forms of upper roof associated with base crucks. A group of them, including Cubbington Manor House (Warwickshire), have crown-post roofs of perfectly orthodox type complete with four struts which would not look out of place in that home of crown-post orthodoxy, the county of Kent. The same cannot be said of all the crown-posts which stand on base-crucks; one in the manor hall at West Bromwich (Staffordshire) is supported in a most unusual way by short passing-braces instead of struts, while at Coningsby (Lincolnshire) two lateral struts have taken on a decorative cusped form unknown in the south-east but widespread elsewhere.

But the upper roof was not necessarily a crown-post, and in two districts particularly, the southern marches of Wales and the counties of Wiltshire and Somerset, base-crucks usually support one of the two allied types: in the former district trusses with principal rafters and in the latter small cruck trusses which give rise to the name two-tier crucks.

Regional differences in wooden architecture extend to decoration as well as structure. From the early fourteenth century, which is the date of the earliest surviving roofs there, there was in the Welsh marches a taste for bold decorative treatment achieved by shaping structural members with cusps so as to form large trefoils and cinquefoils. Perhaps the ultimate in this kind of decoration was reached in the fourteenth century timber-framed refectory of Great Malvern Priory (Worcestershire) where a riot of cusping was used to lighten the appearance of the enormously heavy main trusses. Although this taste found its most dramatic manifestations on both sides of the Welsh border it was widespread elsewhere. A minor instance was noted above from Lincolnshire; a more striking one is the cusped shape given to the base crucks at Mancetter Manor House (Warwickshire) and in the West Country this form of decoration is refined and elaborated to a degree not found elsewhere. Other examples occur in Berkshire and Hampshire but never in the south-east heartland of aisled buildings and crown-post roofs, the counties of Kent, Essex and Suffolk. The most striking example of hybridisation is provided by the use of this decoration at Brinsop Court (Herefordshire); the early fourteenth century hall has a crown-post of impeccably orthodox structure, yet because it was executed in the much larger sizes of timber customary on the Welsh border and given the extremely bold cusping admired there it looks totally alien to its true structural type.

Against this background the varied forms taken by the manor houses of the thirteenth and fourteenth centuries become intelligible. From about 1250 onwards manorial halls progressively ceased to have earth-fast posts and began to be built in the new way with footings and timber sills. Generally they are buildings of less con-

Right: (a) Log-built barn, Valais; (b) farmstead at Livigno, Upper Valtellina.
Page 74: (a) Galleried barn from Satakunta, Western Finland, now in the open-air museum at Ruovesi; (b) farmhouse, Ornäs-Slugan, Dalarne, Sweden, 18th century; (c) barn in Moravia.
Page 75: (a) Reconstructed Viking house, Trelleborg, Denmark; (b) barn raised on posts from Delsbo, Hälsingland, now in the open-air museum at Skansen, near Stockholm; (c) house at Petrosavodsk, now Kizhi, Karelia, c. 1900; (d) Great Russian house, Ladoga-Karelia, beginning of the 19th century (demolished c. 1930); (e) farmhouse, Celadna, Moravia; (f) farmhouse, Zug, Switzerland, 18th century.
Page 76: Houses at Niederwald/Gloms, Valais, 18th century.

a

b

a

b

c

a

b

c

d

e

f

a

b

c

d

a

b

c

d

sequence than Nurstead Court, which must have belonged to a rich minor feudatory, but all are associated with locally important members of the ruling class. Besides being the focus of life for a large household these halls were intended as places of assembly for the transaction of public business, such as that of the manor court; the name of one of the oldest, the mid-thirteenth century Old Court Cottage, Limpsfield (Surrey), signifies both its original and modern functions. What remains at Limpsfield was originally little more than a hall, there being hardly any provision of subsidiary domestic rooms, and this is equally true of Fyfield Hall (Essex), of the end of the thirteenth century, and the somewhat later manor house at Wasperton (Warwickshire). Most domestic and all farm activities were carried on in detached buildings, so that when the surviving halls were built they must have formed a centrepiece overtopping a cluster of smaller structures in the older inferior mode of carpentry. This phase in the development of the house is little represented outside the Home Counties. At both Limpsfield and Fyfield the halls have roofs of the passing-brace type, the latter being particularly remarkable for the duplication side by side of the rafters and all the bracing members of the middle truss; lit during the day only by small, low windows and at night by the flicker of an open fire, this complicated framework soaring upwards in the gloom must have borne impressive testimony to the technical revolution that was taking place.

Development thereafter took three forms. One was to separate the entrances, which were usually two opposite doors set in the long walls at one end of the hall, from the body of the room. It was done by means of a spere-truss, a roof-truss of aisled type which had low screens between its posts and the outer walls to prevent draughts, and its introduction begins a long process of subdivision and encroachment on what was originally a large barn-like room. A second development, simultaneous with the first but not necessarily found in conjunction with it, was to provide additional rooms, first at the lower or entrance end and later at both ends. In early examples this was achieved by extending the roof structure and finishing it off with a hipped end, so that a house with rooms at both ends of the hall must have presented much the same silhouette as a barn. The third mode of development was to give a more spacious appearance to the hall by making the roof construction less cumbersome. In the aisled hall this meant new forms of truss which would dispense with posts; in the base-cruck hall, a lightening of the massive timbers hitherto required for a single span. In either case it was very difficult to achieve this aim in a timber building of wide span, particularly if it had fairly high walls, and hardly anywhere was the carpenter completely successful in combining stability with lightness of appearance. Consequently the most spectacular late-medieval roof constructions are in stone buildings, whether churches, monasteries, or domestic halls, where the greater resistance of the walls to thrust made stability less of a problem.

These developments did not take place uniformly throughout England and Wales. Only at a common social level are plans at all likely to be uniform, and even then only within certain regions. Consequently houses were built contemporaneously to plans at various stages of the typological development outlined above, corresponding to the different requirements and wealth of social classes.

Page 77: Stabbur (barn), Rygnestad, Setesdal, 12th century; (b) porch of the church at Lindsey, Suffolk, c. 1500.
Page 78: (a) Houses at Wurzen (Podkoren), Slovenia; (b) detail of the Nelaski church, monastery of Kirill-Beloserski on Lake Siverski, Vologodsk, 15th century; (c) Jelisarov house, Kizhi, 1880 (after an earlier house); (d) Pirovano house, Cervinia, Val d'Aosta, Franco Albini, 1962.
Page 79: Lüscher-Stauffer house, Muhen, Aargau, mid-17th century.
Left: (a) Farmhouse, north-eastern Bohemia; (b) timber-framed gable, 16th century, with the plaster stripped off, the laths added in the 19th century; Kersey, Suffolk; (c) house of the Jessins, Myakotino, near Gor'kiy, 19th century; (d) barn, Serbia.

83a, b; 94b

An example of the simplest form of development is the manor hall at Wasperton which incorporates a spere-truss but has no other rooms. Only a little later Stanton's Farm, Black Notley (Essex), has an aisled hall of two bays and, beyond the opposite doors, a third bay of two storeys which provided service rooms (pantry and buttery) on the ground floor and a large private chamber (or solar) above. No advance was made in roof construction; an early instance of improvement in that direction occurs at Gatehouse Farm, Felstead (Essex), where the carpenter cleared the hall by standing an aisled structure, complete with octagonal posts, capitals and bases, upon a tie-beam which is hardly more than head-height above the floor. This simple device freed the floor, it is true, but only by destroying the effect of height which an aisled hall had and substituting a structure which lacked both the head room and the visual qualities of a base-cruck. At the same time Gatehouse Farm – another name signifying quite high social status – developed the hall plan by having rooms at the upper end as well as the lower, and again, perhaps, there were storage rooms on the ground-floor and a private chamber over them.

Yet another Essex house – for in this county the evolution of houses is clearer than in any other – advances farther to incorporate, by about the middle of the fourteenth century, all three of the developments outlined previously. Tiptofts, near Saffron Walden, derives its name from a famous family, one of whose members held it by marriage for the twenty years between 1348 and 1367, which is probably when it was built. Its plan was originally the same as Gatehouse Farm with the addition of a stately spere-truss; and the middle of the hall is spanned from wall to wall by an early hammer-beam truss. A hammer-beam roof, in its earlier, fourteenth century form, is simply an aisled roof raised up off the floor on two large brackets which project from the side walls; and its origin, though disputed, is clear enough from Gatehouse Farm; in effect it is an aisled construction raised on a tie-beam of which the ends are supported by curved braces and the middle cut away. An alternative was to set two short principal rafters parallel with the slope of the roof to support the ends of a collar-beam, the latter being exactly like the tie-beam of an aisled construction, even to the extent of carrying a crown-post; Wynters Armourie, in the parish of Magdalen Laver (Essex) is an example.

83b

Towards the end of the fourteenth century aisled halls were becoming obsolete in southern England. One of the latest of them is Baythorn Hall, Birdbrook (Essex), of about 1360–70, where a two-bay hall is flanked, not by rooms partitioned off under one overall roof, but by two two-storey wings built and roofed at right-angles to the hall, and each with the upper storey jettied (projecting) beyond the lower. This combination of aisled hall and jettied wings was sometimes used for domestic buildings in the smaller monasteries, for instance the prior's residence at the Augustinian priory of Dunmow (Essex).

Elsewhere in England fourteenth century timber houses are much less common than they are in Essex. This is due partly to the difference in materials already noted; and even in some counties which are rich in timber-framed buildings, such as Kent and Warwickshire, a manor-house comparable in importance to Tiptofts might well assume a quite different form in stone. Nevertheless the apparent lack of fourteenth

Right: (a) Hammer-beam roof in the hall, Eltham Castle, late 15th century; (b) hammer-beam roof, St. Stephen's Norwich, 15th century.

82

a

b

century timber manor-houses in Kent remains surprising. In the Midlands the lightening of roof construction is shown by the contrast between Martley vicarage (Worcestershire), Solihull Hall (Warwickshire) and Littywood, Bradley (Staffordshire). At Martley, a mid-fourteenth century house, the trusses are all of tie-beam type; the other two houses, which are definitely of the second half of the century, have collar-beam trusses with big arch-braces. The late fourteenth century Lower Brockhampton (Herefordshire) is another west midland house with an arch-braced collar-beam roof. Hand in hand with the improvement of roofs went development of the plan, and it appears that a hall combined with two cross-wings was introduced in the west midlands at much the same time as in East Anglia, although this remark needs to be qualified by saying that close dating of all such buildings is hazardous where, as is usually the case, no documentary evidence is available. The history of the hall and cross wings plan has unfortunately been obscured by the assumption that in such a house both wings are original, whereas in fact many began with an end-hall plan, i.e. with a wing only at the lower end, rather like Stanton's Farm, Black Notley, to which another wing has been added later. Yet even when allowance is made for these difficulties Amberley Court and probably Martley vicarage had this plan before 1400.

On the Welsh border and in the north of England houses datable before 1400 are exceedingly rare and highly individual. Near Oswestry in Llansilin (Denbighshire) stands Hafod, Rhiwlas, the only aisled hall in Wales. Though now greatly altered, this house, put up towards the end of the fourteenth century, seems to have had a large hall, three bays long, and probably a further bay at each end; apart from the size of the hall, not a surprising plan for a house so remote from the centres of architectural progress. It is the quality of its detail that is so remarkable: free-standing posts worked with four half-round mouldings set diagonally and separated by little V-shaped sections, moulded capitals, arch braces with pierced cusps and king-posts with moulded caps and bases; all these make it outstanding among the houses of North Wales.

In plan Baguley Hall, a mid-late fourteenth century house on the outskirts of Manchester, must have been much like Hafod except for the uniquely bowed-out sides of the hall, but the prime importance of this house is the way the wall timbering is worked in the form of planks, all of a uniform thickness of 7 inches throughout and varying in breadth from a minimum of 1 ft. 3 ins. up to 2 ft. 7 ins. – prodigious proportions by the standards of any other British building. It has been argued that this kind of timberwork is linked with Scandinavian traditions, but however this may be, Baguley Hall suggests the existence of a third school of carpentry quite separate from the eastern and western schools further south. Baguley, like Hafod, must have been quite exceptional in its region, from which it may be inferred that both houses belonged to men of greater local importance than did most of the Essex houses mentioned earlier. One other point about Baguley Hall is the curious roof structure, in which the collars of the main trusses support a purlin which runs underneath the collars of the common rafters and is braced upwards to king-posts. This structurally feeble hybridisation may result from copying the collar-purlin of south-eastern

98a

Right: (a) Farmhouse near Slimminge, Seeland, Denmark; (b) barns, Villa di Chiavenna, Val Bregaglia, Italy.
Page 86: (a) Farmhouse from Jaeren, now in the open-air museum at Bygdöy, near Oslo; (b) farmstead, Glaumbaer, northern Iceland; (c) dwelling-house near Cohasset, Massachusetts, 18th century; (d) John Ward House, Salem, Massachusetts, 1684; (e) Lippith Homestead, the Farmer's Museum, Cooperstown, New York, c. 1790; (f) farmhouse from south-western Finland, open-air museum, Helsinki.

84

a

b

a

b

c

d

e

f

a

b

c

d

e

f

a

b

Corner-post supporting jetty of a house at Smarden, Kent.

97d

Page 87: (a) Timber-framed house, La Saussaye, France, 16th century; (b) House, Long Itchington, Warwickshire, 17th century; (c) Dorphof, Epen, southern Limburg; (d) Pelser Farm, Epen, southern Limburg; (e) farmhouse, Elsegård, near Ebeltoft, Denmark; (f) Dick Turpin's Cottage, Hempstead, Essex, probably early 16th century, heightened, 18th century.
Left: (a) Round Shaker barn, Hancock, Massachusetts, beginning of the 19th century (cf. 56); (b) wheat barn, Cressing Temple, Essex, c. 1200.

89

tradition, because something comparable is found in fifteenth century roofs in the West Country.

Only one other timber-framed house in northern England can be dated with any probability before 1400, and that is the now ruinous aisled hall of Broadbottom, Mytholmroyd, near Halifax (Yorkshire). It had a long, tripartite plan originally and the timberwork, which has the Pennine characteristic of being almost totally devoid of ornament or enrichment, depends entirely on qualities of design to achieve its architectural effect. There is no spere-truss, such a thing being unknown in northeast England, where a more complete separation of passage from hall was customary. It was done by utilising a large timber and plaster canopy over the hearth called a fire-hood which needed, to resist the fiercest heat, a stone wall at the back of the hearth, and the wall, forming the lower part of the rear of the fire-hood, backed on to the entrance passage. Thus in this remote district the smoke was removed from a hall open to the roof at a time when the central hearth was universal elsewhere in England and Wales. Moreover the roof of Broadbottom has a kingpost supporting a heavy ridge-piece, to which it is braced, and this kind of roof hardly exists in the midlands or south except in an earlier and different guise. A king-post roof at Hafod, Rhiwlas, the farthest south of its kind, has a highly decorative form quite alien to the purely functional appearance of its counterparts in northern England.

The date 1400, though not a sharp dividing line in English timber architecture, nonetheless provides a useful break in this survey, for during the fifteenth century, nearly everywhere in England and Wales, stone-based timber houses began to be built by a social class or classes which had not built them before. As in earlier periods the difficulties of dating make it impossible to say with certainty when a particular change takes place. It is in the county of Kent that timber-framed houses first appear in numbers which indicate that the technique of prefabrication and the use of stone footings had become available to people who were not manorial lords, however minor. Informed observers agree that Kent has more timber-framed houses of a date prior to c. 1530 than any other English county, perhaps about two thousand, and even allowing for town buildings there are so many others that they must belong to a social class below manorial status. Unfortunately the social structure of medieval Kent is unclear. Among the peasants the custom of partible inheritance (gavelkind) prevailed, whereby a man's goods and property were divided at death equally among his sons, rather than primogeniture which enabled noble and knightly families to maintain undivided estates. This custom encouraged the morcellation of landed property, yet, as another stronghold of gavelkind, Wales, shows, its effects could be minimised if co-heirs agreed to run the whole inheritance jointly, each retaining his title to the appropriate share. This system may well have led to a wider diffusion of wealth than elsewhere and, coupled with the pull which the London market exerted at an early date, may account for not only the numbers of early houses, but, as some say, their actual form.

The most conspicuous house type in Kent is called the Wealden house, from the geographical name The Weald applied to the forest area lying between the North and South Downs. It has a tripartite plan comprising an open hall and a two-storey bay at each end, the whole being contained under a steep-pitched roof hipped at both ends. Houses of this sort fall into two classes; firstly, those in which all the outer walls are flush with each other, and, secondly, those in which only the ground-floor walls are flush, the upper storeys of the end bays being jettied forward at the front and sometimes on two or three sides. It is to the latter type alone that the name Wealden is applied, and which alone has the unmistakable appearance resulting from the upper parts of the walls being in two planes while the whole is covered by a roof of uniform width; consequently the plate at the eaves, which is carried well forward of the hall, is commonly supported by curved braces or brackets, and because there is a gap between this plate and the hall wall, some form of cove is provided to exclude draughts.

89

141a

Connections of some sort can be established between Wealden and earlier houses. Plan, two-storeyed ends, single-span hall, overall hipped roof – all are to be found at Gatehouse Farm before the middle of the fourteenth century, and excavation has revealed a late thirteenth century house rather like it at Joyden's Wood, Sittingbourne. However there is a gap of nearly a century between the Joyden's Wood house and the earliest Wealden house – Wardes, Otham, which is said to be of *c.* 1370 – but most examples of the type are apparently between about 1450 and 1530. One suggested evolutionary sequence, in which the more elaborate examples with end bays jettied on both sides and the characteristic front elevation repeated at the back are early and the simpler ones later, is contradicted by what little dating evidence there is; Pattenden, Goudhurst, which has front and rear jetties, is of the late fifteenth century and perhaps *c.* 1470, and on present evidence there is no reason to think it earlier than some front-jettied houses.

The difficulty of establishing the development of the Wealden house is bound up with a second problem, that of the diffusion of timber-framed building throughout all the strata of the Kentish peasantry. In this county smaller types of house are now being discovered which provide less accommodation and are less impressive in scale and architectural detail than the Wealden house. They belonged, presumably, to peasants of less substance, and despite claims for an earlier date they are likely to be contemporary with the Wealdens or even somewhat later. At Lyminge a fairly small house (by Kentish standards) has plain framing and a simple collar-rafter roof that by then was rather old-fashioned; the bay separated from the upper end of the two-bay hall by a partition wall is of two storeys, but the fourth bay at the lower end is, like the hall itself, open to the roof. It may be of the late fifteenth or early sixteenth century. A smaller version has a two-bay hall and a two-storey bay at the lower or service end, with provision for storing food and drink on the ground floor and a private chamber above. Smaller again (e.g. Winkhurst Farm, Chiddingstone) is a house of two equal bays, one storeyed and the other open and heated by a central hearth. That its smallness denoted a poor rather than an early house is confirmed by the inferior internal finish, so that, for example, the smoke-blackened hall side of the wattled partition between hall and first-floor room was not even covered with daub (tempered clay), let alone plastered. Yet humbler still, and at the bottom of that part of the social scale which is represented by surviving medieval buildings, is St. Mary's Grove Cottage, Tilmanstone, which had only two rooms, one heated by a central

Detail of façade, St. Peter's Hospital, Bristol, 16th century.

90

hearth and both open to the roof.

Thus while Essex, with which much of Suffolk can be linked, illustrates most clearly the evolution of timber-framed building, Kent has the wider social range. Although there is no dichotomy between the two areas one difference is that north of the Thames gabled roofs are commoner than the all-but-universal hipped roofs of Kent. Another is that the long tripartite house, comprising a hall between two end rooms under a hipped roof, appears early in Essex but does not persist there, being replaced in the fifteenth century by a type offering much the same accommodation in a plan of T- or H-form, i.e., with one or two cross-wings flanking the hall. More important than any such structural differences is a feature remarkable by comparison with the peasant houses of western Europe, and indeed of western Britain, namely the complete separation of the dwelling from the farm buildings, so that, as a German reviewer once remarked, you could not tell from the plans alone that these were farmers' houses.

The aesthetic qualities of south-eastern houses vary greatly, and it is perhaps its size and the interest of its main elevation which cause the Wealden house to be the most highly regarded type. Internally all types have much in common. South-eastern carpentry practice of the fifteenth century was rooted in a tradition of using members of uniform size which had not yet wholly yielded to the idea of concentrating the weight and thrust of a roof at particular points in the structure. Not until the sixteenth century did the kinds of roof outlined above culminate in the use of side purlins which were either tenoned into principal rafters or clasped between a somewhat enlarged common rafter and a collar-beam or sloping strut, and even then the new and the old types persisted together for fifty years or more. Against this structural background two contrasting effects are discernible; on the one hand richness, produced by complex and subtle mouldings worked on the main members and running continuously from wall to roof, and on the other severity arising from the use of close-spaced wall studs unbroken by bracing or rails. A second important kind of wall structure, called, from the frequency of its occurrence there, Kentish framing, has two large curved braces from the corner posts of the bay to the sill and is the usual way of framing the upper storey at the ends of Wealden houses. By the end of the fifteenth century these plain external effects were matched by the rich internal effect of linenfold panelling (in the best houses) and wall-paintings in many lesser ones.

Elsewhere in England the manner and pace of development were different. The contrast between the south-east and the rest of the country can be observed in its most extreme form in north-west England, where the timber houses of the Lancashire and Cheshire plain have little but their material in common with those of the Weald. The region was once extremely rich in large timber-framed buildings and despite the growth of industrial towns still possesses the most remarkable group of large timber houses in Britain. The techniques employed at Baguley Hall can hardly be traced in later houses apart from resemblances in the internal timbering of the early fifteenth century hall of Smithills, near Bolton. An early hall of quite different appearance is Samlesbury, near Preston, where a roof of wide span (26 feet) is supported by crucks – massive

81f

139c

27, 96a, b; 114e, f; 151a, b; 171a, b, d; 172a

Timber-framed house, Chester, 1552, rebuilt 1862.

91

timbers rising in a continuous curve from the foot of the walls to the apex – which, though common in smaller houses, are rare in those of this size and importance. More sophisticated in design and execution is a little group of late fifteenth or early sixteenth century halls, comprising Rufford, Speke and Ordsall in Lancashire, and Moreton and Adlington in Cheshire. Adlington is a rare example of a late-medieval timber house which is precisely dated, in this case by an inscription (now destroyed), to 1505, and the others probably fall within twenty years on either side of this date. Like nearly every medieval house of these two counties they have within the hall a spere-truss, a common draught-excluding device which is here developed into an architectural feature of some elaboration. Undoubtedly the finest are the nearly identical ones at Adlington and Rufford, where each face of the posts is worked as a series of trefoil-headed panels and is separated from the adjoining one by a roll-moulding; the posts are linked by a four-centred arch formed of two braces, the junction of which is masked by a carved boss (or rounded projection). These details are characteristic of the profuse enrichment found in many of the north-western halls, whether of the fifteenth or sixteenth centuries. A favourite form was the quatrefoil panel. At Rufford it is used, open, for the upper parts of the speres – the screens between the spere-posts and the side walls – while at the lower or entrance end of the hall similar panels with the quatrefoil shape filled with white plaster occupy the whole end wall above the service doors. Smithills had a row of these bold panels, all that remained of the original wall timbering of the hall, and there are many other instances of its external use. On a smaller scale they are found at Tatton Old Hall, near Knutsford (Cheshire), where they occur on the collar-beams facing the seat of honour at the upper end of the hall. At Tatton, Rufford and many other halls the quatrefoil motif is repeated on a large scale in the roof, by shaping each of the wind-braces with a cusp – a projecting member formed by two shallow curves. Here, too, on the tie-beams, is another favourite north-western ornament, the battlemented moulding, the upper part of which is like castle battlements in miniature. Rufford has this too on the tie- and collar-beams, and, indeed, on most other horizontal timbers. At Adlington a battlemented moulding decorates a beam which spans the hall above the dais or high seat, and which provides a housing for the great panelled canopy, of coved (quadrant) shape, whereon are displayed the arms of many Cheshire families. While this particular canopy is unique in its size and rich heraldic display many of the northern halls possess a more modest version of it, although unfortunately the most fully developed examples have been destroyed. One of those now lost was at Samlesbury, where the high seat and table, besides being under a canopy, stood between two side screens which shielded those seated there from draughts coming from two flanking doors leading to rooms in the upper end of the house. This arrangement suggests the interesting possibility that the upper and lower ends of the hall were symmetrically planned, the posts for the side screens of the dais being matched by the spere-posts at the passage end.

Another regrettable loss at Samlesbury was the massive panelled moveable screen which stood between the spere-posts and provided further protection from draughts; it was of late-Gothic appearance, bore an inscription stating that it was

139a
70

1

Right: Portau house, Jork, near Hamburg, 17th century.
Page 94: (a) Crown-post roof in a Wealden house, Harrietsham, Kent, end of the 15th century; (b) proto-hammer-beam roof, Bishop's Palace, Chichester, Sussex late 13th or early 14th century; (c), (d) timber-frames of houses in process of rebuilding; (c) Heydenreich farm, from Herzhorn, now in the open-air museum, Kiel, 1711; (d) Jagerspad house, Zaanse Schans, near Amsterdam, beginning of the 17th century (cf. 121, 193 c).
Page 95: Barn from southern Dithmarschen in process of re-erection, open-air museum, Kiel, 1782.
Page 96: (a) Brishling Court, near Maidstone, Kent, end of the 15th century; (b) the Swallows, Boughton Monchelsea, Kent, 1474.

a

b

c

d

a

b

a

b

c

d

a

b

c

d

a

b

c

d

built in 1532, and resembled closely the undated and slightly later screen which survives at Rufford. Both were capped by tall, boldly carved pinnacles as high again as the solid panelled screen itself, and since these occur on the screen at Pentre-hobyn (Denbighshire, North Wales) and in modified form at Worthiam Manor (Devon) they are likely to have been customary wherever such screens were used in western and northern England, and in Wales. Their aesthetic purpose was to fill the upper part of the opening between the spere-posts and so achieve an effect comparable to that of the speres themselves, which also had a solid screen below and an open one above.

While the planning of the hall itself did not differ greatly in Lancashire and Cheshire from the rest of England and Wales the houses there are often distinguished by an unusually long two-storeyed range of timber building at right angles to the hall block and sometimes now forming one wing of a square courtyard enclosed on three or four sides. In some cases a range of this sort is or was completely detached from the hall; thus all that remains of Denton Hall, Hyde (Cheshire) is a well-finished block of two storeys which stood near – but detached from – the upper or dais end of the old hall and has long been used as a barn. Agecroft and Speke Halls, near Manchester and Liverpool respectively, incorporated long wings with internal corridors on the courtyard side and generally plain timberwork enriched by the occasional splendidly detailed oriel or doorway. They seem too good and too large for servants and were perhaps ranges of lodgings for guests, or even virtually independent dwellings for members of an extended family, of a kind familiar at Gwydir and elsewhere in North Wales. The problem serves as a reminder that these houses, though built by some of the most important members of local society, were among the earliest domestic buildings thereabouts to use the technique of framed timber construction, so that in this respect Lancashire and Cheshire reached a comparable stage of development a clear century later than the south-eastern counties.

The contrast between north-west and south-east which emerges clearly in the fifteenth century is expressed in aesthetic and structural as well as economic and social terms; the two regions are poles apart. What of the rest of England? It is time to take up again the notion advanced earlier, that there are three distinct regional traditions or schools of carpentry in the country, overlapping with one another and interacting, each with its own characteristic structural and decorative forms and each containing the seeds of its own particular development. The first and most important aspect is that of roof structure. Excluding south-east England, which for this purpose embraces Norfolk, Cambridgeshire and all the Fens, and excluding also the county of Northumberland, cruck roofs are found everywhere in the earliest peasant houses, whether they are of late medieval or later origin. For the larger houses of the region the picture, though confused, is certainly different. For them, with rare exceptions, some kind of roof other than a cruck is used. Over the whole vast area, excluding only some northern counties, virtually all big roofs have principal rafters and purlins. Broadly they fall into two classes. There are those in which the purlins are fairly long timbers slotted into the backs of the principal rafters; and those in which the purlins are shorter timbers, each length being tenoned into the

Page 97: (a) Timber-framed house, Raren, Limburg, Netherlands, 16th century; (b) church at Greenstead, Essex, 11th century; (c) store-house, Rauland, Norway; (d) Manor House, Leeds, Kent, end of the 15th century. Page 98: (a) Baguley Hall, Cheshire, cross wall seen through spere-truss; 14th century; (b) crown-post roof, Nurstead Court, Kent, 14th century; (c) interior of barn (ridge supported by post to the ground) from Süderstapel, open-air museum, Kiel, 17th century; (d) posts resting on stone footings, town apothecary's, Tondern, Denmark, c. 1500.
Page 99: Roof-timbers: (a) Great Tithe Barn, Great Coxwell, Berkshire, mid-13th century, with alternating aisled and base-cruck trusses; (b) Barghus (granary), open-air museum, Kiel, 17th century; (c) cloisters of the ossuary at Montvilliers, 16th century; (d) Kapellbrücke, Lucerne, 16th century. Left: room from an Alsace farmhouse, now in the Musée d'Alsace, Strasbourg, 1796.

101

principal. Minutely technical though this differentiation is, it is important because the two types are differentiated geographically, the latter occupying a broad swathe of country from the south midlands to the south coast, along which it extends westwards into Devon, while the former occupies the remainder. Consequently the technical distinction has an important bearing on the origins and diffusion of roof structure and therefore on the way ideas and techniques were transmitted, and the limitations of their transmission, in the Middle Ages. Visually the importance of both these

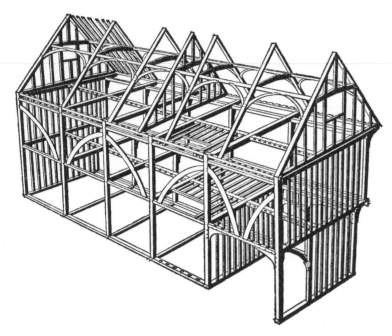

Timber framework of Paycocke's House, Coggeshall, Essex, c. 1500.

categories of roofs is that the general use of windbraces to form rigid triangles in conjunction with the principals and purlins permits – but it does not demand – decorative efforts of the Lancashire kind, though usually on a more modest scale. As already hinted, northern England must be partially excepted from these generalisations. In West Yorkshire, Westmorland and Cumberland the king-post roof is the usual thing, and whereas the finest examples in the first-named county are all severely plain and entirely lacking in ornament, those of the other two (where all medieval buildings have stone and not timber walls), show a paler version of the exuberant taste found in Lancashire. Therefore, excluding the characteristically plain roofs of West Yorkshire, and perhaps Durham and Northumberland as well, the whole of the western half of England and much of Wales forms one big region in which, over at least two centuries, a taste for particularly bold decorative effects appears in the larger roofs; and neither the taste nor the structural form it accompanies is found in the rest of the country. It is not, of course, found in every roof, and indeed some severely plain roofs with little even in the way of mouldings can be found throughout the whole area.

This geographical basis of styles is paralleled in timber-framing, where its most striking manifestations occur in the late sixteenth and early seventeenth centuries; and it may not be coincidence that by this time the use of roofs as a vehicle for architectural display had almost ceased. The fundamental structural division is

27

102

151a, b; 105

97d

141a

139b

142a

238c

102

144c

between eastern and western England, between walls which are essentially a succession of closely-spaced studs and those conceived as a series of squarish panels. In the latter type the wall is divided horizontally by at least one rail; in the Middle Ages there seem to have been two in the full wall height of an open hall, whereas in storeyed buildings there would only be one at mid-wall height in each storey. This rail, always perfectly plain, was incorporated into the framing as a structural member and served as a window sill where necessary. It is to be distinguished from the moulded timber found in a comparable position in Kentish and Essex houses, which is in the nature of an applied cornice without structural function, being halved on to the wall studs from the outside.

As with roofs, hybridisation occurred. In the midlands, and especially in the Severn valley and Warwickshire, close-studding began to be copied as a fashionable thing. Early examples of this spread of 'metropolitan' taste show close-studding much as it was in, say, Kent; but by the late fifteenth century it had become common to break the line of close studs by a middle rail, in what may be regarded as the native midland way. Close studding in this form became very popular and lasted far into the seventeenth century, long after its disuse in the south-east. Soon after the middle of the sixteenth century, more decorative kinds of framing began to be developed in the west. The change, following the abandonment of the open hall in which the roof was a principal means of architectural display, may have been due to the fact that the wall framing was then the only possible vehicle for large-scale ornamental effects. In the better two- and three-storey buildings of the Elizabethan age walls were divided into three heights of panels instead of two, and the first decorative treatment applied to them, in the 1560s, was a series of short diagonally-set timbers forming a herring-bone pattern. A decade or so later the square panels were filled with curved timbers to form a concave-sided diamond shape, which could be enriched by shaping each timber with cusps on both sides, and from then on for the next thirty or forty years the shaped infillings of the panels defy description as they become ever more elaborate. In the early seventeenth century there appears a taste for a more architectural kind of ornament, employing studs of the same outline as a stair baluster, and panels with the round-headed arch found in contemporary pulpits. The interior panelling which is so common at this period is normally plain but sometimes has miniature architectural forms of this sort. All these types of Elizabethan and Jacobean ornament persisted along the Welsh border and in central Wales to the middle of the seventeenth century.

It was in these remote borderlands that timber-framed building of the western school found one of its latest and most remarkable expressions. Here the cruck remained in use for large open halls long after it had been relegated elsewhere to the peasant house, so that a house of this type at Newchurch (Radnorshire), which may be of the late fifteenth or early sixteenth century, had the astonishing internal width of about 27 feet. In other houses the framed walls were variously ornamented with patterns designed to express the relative importance of the several parts or storeys. All this contrasts strikingly with the more restrained and sober timber framing of eastern and south-eastern England. There, by the second half of the sixteenth century, the open hall had everywhere been replaced by storeyed construction and in the countryside timber-framing was gradually falling out of use for manor-houses in favour of brick. The tradition of timber construction was carried on and developed by an emergent class of yeomen – farmers who were virtually freeholders – who, in East Anglia and the southern counties, built large numbers of rectangular internal chimney houses with either two or three ground floor rooms. This is a type of very distinctive appearance, so called because the chimney-stack does not touch any of the outer walls. The three-room version appears to be the earlier, those with two rooms being characteristic of the first half of the seventeenth century. All of them have perfectly simple framing, usually close studding, and the resulting architectural plainness is relieved by bay windows with carved or moulded sills, or by ornamental brick or terra-cotta chimney stacks. A very common feature is the placing of the front door directly in front of the chimney-stack, so that it opens into a little lobby between the two heated rooms (hence, 'lobby-entrance' type). Both two- and three-room forms seem to have been built in somewhat smaller versions, without embellishment, into the early years of the eighteenth century; but by this time timber-framing in southern and eastern England had run its course as an architectural style.

The beginnings of decline are observable after the Civil Wars with the spread throughout East Anglia of a fashion for boldly modelled decorative plasterwork called pargetting, which was an external manifestation of a general taste for high relief that appears in contemporary plaster ceilings, fireplace-surrounds, panelling and staircases. In the best examples human figures appear; generally, though, swags and fruit, with the occasional use of mouldings in relief to break up an elevation into panels, were the limits of the plasterer's ambition. The fact that some of the earliest and best work appears on medieval buildings which were altered in the middle years of the seventeenth century to bring them up to date suggests that pargetting was a device to conceal the resulting irregular and interrupted patterns, and for this purpose plainer styles of it continued in use throughout the eighteenth century. Commonly a plain surface was enlivened by inscribing combed patterns on it, and as the taste for plain frontages, relieved only by excellent proportions and carefully chosen architectural detail, grew throughout the eighteenth century, even these were abandoned. One factor in favour of plaster was that the increasing cost of wood caused builders to reuse old timbers so disfigured by mortises that they had to be covered up for appearance's sake; consequently from the middle of the seventeenth century onwards much new construction had to be plastered. The exceptions were the cottages of the smallholders and prosperous labourers in the west midlands, where sturdy exposed framing, reduced to its bare essentials, continued to be used well into the eighteenth century. By this time brick was universally used for all but cottages in those areas where timber had been common a century before, and the aesthetic effects which the rule of taste among patrons and operative builders produced in this material made the older framed houses look old-fashioned. To this most deadly sin in architecture was added the practical inconvenience of the small and heavily-mullioned windows on old houses, with the consequence that throughout the second half of the eighteenth century and the first half of the nineteenth there was a

183d

87f

Right: The Old Trumpet Inn, Pixley, near Hereford.
Page 106: (a) Room panelled in pine in the Gasthof Elephant, Brixen; (b) dining-room at The King's Head, North Weald Bassett, Essex (cf. 166).

a

b

a

b

a

b

c

d

great wave of refronting in brick. It was so common that west-midland towns such as Pershore (Worcestershire) and Alcester (Warwickshire) look brick-built, whereas they are to a large extent only brick-fronted. But even when a house was not refronted, in country and town alike, exposed timberwork was plastered over to meet the demands of fashion or to make it weathertight, with the result that today a great part of the wealth of seventeenth century and earlier timber houses with which England is endowed is hidden from all but the architectural historian.

Even then the tale of rural timber building is not quite told. In the Lincolnshire Fens and West Lancashire most of the seventeenth century farmhouses are of only one storey and attics, with a simple and often crudely built timber framework reduced to its bare essentials of principal posts (to support roof-trusses) and wall-plates, and the minimum of bracing to keep them upright. The thin walls are made up of rough untrimmed poles and twigs tied together and set directly on stone footings, the whole being rendered with clay and then skimmed over with plaster. Crude though such construction is it perpetuates an ancient method of building used in peasant houses before the introduction of timber sills and stone footings.

The structural and stylistic development of timber-framing in the countryside holds good for towns too, and with the same regional variations, but with differences of emphasis arising from the different functions of town buildings. Thus it is hardly surprising that aisled halls are unknown in towns because very little urban timber construction has survived from before the fifteenth century; and, as before, the reasons are to be found in economic and social history. English towns fall, very broadly, into two classes. On one hand there is a relatively small number of ancient towns founded before the Norman Conquest, most of which were from the first centres of local government as well as of trade, and on the other the great mass of post-Conquest towns founded purely for trade, and the two classes seem to have had different social structures which are reflected in their buildings. Many of the large towns in the first class had a few big stone houses in the thirteenth and early fourteenth centuries, some of them with a ground-floor hall and some with an upper first-floor hall. These are not likely to be merchants' houses but rather the town residences of locally powerful feudal families. By the late fourteenth century these towns have some large timber-framed halls, comparable in size to a manor-house, which may be successors of the earlier group and were perhaps built for a somewhat similar class; if not, for merchants of a very superior kind. The problem is complicated by the loftiness of these halls, some of which stand twenty feet high or more; thus one at Shrewsbury (in Castle Street – demolished) was a cube with sides of about twenty-one feet, and another at York (latterly known as the Fox Inn and also demolished) had its wall-plates at a height of twenty-six feet from the ground. In the latter case, and perhaps in the former, there must have been an upper floor about seven feet from the ground on which the open hearth stood, so that they resembled their stone predecessors in at least that respect. Other timber halls of the fourteenth and fifteenth centuries which stand well away from the street in a court-yard have all the appearance of a manor house transposed into a town setting except that where a gatehouse and its attendant buildings would be there is a row of shops

Page 107: (a) Hall at Harts House, Boughton Monchelsea, Kent, end of the 15th century, showing fireplace and ceiling inserted in the late 16th century; (b) hall at Paycocke's House, Coggeshall, Essex, c. 1500.
Left: (a) House with front loggia, west Prussia; (b) house in Saffron Walden, beginning of the 16th century; (c) farm-building from Cimpeni, Romania; (d) farmhouse, Emmental, Switzerland.

109

pierced by a wide opening in the middle. Houses like this in Shrewsbury are associated with burgesses rather than landowners and occasionally architectural detail suggests that a house was built at about the time when some member of the family presided over the town council as mayor or bailiff, or, in other words, that house and civic dignity alike express a peak in the family's importance.

In some towns of the second category there are timber-framed halls of the fifteenth century built on the street and parallel to it. Almost invariably the house is simply a straight range incorporating a small open hall and a two-storey bay of which the upper part is a 'solar' or private chamber. This is like a miniature version of the end-hall houses in the countryside at the same period, and it is puzzling that this type should have suited town dwellers so well, for they were evidently very common. In eastern England they may be found at Saffron Walden (Essex), right in the heart of the town next to the market place; in the midlands at the ancient cathedral city of Lichfield (Staffordshire), where in at least one case a pair of semi-detached cruck-houses was built; and in Weobley (Herefordshire), where there are two separate pairs of semi-detached Wealden houses, each house having a simple two-storey bay rather than the two usual in rural Kent. Most remarkable of all is a range of six Wealden houses in Spon Street in the much larger town of Coventry (Warwickshire), so that this particular house-type was built in big and small towns alike wherever land prices were low enough to make it worth while doing so. Besides these urban versions of rural house-types there is one peculiar to towns, a type with a two-storey range facing the street and, contiguous and parallel to it, an open hall. So far it has been found only in west midland towns, at Oxford, Shrewsbury and Coventry.

The existence of a range of identical houses implies speculative development, building in advance of specific need and without tailoring the plan or structure to individual requirements. It is very common to find building of this sort at the street corners of medieval towns, always of at least two storeys throughout and with each upper storey jettied out beyond the one below. Often there are four or five houses, three along the more important street and one or two at right angles to it; they are usually of two storeys, sometimes of three, and in the more ambitious projects the massive corner post was either enriched with architectural details like a contemporary church screen or, in some East Anglian towns, such as Lavenham, carved with human and animal figures. A particularly fine example in Ipswich (Suffolk) was a carving of the fox preaching to the geese. In these ranges each unit comprised either one room or one room and a lobby, or two rooms on each floor, and everywhere the top floor was open to the roof, i.e., the roof space was not used for attics. Development of this simple type in the sixteenth and seventeenth centuries took three forms. Generally, the frontage was reduced in width to one room and a passage at the side of it leading to a second room at the back, both rooms having fireplaces discharging into a common chimney-stack; and, with the passage replaced by a lobby, this was the plan of each of the upper storeys. During the last quarter of the sixteenth century use began to be made of the roof space, whether in the simplest way by flooring it over at the wall top and using gable windows; by putting in dormer windows to

144c

108b

141a

144f; 151a, b

171b

Right: (a) Nonsuch, the timber-framed pleasure palace built for Henry VIII of England, 16th century (after Speed's map of Surrey, 1611); (b) Palace of the Tsars, Kolomenskoye, 1667—81, log-built by Semyon Petrov, Ivan Michailov and Savva Dementiev, demolished in 1768 (after the engraving by Hilferding).

110

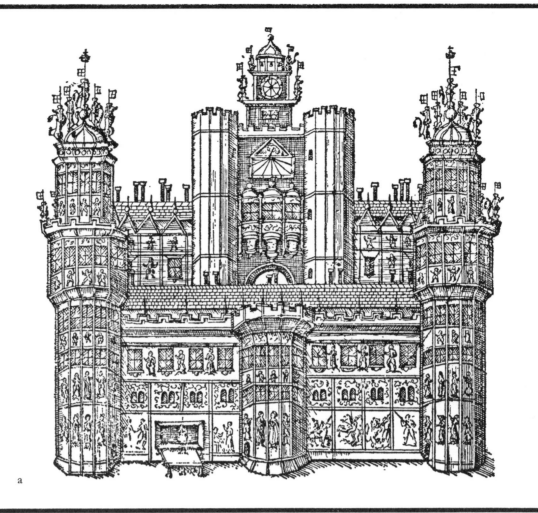

a

b

increase headroom and light at the same time; or by making the top storey into a
semi-attic, that is, with walls about three feet six inches high and with openings
contrived in the roof trusses so as to give easy access from one bay to the next. A
third way was to increase the height of a building, so that in the most flourishing
towns such as London, Bristol and Exeter four and even five storeys and attics were
not uncommon.

105

143; 184a

Use of the roof space produced one distinctive change of appearance from the
late medieval house; another was the proliferation of projections such as bay windows, which could be square, semi-octagonal or even semicircular in shape. A third
fashionable kind of projection in the early seventeenth century was the two-storey
porch, a feature now almost totally removed from town streets by two centuries of
schemes to produce 'regular' or 'polite' elevations or to ease the passage of pedest-
rians. Evidence of them comes largely from fines recorded in borough accounts for
posts encroaching on the pavement, and from empty mortises in Jacobean timber
houses; and in the smaller towns a few such porches yet remain. Something of the
effect of this fondness for projections can be gathered from a late sixteenth century
house in High Holborn and from its even more striking contemporary, Ireland's
Mansion in Shrewsbury. The latter is a building of three jettied storeys and attics,
and four bays wide; occupying the middle two bays was Thomas Ireland's own
house, each bay having a boldly projecting square bay window on the two principal
upper storeys. Flanking his own residence were two one-bay houses, each with a bay
window of semi-octagonal plan. Its several planes, the successive projection of the
storeys, and the proliferation of herringbone and other patterns combine to produce
an extremely rich and lively effect quite in harmony with the lavish, ostentatious,
yet withal dignified way of life expected of an Elizabethan burgess.

182c; 183d

175

172a, b

In the towns of western and northern England and Wales are to be found the
most striking evidence of the hold which timber-framing had over the imagination
of townsmen. It is the type widespread in western Europe which is known to Dutch
researchers by the useful name of the three-quarter house, from its having three
walls of stone and a timber front. How important the aesthetic effect of the timber
was can be seen from the fact that in the larger houses the principal elevation of a
rear wing facing a courtyard was also timber-framed. Examples are to be found in
south-western towns such as Launceston, Plymouth and Dorchester, where they
may be picked out by the use of massive moulded corbels carrying the gable-end walls
forward to match the timber jetties. Where freestone was not available for corbels
such houses are less conspicuous, as in Herefordshire, South Wales and the Lake
District.

184b

The last development of town architecture occurred in London and a few nearby towns, particularly Guildford (Surrey), where some imposing houses c. 1650–80 incorporated classical details in timber. Pediments over windows and doors were the
most conspicuous feature, the usual triangular shape being varied occasionally by the
introduction of a curved one, and always in conjunction with mullion-and-transom
windows. It never developed very far. In 1666 the great fire which destroyed the
City of London dealt urban timber architecture a blow from which it never recover-

*Right: (a) Post mills near Störlinge,
Sweden; (b) windmill, island of Am-
rum in the North Sea, 1771; (c) oil mill
'De Ooievaar', Zaandam, North Hol-
land, mid-19th century; (d) mill near
Hedsted, Denmark.*

a

b

c

d

a

b

ed. It was not so much the destruction caused by the fire itself as the subsequent building regulations drawn up to prevent its recurrence. The brick architecture they imposed produced new aesthetic standards at much the same time as the cost of timber and difficulties of supply were causing men to look to the new material for purely economic reasons; and by the end of the century the town house of timber was everywhere outmoded for new construction.

139d

A conspicuous feature of the smaller English and Welsh towns is the two-storey timber market hall which still exists in considerable numbers, especially in the west midlands; Ledbury is one such. The finest (its original purpose changed) is at Leominster (Herefordshire). As with all of them, the lower storey was originally open; its twelve Ionic columns support an upper storey projecting on all sides, which has decorative details of a quite unclassical kind including mermaids, grotesques and the various kinds of ornamental framing found locally. The upper chamber was used for meetings of the town council or by the magistrates, or both. But probably the *111a* finest and most monumental of the timber-framed buildings of England was Henry VIII's pleasure palace of Nonsuch, now demolished.

There was a lack of indigenous building timber in Scotland and as a consequence timber-framing disappeared after the seventeenth century. Buildings such as the Old Dow House in Perth, erected in the late sixteenth or early seventeenth century and demolished in 1896, and John Knox's house in Edinburgh are rarities.

Left: (a) Windmills on the 'Mill Hill', near Uusikaupunki, western Finland; (b) post windmills near Worms.

The King's Head, North Weald Basset, Essex, 16th century (cf. 106b).

The north-western part of the Netherlands, near the sea, was occupied by the former county of Holland, whose name foreigners always equate with the Netherlands. The name is supposed to be derived from *Holtland* (= wood land). During the Middle Ages large areas of the Rhine, Meuse and Scheldt deltas were covered with forest. In an area which was poor in natural stone, wood would obviously become the prime building material. The art of firing bricks was later discovered in regions where the soil was clay, but in many regions wood remained the material most commonly used for building. Throughout large areas of the country the soft subsoil did not permit excessive loading, so that wood represented the most suitable building material.

The early Christian churches were built of wood, and churches made entirely of wood were still being built in country districts into the late Middle Ages. In the town of Delft a temporary wooden church with a reed roof was put up as late as 1381. Throughout the whole of the coastal region wood continued even longer to play

26a; 34a, b an important part in church building, for medieval churches almost everywhere were roofed with wooden barrel vaults forming part of the external roofing of the building. The roof was held together at its base by tie-beams which spanned the space horizontally and were supported by masonry columns. The tie-beams usually have wall-posts and there is a rigid triangular structure between beam and post. This wooden framework prevented the walls from being thrust outwards.

The softness of the subsoil accounted also for the fact that wood was often used for the topmost part of the tower; the wood was sometimes then sheathed with

54a lead and the lead often painted in the colours of stone. The sequence of events during the building of the tower of the crossing in the church of St. Bavo in Haarlem is characteristic of the way work was done. First, in 1500, a stone tower was erected. Disquieting subsidences showed themselves during building, however, and it was taken down and replaced by a wooden structure which was completely sheathed with lead. The plan of the church called for stone vaulting, but the interior was roofed with imitation vaults made of wood. In the west and north Netherlands, too, a series of bell-towers were built entirely of wood. They are sometimes free-standing, near a church, and sometimes they form an integral part of the church.

The great spans of the roof structure in the halls of the nobility and of the monastic orders which were being built in Flanders and the western Netherlands even before 1300 are further examples of the quality of carpentry in the Netherlands. These buildings, and, indeed, many others, are comparable with similar structures in England. Here, however, there are no tie-beams, so that most of the lateral thrust has to be carried by the heavy wall posts. This remained the usual method of building in

117 the south-western Netherlands throughout the Middle Ages.

During the Middle Ages the dwelling-houses in the towns were built of wood, with the exception of the most important ones. As a result of serious fires the civic administrators issued strict regulations requiring the outer walls of houses to be built of stone. The main structure, however, remained the same as in all-wood buildings. In practice wooden side-walls and gables were replaced by a thin infilling of stone, but the weight-bearing structure and the back and front continued to be built of wood in the traditional way. Most of the partition walls inside the houses were 192; 284c

Left: timber-framed house, Mecheln, Belgium, 16th century; right: wooden house, Netherlands, 1530.

also made of wood. Only a few all-wood houses survive today in the cities of Flanders and the Netherlands, including Amsterdam, Antwerp and Bruges. Early engravings of cities such as Utrecht or 's Hertogenbosch depict many wooden façades in which each storey projects a few inches above the one below. This may account for the fact that the stone façades built later in the Netherlands were made to slope slightly forwards. 118; 119; 131a; 193b

Nearly all the houses built before 1650 in the west of the country have an internal wooden framework which served to keep the thin walls upright. This applies also to churches.

The tradition of building in wood persisted for much longer in the country. The houses in the small towns and farmsteads of the east were built with timber frames in a tradition dependent upon that of the neighbouring regions of Germany. The method of building in the extreme south-east is related to that of the bordering districts of the Ardennes and Eifel. The walls of these timber-framed houses were formed by filling the bays with wattle and daub, though at a later date these infillings were usually replaced by bricks.

A completely individual type of building in wood grew up in the province of North Holland. The regulations concerning fire prevention were less strict in the country than in the towns and it thus remained possible to build houses entirely of wood.

After 1600, thanks to the windmill, the area saw a great increase in the wood trade and the wood-sawing industry, both of which had been mainly centred in Amsterdam during the Middle Ages. The buildings of the district were not timber-framed but were wooden skeletons completely clad with wood. Side-walls were

121; 193 a, c, d

usually clad horizontally and gables vertically. The interiors of the living-rooms were also lined with very thin oak. Especially in areas north of Amsterdam, Zaanstreek, Waterland and the island of Marken, this method of building persisted into the second half of the nineteenth century. In the Zaanstreek, in particular, to which the windmills had brought a diversified and flourishing industry, the inhabitants

194 a; 195

went in for richness of workmanship in their houses, both inside and out. Façades erected during the eighteenth and early nineteenth centuries were showy and over-

258 a, b, d

decorated. They were usually painted green with white decoration and were in the current style of fashionable architecture. The interiors were extremely colourful, being painted blue, green and purplish-pink. Gazebos and garden pavilions were also built of wood. The wooden houses in the prosperous village of Broek in Waterland were much more restrained in form and architecture. Formerly the homes of shipowners and shipbrokers, they were all painted in light colours, and many of them were built on the medieval principle of the hall-house, in which the columns of the supporting structure are placed at a distance of more than a yard from the side-walls under the deeply overhanging roof. This method of building may go back to early medieval and even older types of house, such as excavations have uncovered throughout the Netherlands. The curious thing is that in the houses at Broek the rear part usually resembles the farmsteads of North Holland (which will be discussed later) but was still a dwelling-house. Most of the fronts of the houses were modernised during the eighteenth century, though they were not given as spectacular an appearance as those of the Zaanstreek. The small black tarred houses on the fishermen's island of Marken were even simpler. They stood close together on wharves, because of the floods which used to be a regular occurrence. Until the present century most of these houses had no chimney, unlike the other wooden houses of North Holland. The smoke rose through a hole in the loft and disappeared through an aperture in the roof. The wooden houses of the whaling village of De Rijp mostly have an upper floor in the manner of the earlier wooden houses in the towns. Elsewhere in the country this type is rare.

The Netherlandish manner of building houses in wood found its way as far afield as the New World, where houses of this kind were built in the Dutch colony on the banks of the Hudson River.

Warehouses too, in Amsterdam, the Zaanstreek, De Rijp and elsewhere, were

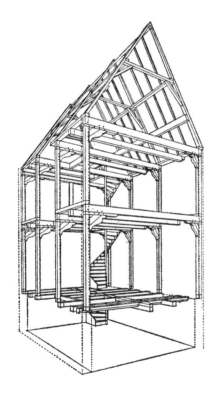

Timber framework, Groenburgwal house, Amsterdam, 16th century.

119

built of wood. Along the former sea-dike in a village in the northern part of North Holland there are still a number of storage-places for peat built entirely of wood. Seaweed was stored in this district in wooden barns.

194b

The farmsteads of North Holland were usually built of wood. In fact they consist of an enormous hay-shed, round which men and animals were housed, the whole under a pyramidal roof. In this district free-standing hay-sheds too were clad with wood to protect the precious winter cattle feed from wind and weather.

Further south, in Zeeland, Brabant and Flanders, the farmsteads have long barns under deep continuous thatched roofs; their walls consist of wooden posts and are mostly clad with black tarred boards. The white surrounds which appear on many doors are characteristic of this region. These large barns with their wooden weight-carrying structure evolved out of the vast barns of the medieval monasteries. Here also there are great similarities between the Flemish and English barns, Normandy perhaps being the intermediary. The large tobacco barns which until the nineteenth century continued to be built in the south-eastern part of the province of Utrecht are characteristic, and their construction is related to the method of building found farther east, where a series of tie-beams carries the weight.

After the Reformation in the second half of the sixteenth century wood remained an essential factor in church building. Roof-frames, vaults and towers were the parts most often constructed of wood. Bricks were the accepted material for the walls of the buildings of the state-recognised Reformed Church, but the exteriors of the churches of denominations which were tolerated only from sheer necessity were made to resemble barns. In North Holland, where in country districts everything was built of wood, there are many such barn churches; they are simple but their proportions are always very pure. The interior architecture is plain too, being entirely of wood, and has great charm. The wooden floors, which are usually strewn with sand, the seats, and the church furniture, such as pulpit and font, are all most carefully carpentered. The body of these churches differs greatly from the elongated medieval type. They are sometimes almost square in plan, with galleries, and the seats are grouped round the pulpit, whence the word is proclaimed. There are also a few rather small Catholic churches that were built in this spirit. Even the altar is wooden, although it is painted to look as though it were made of marble. The same applies to many painted wooden inner walls, floors and ceilings in houses in North Holland.

38a, b

A few seventeenth century churches of the state-protected Reformed Church were also built of wood. Thus the church of the fishing village of Volendam resembles a barn in structure and form. The same type is found in other places. A wooden church of this kind was even built in Amsterdam in 1750, although with the idea that it would soon be pulled down. It is, however, still in use. The interior was altered in the nineteenth century in the spirit of the Gothic Revival.

A wooden theatre in the neo-classical style was erected in the same city in 1773 and remained without a stone cladding until 1872. It was burnt down in 1890. One of the last wooden orphanages was burnt down in the Zaanstreek in 1967. The last wooden orphanage was erected in the Zaanse Schans, a reserve where important specimens of the wooden architecture of the Zaan have been assembled. The whole area has been reorganised as a quarter where people live in old restored houses surrounded by other wooden buildings, in which the Zaanstreek is so rich. There, among other things, is the shed of a shipyard where wooden ships used to be built. In the immediate neighbourhood too there are many windmills of widely varying types. It was the windmills with their diverse functions which once brought such great prosperity to the Zaanstreek.

113c; 117; 123c; 124a

The first windmills made their appearance, probably in the southern Netherlands or in England, in the thirteenth century. The veering winds of the coastal regions compelled their builders from the beginning to equip these great apparatuses with a machine to bring the sails to face the wind. Thus it was that in the course of time various types of mill evolved. The earliest, meant for grinding corn, consist of a large body which can rotate on a wooden axis, is supported by four struts and stands on the ground. Because of its structure this type is known as a post mill. The rotating part was later made smaller and smaller, until finally only the head with its cross of sails could be turned. Mills were used for various industrial purposes. They

123c

often stand on a long wooden shed in which the work is done and the material stored. Wooden sawmills made their appearance in the Zaanstreek in about 1600. The whole vast wooden structure stands on a circular track of hardwood rollers. These so-called smock mills formed the basis for the Dutch wood industry which was developing at that time. Other types too were later used as sawmills. Large tracts of the low-lying coastal areas of Holland were reclaimed from the sea with the aid of mills, the water being brought up with scoop-wheels or wooden screw jacks.

A country with as much water as there is in the Netherlands will obviously have many bridges. Many of them are made of wood. It was essential that those in the shipping-lanes should be movable. Thus the quite individual form of the Dutch drawbridge evolved. One of these drawbridges is preserved in the open-air museum at Arnhem which exhibits examples of the rural architecture of the Netherlands. Many aspects of the wooden architecture of the countryside are represented there. The rural architecture of the Flemish-speaking part of Belgium has been most carefully assembled and grouped according to district in the open-air museum at Bokrijk.

124a, b

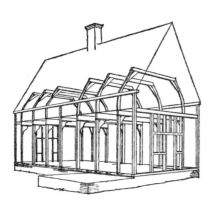

Timber framework of the Jagerspad house, Zaanse Schans, north Holland, beginning of the 17th century (cf. 94d, 193c).

Wood is a perishable and inflammable material. This is why only a fraction of the architecture in wood of past ages has survived. With wood, however, buildings can be erected which form a durable whole on a unstable subsoil. It is true that wooden piles were rammed into the soft ground for support, but they were not strong enough to bear much weight. Massive subsidence in medieval church buildings remained without serious consequences because the wooden structure of the roof-frame was sufficiently elastic to absorb changes of shape and sufficiently rigid to support the walls. Today, as in the past, wooden houses and mills are often taken up and moved. That is practically impossible with stone buildings. The people of the Netherlands have learnt all this by experience and extensively put it into practice. Which is why in a country so poor in building materials they have usually chosen wood: it is not very heavy and it withstands both tension and compression, whereas stone, which is much heavier, can only withstand pressure. Because the people of the Netherlands have had so much experience over the centuries in the handling of wood, their carpentry has always been of a high quality. It is still true that Holland = *Holtland* = wood land.

One of the earliest representations of a post windmill in the Netherlands or England, from Stowe MS 17, in the British Museum, c. 1300.

Right: (a) Post windmill, Ouarville, near Chartres; (b) windmill, Tibberup near Copenhagen, mid-19th century; (c) sawmill 'De gekroonde Poelenburg', Zaandam, north Holland, 1867; (d) windmill Kizhi, Karelia.

122

a

b

c

d

a

b

V Wood Building in France

Timber-framed Buildings, Churches, Charnel-houses and Chalets

In earlier times building in wood was common throughout France, except on the Mediterranean coast. In the course of centuries, however, it has greatly diminished and is now confined to certain distinct regions. Thus many wooden buildings are still found in the villages and towns of Normandy, Champagne, Alsace, in the Loire valley and in many towns of Picardy and Burgundy, and in western Brittany and the Massif Central. They have a character of their own in the Pays Basque, Bresse and the Alps.

In a timber-framed house, in the full sense of the word, the exterior and interior walls, ceilings and floors, are supported by a wooden frame. Posts, joists and plates and the rest of the frame are so jointed together as to make it impossible for the whole thing to go out of true, or 'roll'. Posts, main joists, tie-beams and roof-trusses lie in the plane of the gable, other posts and plates in the plane of the lateral walls. Anchor-beams and keys lock the various members together at the joints, while the studding contributes to the rigidity of this kind of cage.

The earliest surviving timber-framed houses in France are in Normandy and were probably built at the end of the fourteenth century (Rouen: the houses at 139 and 141 rue de la Grosse Horloge, 85 and 133 rue Saint-Hilaire, 52 and 54 rue Saint-Romain; Caudebec-en-Caux: the house called La Corroirie). The timber-framed houses of Bourges and Alsace appear to date only from the beginning of the sixteenth century.

From the fourteenth century onwards the carpenters were masters of their craft. They had improved upon the simple trussed-rafter roof in introducing wind-bracing between the trusses, in the form of a ridge-piece and, lying parallel to it and lower down, a collar-purlin, both of them being strutted by braces which were often in the form of a St. Andrew's cross (saltire). Finally, in the sixteenth century – though it was considerably earlier in Rouen – purlins made their appearance and altered and simplified the truss. We have only to think of the number of different ways of jointing wood which the carpenter already had at his command – the dovetail and the half dovetail, the plain lap-joint, the notched lap-joint, the mortise and tenon, the through tenon using the full thickness of the beam, the slotted tenon, the single tenon, and so forth. Equipped with these he could solve the most difficult problems. So solid were the joints that often nowadays when a building has to be demolished it is necessary to saw through the posts and beams because the joints cannot be parted.

Usually only oak was used, except in the case of alpine chalets, for which conifers – fir or spruce – were used because they were lighter and more weather-resistant.

As long as the forests were able to produce timbers of large dimensions, posts extended from ground to roof. Joists and plates were grafted together by tenons which were secured by wooden keys or pegs, reinforced by rails and braces. The

Left: (a) Post windmill from Mol, now in the open-air museum, Bokryk, Belgium, 1788; (b) Haspengau farm, open-air museum, Bokryk, Belgium.

125

earliest and most solid ridge-joints were T-shaped.

Long timbers are found in widely separated localities – in Lisieux, Honfleur, Caen, Louviers, Vernon, in the Pays d'Auge, in the Landes, the Ardennes, on the Meuse and the Marne, and in Savoie, Alsace and elsewhere.

By the second half of the fourteenth century and the fifteenth century, however, full-grown trees had become so scarce that the use of short posts became general. This was why multi-storeyed buildings made their appearance at this time (in northern France, Saint-Jean de Dijon, 1468); and Philibert de l'Orme in his work *Nouvelles inventions pour bastir à petits fraiz* (1561) explained the system of planks set on edge and pegged together which he himself employed in the châteaux of Anet and La Muette. Nevertheless, in his book of 1623, *Masnière de bastir pour toutes sortes de personnes,* Le Muet was still explaining how to build wooden houses that rise from the ground.

Structures in which short timbers were used required different and more complicated framing than did houses with long timbers. Much more care was needed to ensure the rigidity of the whole. Besides the braces which were already in use, brackets now made their appearance: in Rouen they were called *pigearts* or *pigeatres* and were a kind of triangle made of wood used to strengthen the internal angle between the posts and rails. Besides this the carpenters now left a thickening at the top and sides of the posts, called a shoulder (or jowl), which would prevent the beams slipping down should the tenon on the post give way; this was the joint *à demi-enfourchement.* Dovetailing was used to prevent the horizontal members, plates and bearers, from parting company.

One particular kind of jointing *en enfourchement* has yet to be described. It made its appearance in Rouen in the seventeenth century and remained in use throughout the eighteenth century. The end of the beam was tapered to form a trapezoid and was then fitted into the head of a post which had been hollowed out to receive it. Judiciously placed tenons ensured that beams and rails remained rigid.

Construction became yet more skilful when – probably during the fourteenth century – houses began to be built with oversailing upper floors (jetties); this was in fact the period when urban civilisation began to evolve in walled towns. The successive projections increased the area of each storey to a small but nevertheless useful degree which was most welcome to the members of a crowded community. However, these projecting storeys made the narrow streets dark and unhealthy and, towards the end of the fifteenth century, the authorities felt obliged to prohibit them. But so little attention was paid to the regulations that they had to be repeated several times and it was not until 1532 that builders began, reluctantly and with many deviations from the law, to comply. Houses with jetties were rebuilt in Troyes after the fire of 1524 that destroyed the greater part of the city; and very fine jettied seventeenth-century buildings exist in Strasbourg to this day.

131c; 162a, b, d; 163; 164b; 174; 182a; 184c; 232d

During the eighteenth century the jetty gradually disappeared, but wooden buildings continued to be put up throughout the nineteenth century. When from about 1875 onwards, however, the use of timber from the north made it possible to build extremely light frameworks, timber framing in the old sense quite lost its point.

Gable in the rue des Boucheries, Lisieux.

In jettied houses built with short timbers it no longer sufficed simply to tenon the main and common joists and the plates to the posts; much more complicated methods were needed to hold all these superimposed members in position. We may distinguish three different forms of jettying: with main joists or bearers; with common joists; and with *pigeatres.*

With the first type the main joists oversail the posts and are visible outside. Their ends support the sill-beam into which the posts and studs for the upper storey are tenoned. Behind the sill-beam of the upper storey lies the wall-plate of the lower storey, in which the upper ends of the studs and posts of the lower are housed. The main joists may be strengthened either inside or out by braces, brackets or *pigeatres.*

The method using common joists is similar to the previous method, only they are laid closer together than main joists. It is found in Brittany and in central and eastern France.

Oversailing storeys on *pigeatres* seem to have been restricted to Rouen and were clearly systematically employed in order to avoid the necessity of using common joists. In this case the outer ends of the posts were strengthened by triangular brackets tenoned into them. The wall-plate of the lower storey rested on the post, the sill-beam of the upper storey on the *pigeatre.*

In the second half of the fifteenth century, builders began to place the beams of floors and ceilings at such a height that it was possible to fit another rail between them. This intermediate rail was tenoned to the posts and increased the rigidity of each bay, gave the façades greater solidity, emphasised the overhang and made it possible for decoration on the projecting storey to extend from the wall-plate to the sill-beam. It represents the culmination of jettied construction.

Jetties carried on braces continued for centuries to be used for the important fronts of buildings and rural dwellings; in Rouen they ceased to be fashionable during the sixteenth century, but reappeared during the eighteenth.

Probably the earliest houses, which consisted only of a ground floor, had no stud-work but the bays between the posts were filled by a thick layer of cob. This method can still be seen in certain cottages near Caux in Normandy.

In storeyed houses, though, studding was indispensable for supporting the wall-plates as well as the infilling. This, however, was made thinner so as to be lighter. Triangulation was achieved by the use of braces – small, slightly inclined timbers – to maintain the right angle between vertical and horizontal members. They were usually placed near the corner-posts in order to leave the central area of the façade as free as possible from windows, which were often very numerous.

Triangulation was logical if the brace joined a plate and a post; the rigidity of the angle was mathematically assured. Structures of the kind are found in Normandy, west of the Seine in the Lieuvin – where, sometimes, three braces, one above the other, cut across a right angle – and also in the Loire valley. In Rouen, on the other hand, the braces connect only the wall-plate with the sill, consequently resistance to wind-pressure is less, but the vertical posts are not weakened by mortises. It is also the braces that give the façades of Alsace a character of their own: in each bay of a storey a long brace cuts across the lower angle, and a short brace across the upper

196b

127

one; the two mortises which receive them lie side by side on the post. This method is found throughout western Germany, too.

141b, c, d; 162c; 174; 196b

Saltire-braces are just as common as simple braces. They were tenoned into post or plate and the point of intersection was secured by halving. The earliest saltire known in a French timber-framed building is depicted on a Gallo-Roman bas-relief in the museum at Vienne (Isère); such representations of timber-framed houses of a period from which no actual buildings have survived are extremely rare.

The intermediate rails forming continuous lintels and sills to the windows also helped to stiffen the façade.

The wall-space below the windows was invariably filled by V-shaped saltire braces but when, during the seventeenth century, windows became larger, this framing became more complicated. To provide support and to decorate the façade a new element made its appearance and became a test of the craftsman's skill; it was ornamentation, which was first restricted to two kinds of motif. One consisted of a lozenge supported by two uprights and containing a cross; and the other was a *rayonnant* motif made up of four sets of two parallel braces forming a small lozenge at the centre. The first of these ornaments appeared over a wide area, the second more particularly in western Normandy and in Picardy.

Décharges couplées or paired braces made their appearance in Rouen in the seventeenth century and remained in use until the end of the eighteenth. The braces are inserted quite far down into the posts, pass obliquely in opposite directions under the window and finish far along the sill-beam of the wall.

In Alsace the arms of the saltire were bent into elegant curves and reverse curves, sometimes with a kind of branch as well, so that the triangles of the infilling took on the shape of clover-leaves. This pattern, occurring only in Alsace and western Germany, was also used with very large saltires which extended to the full height of a storey.

137

The greater the number of storeys the more important did the studding become as a form of support. Usually the number of studs was increased (Rouen: houses at 72 rue Beauvoisine and 50 rue Saint-Nicholas; Strasbourg: Maison Kammerzell); sometimes they were assembled in a trellis forming either squares (Vitré, in Brittany) or lozenges (Anjou, Touraine, Berry: house in the rue Cambournac and Maison Pelvoysin and others in Bourges), or even a radial motif (Picardy). In Alsace, where timber-framed houses were larger than in any other French province, builders were content to increase the size of posts, braces or saltires.

The spaces between the studs were at first filled with clay or earth tempered with chaff, which gave a fairly thick wall, such as can be found today in the countryside of Normandy, the Landes, and Bresse. When the number of studs was increased the wall thickness was reduced and the puddled clay was reinforced by a trelliswork of thin branches (i.e. wattle and daub). In town houses, however, plaster quickly replaced clay. The infilling was now little more than ten centimetres thick and was sometimes fixed to the frame with wooden pegs. Infillings of tiles and bricks – sometimes very thin – occur frequently in manor-houses and rural buildings in Normandy, the Basque country, the Loire valley, Bresse and Picardy. The bricks were

Right: (a) Kitchen, Rygnestad farm, Setesdal, 16th century; (b) room from a farmhouse at Pettnau in the Arlberg, now in the Österreichisches Museum für Volkskunde, Vienna, c. 1700; (c) living-room in the Old Friesian House, Keitum, on the island of Sylt, 18th century; (d) royal chamber in the Freuler Palace, Näfels, Glarus, 1642–1647.
Page 130: (a) Courtyard of the Alte Hofhaltung, Bamberg, 1576; (b) inner courtyard, Lord Leycester's Hospital, Warwick, mostly 15th century.

128

a

b

c

d

a

b

a

b

c

d

a

b

c

d

often laid in a herring-bone pattern, but their arrangement can vary and produce original designs, as in Picardy. In other districts, however, as for example the Basque country, the bricks were covered over with mortar.

137

In the fifteenth century, instead of plaster, well-to-do patrons commissioned richly-carved wooden panels. Celebrated examples are the Maison Kammerzell in Strasbourg and the house of Diane de Poitiers at Rouen, which was destroyed in the Second World War. Plaster remained in use, even so, during the seventeenth and eighteenth centuries because it lends itself well to carved or moulded ornament.

Gable-ends and longitudinal walls were protected by the roof, which as a rule, especially in rural buildings, had a wide overhang. Sometimes, however, the walls were clad from top to bottom with wood panels or slates; these were sometimes arranged in simple patterns such as squares, lozenges and zig-zags (Morlaix, Rouen). Sometimes the covering protected only the timbers to which it was nailed and the masonry of the infillings remained visible (manorial dovecot at Fay, by Bourg-

144d

Achard and the Auberge du Vieux-Puits at Pont-Audemer (Eure); manor-house of Pierre Corneille at Petit-Couronne (Seine-Maritime) and others).

171c; 183b

Decoration was usually confined to the frame and only exceptionally extended over the infilling. It made its first appearance at the beginning of the fourteenth century and developed during the Renaissance. The carved ornament hardly differs from that on religious or secular stone buildings. Plates, sills and rails are often worked into convex or hollow mouldings, beads and cavettos which catch the light and give the overhangs in Rouen and Morlaix their finely articulated outlines. In the Loire valley and at Lisieux and Macon no great store was set by the decoration of the horizontal members; but here more often than in Rouen posts and brackets are carved in high relief, with Gothic pinnacles, Renaissance candelabra, human figures and whole scenes, and there are ornaments such as scale patterns, cable moulding, leaf-stem patterns and fluting. When the infilling was faced with wood, panels were always richly carved; when bricks were used they were often laid in geometric patterns. In Caen there are buildings where the plaster is inlaid with coloured cement; in Beauvais square varnished plaques were applied to the rough infilling; in Alsace the infilling was sometimes painted.

There are few timber-framed churches in France. They number about twenty in all and, except for the church of Sainte-Catherine in Honfleur (Seine-Maritime), all are in the departments of Aube, Marne and Haute-Marne, that is, in the southern part of Champagne near the great forests on damp clay soil. Generally these churches are fairly small.

Page 131: (a) Street in Titograd, Yugo-slavia; (b) 'Het Houten Huis' in the Beginenhof, Amsterdam; (c) street in Vannes, Britanny; (d) street in the old town, Plovdiv, Bulgaria.
Left: Interiors: (a) Satakunta, Finland; (b) open-air museum, Bygdöy, near Oslo; (c) Grimstrup, Denmark; (d) Grenjadharstadhur, Iceland.

When Sainte-Catherine was built, towards the end of the fifteenth century, the church comprised a nave and two aisles; but it was enlarged later and today has two adjoining naves of uniform height and of twelve bays, each flanked by an aisle. Each nave has a wooden pointed barrel-vault like an upturned keel, worthy of a Norman ship-builder. Sturdy octagonal posts rise from the ground to support the plates and the exposed tie-beams carrying the king-posts. The wooden apses were rebuilt in brick when the church was thoroughly renovated in 1879.

28

The ground-plans of the churches of southern Champagne vary: aisleless nave and polygonal apse at Chatillon-sur-Broué (Marne), Morembert (Aube), La Loge-aux-chèvres (Aube), the chapel of Saint-Gilles at Troyes, now destroyed, the chapel of Saint-Jean at Soulaines (Aube); aisled nave and polygonal apse at Lentilles (Aube), Bailly-le-Franc (Aube), Drosnay (Marne); aisleless nave and transept at Perthes-les-Brienne (Aube), Saint-Léger-sous-Margerie (Aube), Dammartin-le-Coq (Aube); aisled nave and transept with a polygonal apse at Oustine (Marne) and with a square-ended chancel at Longols (Aube). Mention should also be made of the churches of Chauffour-les-Bailly, Epagne, Epothémont, Juzanvigny, Mathaux, Pars-les-Chavanges and Villiers-le-brûlé, all in the department of Aube.

The sill-beam was usually laid on a masonry footing and the posts rising from the ground were jointed into it. The posts support a trussed-rafter roof with tie- and collar-beams. A plate joins the posts and an outer plate resting on the ends of the tie-beams, which are supported by braces, carries the wide roof. The roof, incorporating ridge-piece and collar-purlin, is reinforced by struts, braces or saltires. Sometimes – as at Dammartin-le-Coq or Perthes-les-Brienne – the roof is panelled, or hidden by a ceiling on joists, as at Oustine, Lentilles, Chatillon-sur-Broué, Bailly-le-Franc. The wall-posts have braces, saltires or cruciform ties. Simplicity is the rule in the arrangement of the timbers.

In some churches the roof covers both nave and aisles so that there are windows in the aisles only (Oustines). Sometimes, however, the nave and aisles each have their own roof and the nave windows open high above the roof of the aisle (as a clerestory) to light the church from above. The windows are in general undecorated. But mention should be made of the church of Lentilles where the chancel and apse are lit by circular windows above rectangular ones.

These churches were obviously built economically. The infillings of the wall were held by laths forced into the panels and consisted of a mixture of earth, chaff and plaster, whitewashed over.

The churches were sometimes embellished by a timber porch which ran the length of the west front: e.g. Saint-Jean de Soulaines, Bailly-le-Franc, Drosnay, Longsols and others. The naves of Lentilles, Oustine, and Longsols, among others, are surmounted by a sharp-pointed wooden spire astride the ridge. Little fantasy went into the building of these small churches; their appearance is humble and modest, though they are well constructed.

Timber-framing includes a whole gamut of buildings ranging from the mean little house which looks more like a hut to the tall building with many windows and a superabundance of carving.

The façade may be flush or jettied, the framing may be exposed or covered by shingles or slates, the gable on the street may reveal the whole width of the roof or the roof may project far beyond the long walls – but in every case these houses have a medieval air, and indeed this is literally true, for not only were they very numerous in the Middle Ages, they were also the predominant type of building then. Timber-framed buildings were still being erected in the nineteenth century though the last ones were small and insignificant, wood having long since been replaced by stone.

Wood evokes the forest and the forest was of exceptional importance during

134

Detail of the façade of a house in the Grand-Place, Roye, 16th century.

the Middle Ages. It is true that robbers had their hiding-places in the dense forest but it also kept over-turbulent neighbours and plundering bands at a distance. If it was frightening, it was still a comfort to have nearby, for it provided part of the daily food as well as wood for heating and building. The wood which the carpenters hewed and cut with their great axes seemed to bring the forest itself into the city; and the urbanised and domesticated forest, for all that it had been forced into geometric forms, still retained something of the feel of organic life. We find this air of primal nature in beams which have sagged, in posts which have begun to lean, in roof-beams which are no longer level, as though, still animated by a breath of their forest life, they refuse to accept the immobility which spells petrification and death.

This feeling of the nearness of nature is one of the forms of Gothic sensibility and an expression of a social life which was simple in organisation but solid; it is evoked by the very names of the streets in which timber-framed houses once stood – everyday names, but ones which have not lost their evocative power: rues des Bateliers (boatmen), des Dentelles (lace), du Fossé des Tanneurs (tanners) in Strasbourg; rues des Marchands (shopkeepers), des Serruriers (locksmiths), des Tanneurs in Colmar; rues du Pont-des-Brouettes (wheelbarrows), des Teinturiers (dyers) in Abbeville. In Morlaix there are the Grande Rue, the rue Basse, rues des Bouchers (butchers) and des Vignes (vines); in Rouen the rues de la Grosse Horloge (clock), de la Tuile (tile), de la Pie (magpie). Caudebec-en-Caux has the rue de la Vicomté, de la Cordonnerie (shoe-making), des Halles (market), de la Boucherie; Angers the rues Beaurepaire, des Filles-Dieu, de l'Oisellerie (bird-selling). In Lisieux we find the rue des Fèvres (metal-workers), in Blois the rue des Orfèvres (goldsmiths). There is a place de l'Herberie (grass market) at Macon and a place du Vieux-Marché, rue Mercière (haberdashers) and des Bouchers at Billon.

The names that were given to specially handsome and richly decorated houses are just as much alive – names inspired by history or legend and also by everyday life. There is a Maison d'Adam in Angers, a Maison de la Reine Bérengère in Le Mans; maisons du Carroir Doré and de la Chancellerie in Romorantin; de l'Homme de Bois (the wooden man) and des Péchés capitaux (the deadly sins) in Thiers. The Maison de la Reine Berthe is in Chartres, the Logis de la Duchesse Anne in Morlaix, the Hôtel du Grand Cerf in le Grand Andelys; the Maison de la Salamandre in Lisieux; the house of Diane de Poitiers and the Logis de Saint-Amant in Rouen; the Maison de l'Image de Saint-Jean is in Beauvais. Narrow streets where the houses draw closer together the higher they rise, where windows increase as the light gets less, where storeys rise irregularly tier upon tier, where brackets emerge from the shadow and weather-boards reflect the light – everything seems to live and move and adds to the atmosphere of that warm, crowded life our ancestors lived. We have only to shut our eyes to see it all before us.

Sometimes at a street-corner or in a little square we come upon a façade more richly decorated than the others. This was once the home of a prosperous merchant or of a noble family. We will describe three of the best known.

The so-called house of Diane de Poitiers was unfortunately destroyed during the Second World War. It stood in the Rue de la Grosse Horloge in Rouen. It was

164b; 174

163

built after 1525 and had a façade of which the whole length was taken up by Renaissance windows with mullions and transoms. The windows of the upper storey were less conspicuous and on the top floor there was only one. The plates and sills were decorated with a frieze of foliate design, while the brackets of the jetties were carved with all kinds of grotesques and human figures. The little columns under the window-sills were in the form of slender balusters. The infilling of wooden panels was covered with carvings and the windows of the second storey were framed by two medallions. The history of this house is unknown, but it was the most richly decorated of all the houses in Rouen.

We know that the Maison Kammerzell in the Place de la Cathédrale in Strasbourg was rebuilt by Martin Braun, a cheese-merchant, in 1589 and that it was heavily restored in 1892. It consists of three oversailing storeys above a ground-floor of ashlar stone. Transomed Renaissance windows occupy the full length of both façades; the timber-framing consists only of posts stiffened by very short braces. All the timbers are covered with carving. The sills and plates are moulded and foliage friezes run along the window-sills. The vertical members are even more richly decorated: on each floor there is a large corner-post carved in the form of a human figure. One represents Faith standing on an eagle, another Hope on a gryphon and the third Mercy on a pelican. The other posts are in the shape of herms or of very much elongated human figures or animals; there are shell motifs and inscriptions. The little posts below the window-sills have been carved in a richly realistic manner: there are musicians, signs of the Zodiac, old men, dogs and so on. Although it was over-restored in 1892 (the paintings date from that period), the house remains one of the jewels of Renaissance timber-framed architecture.

137

La Maison de la Salamandre, which before the Second World War stood in the Rue aux Fèvres in Lisieux, was also remarkable for its decoration. The carving of the vertical members was even richer than that of the horizontals: the great posts carried animals, birds, monkeys and human figures, including soldiers, savages and musicians, all powerfully carved in broad planes out of the solid oak. The brackets were similarly decorated. Small posts were carved into pinnacles like little bell-turrets and were covered with motifs such as shells, stars and cable-moulding, broken here and there by human masks, sinuous beasts or shields. The door with its Flamboyant (ogee) arch was surrounded by sculptures and the door itself was decorated with full Gothic infillings. Many of the houses in Lisieux were highly ornamented but the Maison de la Salamandre was one of the finest.

In addition to the private houses – a few of which survive – there are the public buildings (market halls were basically only free-standing timber frameworks). One example is the charnel-house of Saint-Maclou belonging to the old cemetery of this Rouen parish. Charnel-houses, where exhumed bones were housed when a new grave was dug, were not rare in the Ile-de-France, and are still more numerous in Italy. They developed along individual lines in Brittany, and are known there as ossuaries. The charnel-house of Saint-Maclou was begun in 1526, but was not finished until 1640 with the completion of the south side. It is a kind of cloister which surrounds the whole rectangle of the churchyard and comprises a ground-floor and upper sto-

Right: Maison Kammerzell, Strasbourg, 1589.
Page 138: (a) Town-hall, Esslingen, c. 1430; (b) timber yard, Geislingen, 15th century.
Page 139: (a) Little Moreton Hall, near Congleton, Cheshire, 1559; (b) the Old House, Hereford, 1621; (c) the Old Wool Hall, Lavenham, Suffolk, c. 1500; (d) market-hall, Ledbury, Herefordshire, late 16th century.
Page 140: (a) Wooden bridge over the Brenta, Bassano, Andrea Palladio, 1569; (b) ossuary of St.-Maclou, Rouen, 16th century.

99c; 140b

a

b

a

b

c

d

a

b

a

b

c

d

e

f

rey. The open ground-floor has a wall with saddleback coping. Ashlar columns stand on the wall and support the sills and beams of the timber-framed upper storey, which forms the charnel-house proper. It is very simply constructed but the macabre decoration deserves attention, for the ornaments represent the gravedigger's tools, objects used in services for the dead and the obsequies, and a variety of bones.

Another public building deserving mention is the canons' library at the cathedral of Noyon. Here again the structure is an extremely simple one of a ground-floor and upper floor. The upper floor projects and is supported by short, strong posts terminating in three brackets, of which the one facing the street is carved. On the upper floor there is a rectangular window between each pair of large posts and the heavy brackets on these posts support a very thick plate decorated with a simple moulding that emphasises the eaves of the roof. This sober and solid building dates from the year 1507.

An account of upper-class houses would be incomplete without mention of their rural version, the Norman manor-houses. Normandy is probably the only part of France where such buildings are found in any number. Very occasionally one finds true castles of vast dimensions, such as Courpesante, the long façade of which is defended by watch-towers, or Canapville, a somewhat disorderly agglomeration of buildings disposed round a stone stairway. Some of these castles – including Grandchamp, Saint-Germain de Livet, le Mesnil-Guillaume – are built partly of stone and partly of wood. But the true Norman manor is a large country house, elegant and simple. The upper floors are sometimes jettied; the studding usually consists of fairly closely set posts and a few braces (these are more numerous in the Lieuvin). The dark wood stands out sharply from the white infilling. And these bright, trim manor-houses which stand out among the pastures dotted with apple-trees, are part and parcel of the Normandy countryside. The Basque house too is inseparable from its dry and hilly landscape. The Basque method of building is technically less complicated than that of the Norman manor-houses and the different architecture produces a totally different impression. Three of the walls are built of stone and only the façade – which always has a projecting gable – is timber-framed. The wall-plates, therefore, rest on masonry and all the problems that might be raised by the "rolling" of the timbers are avoided. Sill-beams are easily prevented from sagging by the erection of posts and studs. Jetties, when they occur, are not very pronounced; they are constructed by bringing forward the longitudinal wall on a corbel which at the same time supports the first-floor sill. The façade may have several projections. Sometimes a balcony supported on the ends of the joists runs the whole width of the façade often on several storeys. The infilling is of carefully laid bricks that are always whitewashed, whereas the framing is painted red or green. Animals and farming equipment are housed on the ground-floor of the house, which usually has a wide door. The windows of the upper floor are generally placed symmetrically in relation to the axis of the gable. There is carved ornament on the sill-beams: gadrooned and ovolo moulding, dentils, scroll-work of Renaissance or Hispano-Moresque origin; on the posts there are geometric and cusped motifs, faceted spheres and so on. The decoration is restrained. These Basque houses with their extremely aristocratic air are not found all over the Basque country, however, but only on the coastal plain known as the Labourd.

The house of the Landes, on the other hand, is low and has kept its peasant, primitive character. There is nothing except a barn above the ground-floor. The posts are tenoned into the plates and tie-beams. There are a few braces to stiffen the walls, which are filled with puddled clay, cob, or, more rarely, brick. The façade is under the gable and the roof oversails widely on all sides.

The houses of Bresse are closely related to those of the Landes. They too have only a ground-floor with a barn above. Buildings with one or two upper storeys – a rare phenomenon – are not farm-houses but middle-class country houses, like the manor-houses of Normandy. The boldly-projecting eaves of houses in Bresse are supported on a system of timbers that, seen in cross-section, take the shape of a figure 4, or by posts placed on stone bases. Firewood and maize-cobs were dried under these great eaves. Another distinguishing mark is the chimney known as a *sarrazine*. The chimney forms a large rectangular opening in the middle of the ceiling of the communal room. The flue is supported by two great ceiling beams on which rest four vertical posts; between the latter is an infilling of wattle and daub. The chimney-stack rises from the roof and is built in brick to a very characteristic design that is found only in La Bresse.

Another farmhouse with an individual character is the Savoyard chalet. It is found particularly in Haute-Savoie and in the north of Savoie, and differs from all the buildings so far described in that it is log-built. In former days the walls were of rough-hewn logs laid one on top of the other. Today, however, the timbers are trimmed with an axe or sawn, and in some districts – among them Le Chablais and La Maurienne – plain boards are laid on edge and slotted into grooved posts.

A chalet is usually a spacious building because it is designed to house people, cattle and provisions during the long winter. It stands on a masonry footing that may extend to the full height of the ground-floor. The wooden framework rises from it through one or two storeys. The roof projects on all four sides far beyond the walls and the bold overhang of the gable also protects the wooden balconies which run the whole width of the façade and sometimes round the corners on the lateral walls. The dwelling occupies part of the ground-floor and the upper floor adjoining the gable with the most favourable aspect; the barn and cow-house take up all the rest.

The logs forming the walls are very long and are fixed together at the corners by T-shaped joints or by dovetailing. Further, in the centre of each wall the ceiling-beams and tie-beams project beyond the wall and are securely jointed to two posts which rise to the full height of the wall and enclose and stiffen the logs. Sometimes the wooden walls are further protected against the weather by vertical boards that are nailed to them, and this also means, of course, that they are better insulated from the cold. Roofs are found even today that are covered with wooden shingles (known as *bardeaux, essentes* or *essendoles*). The chimney is a variant of those of Bresse. It is made entirely of wood and opens as a rectangular hole in the kitchen ceiling, from which rise four grooved uprights to hold the board forming the four sides of the

146

Carved timber frame, Morlaix, Brittany.

flue. The chimney rises through the fodder barn and small wooden tiles are nailed to the stack above the roof to protect it. The aperture can be regulated by hinged boards which are raised or lowered at will by means of a rod reaching down into the kitchen. These chimneys, known in Savoie as *bornes*, are rapidly disappearing.

There is great risk of fire in the Savoyard chalet. The main concern of the inmates is to put their most precious belongings – seed for the coming year, bread corn and their expensive clothing – in a safe place. This anxiety was behind the evolution of the Savoyard barn, which is commonest in the valley of Abondance and of which the earliest specimens date from the eighteenth century. The barns are like small chalets but are built of specially durable materials: thick boards or planks dovetailed at the corners and reinforced by pegs. The joints were filled with moss to ensure that the construction was perfectly watertight and the corners were often raised on stone or wooden platforms to lift it off the ground and give it greater protection against damp and rodents. The barn had a ground-floor and an upper floor and the openings were under the oversailing gable of the pitch roof. The door in the ground-floor always had an arched lintel since it led into the granary and had to be tall enough to admit a man carrying a sack. The upper floor was reached by an external staircase ending in a little wooden balcony, from which a door led to the room where clothes were stored.

We have described the smallest of the Savoyard barns. There are other, larger ones, some of them built of different materials. But those we have described, that are built entirely of wood, were like dolls' houses and, as precious as miniatures, seem fittest to exemplify the simple beauty of wooden houses and bring this rapid survey to a close.

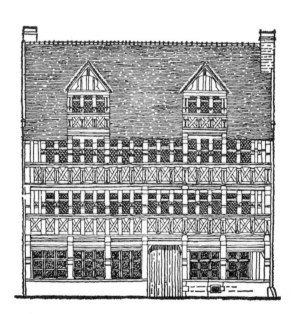

Timber-framed house, Caen, Normandy, 16th century.

Right: (a) Carving of the portal of the Butchers' Guildhouse, Hildesheim, 1529 (destroyed in 1945, cf. page 165); (b) figures on the brackets of a timber-framed house, Duderstadt, beginning of the 17th century.
Page 150: (a) Interior of a house from Nieblum on the island of Föhr, now in the Städtisches Museum, Flensburg, 17th century; (b) linenfold panelling in hall, Paycocke's House, Coggeshall, Essex, c. 1500 (cf. 107b, 151b, 171a).

148

a

b

a

b

a

b

VI Wood Building in Central Europe

Timber-framing in Germany, Wooden Buildings in the Austrian and Swiss Alps

In central Europe, too, the earliest building material was wood. Excavations at the Stone Age settlements on the Federsee, and those at Haithabu which shed light on historical times show this to be so. Tacitus in his *Germania* bears witness to the fact. He does not, however, appear to have been specially impressed by wooden buildings, despite the fact that they offered the most varied possibilities to have emerged since the Bronze Age: buildings constructed of squared logs laid one on top of the other, buildings constructed of posts with perpendicular frames, houses built of thick boards with infillings of planks between grooved posts placed at intervals, and finally houses with wattle and daub walls. There were wattle and daub walls on the Federsee and there are wattle and daub houses today. All these forms could exist in close proximity to one another, as is demonstrated by the excavation of the Stellerburg in Holstein (1934–36). But Tacitus was presumably familiar only with the everyday scene and with strictly functional buildings. While visiting certain cities of the Rhine in about 560 Venantius Fortunatus, bishop of Poitiers, saw more ambitious works, and the lines he wrote about them are eloquent and somewhat belittle the much-praised walls of Rome:

> 'Away with you, walls of square-hewn stone.
> Nobler far, I find, a masterly work, the carpentered building here.
> The panelled rooms give shelter, thwarting wind and weather,
> The carpenters's hand permits no gaping split.
> Fine airy arcades squarely surround the house,
> Richly carved by the master's hand in playful, inventive mode.'

Carpentry of this quality called for special skill and carpenters soon became an independent trade guild, as Bishop Wulfilas stated in about the year 350 in his translation of the Bible for the Goths; and Socrates Scolasticus admiringly wrote of the Burgundians, while they were still at the Rhine, that they had been trained as carpenters and were well versed in that art. We read in all the known Teutonic laws that wood building was of fundamental importance to these people and was protected. Not only were the modest houses of the vassals of necessity made of wood, which was found at their very doors, but so too, according to Priscus's account, was the palace of Attila, where the Nibelungs met their end, and the fortresses of the Teuton kings.

We know from many sources that the first Christian churches in central Europe were built of wood. As conversion to Christianity advanced, churches came to be built according to the promulgations of Rome, and as they were supposed to be the Rock of Christ the most appropriate material was stone, with which an effect of monumentality could be achieved. Wooden churches were allowed to last as temporary buildings until the lengthy business of erecting a large building in stone was

Page 151: (a) The Little Hall, Lavenham, Suffolk, with old shop-front, c. 1500; (b) Paycocke's House, Coggeshall, Essex, c. 1500 (cf. 107b, 150b, 171a).
Left: Butchers' Guildhouse, Hildesheim, 1529 (destroyed in 1945, cf. 149a).

153

completed. Thus the stone basilica of Chancellor Einhard at Steinbach near Michelstadt was preceded by a wooden church that was specifically mentioned by Louis the Pious in his deed of gift to Einhard. But these wooden churches were in no sense mere makeshifts. Adam of Bremen describes the wooden church of 789, which Bishop Willehad of Bremen used as a cathedral and which Willerich, his successor, replaced by a stone one, as a building 'of astonishing beauty'.

Many of the decorative elements of stone building – little columns looking as though they had been turned on a lathe, forms reminiscent of chip-carving, fluted posts and much else – undoubtedly derive from wood building. This can be seen more clearly, perhaps, in the early English churches – for example, Earls Barton of the tenth century – than in German ones, but it can be recognised in the gables above the little pilasters of the upper-storey of the porch at Lorsch, built before 800.

The wooden churches were obviously smaller than the stone buildings that replaced them, but it would be wrong to regard them as simple. We must not criticise the meanness with which Michael Ostendorfer represents the pilgrimage church 'Schöne Maria von Regensburg' in a woodcut of 1519, since this boarded building was only meant to stand for a year. The artists round Albrecht Altdorfer, who come to mind in this connection, were in fact interested in highly decorative pieces of architecture like those contrived by carpenters and joiners. Both elements, small size and cramped and limited decoration, have contributed to the opinion that since wood building lacks monumentality it is therefore inferior to stone building. Augustus the Strong was of this mind when he boasted that he had 'found Dresden small and made of wood and had left it large, splendid and made of stone.'

If monumentality means mere size, there is from the outset no justification for denigrating wood building, for wooden beams of up to eighty feet in length are by no means rare and some of the spaces spanned are wider than those of most stone buildings. We have only to recall the daring height of the Guildhall in York (destroyed in 1942), or the dormitory, extremely simple but immense, of the monastic church of Saalfeld an der Saale. If, however, monumentality implies a degree of inflexibility, wood fails to achieve this, for it remains a living material, but pays the price of being less durable than stone.

The wooden churches erected in Silesia to commemorate the peace of 1648 – Schweidnitz, Jauer and Glogau – are impressive, and their interiors have a certain monumentality. The pilgrimage churches of Sagan, Militsch and Freystadt are very large. Yet they may only have been built of wood from sheer necessity, for the other pilgrimage churches are built of stone, a material always used by the Catholics, who were in the majority in Silesia.

During the seventeenth century princes chose timber-framing for their palaces, too. Besides Weilburg an der Lahn, Giessen and Coburg, special mention should be made of Wolfenbüttel and Salzdahlum – as pretentious as it is famous. The large palace of Salzdahlum, built in 1691, was a timber-framed building, although its builder, Hermann Korb, based his designs on French and Italian models and finally whitewashed over the characteristic structure of the building. Another celebrated palace was Kolmonskoye, near Moscow, built for Tsar Alexei between 1667 and

110 b

154

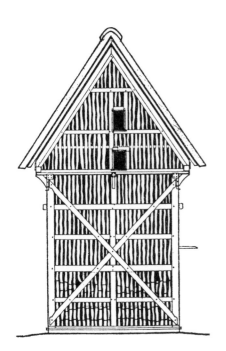

Wattle and daub barn from Donstorf, now in the open-air museum, Cloppenburg, c. 1525.

1681, a many-coloured agglomeration of basic, undecorated log-buildings. There was no feeling against wood building in Russia before Peter the Great, despite the Italian fashions of Moscow.

The criteria for stone architecture should not be applied to wooden buildings. It is true that timber-framed buildings imitated stone ones, and that the distinctive features of wooden building – overhanging upper storeys, protruding beams and closely set windows – became less and less apparent until finally during the nineteenth century timber-framed buildings were dressed up to present a 'polite' frontage to the street and ceased to be distinguishable from the universal house. Nevertheless, wooden building is essentially quite distinct from stone, as can still be seen in the wooden buildings of the country districts of Switzerland. The former house of the Butchers' Guild at Hildesheim (Knochenhaueramtshaus) and the Wehlburg near Quakenbrück, the one a town house, the other a farmhouse, are both equally splendid, so it would be wrong to compare their relative merits; and any comparison with solid stone building would be absurd. From the fifteenth and sixteenth centuries onwards wood building is sharply differentiated from region to region and it can be stated with certainty that these two tall timber-framed buildings are unmistakably Lower Saxon in inspiration. In reality it is only from this period onwards that we can consider central European wood building, although there is earlier evidence in Scandinavia and England. The Schober house at Pfullendorf in Baden is indeed dated 1317 in the literature; even so, all its individual forms suggest that the date should be 1517. The differentiation according to region which enables the art historian to write an 'art-geography' only became clear-cut in the fifteenth century.

Log-building predominated in Scandinavia, but in central Europe, with the exception of Austria, timber-framing was the common form. As we have already seen, timber-framing with stakes covered with clay between posts and rails was already known in prehistoric times; however, differentiation does not depend upon whether the infilling is of clay, boards or brick, but upon the structure of the frame. This point has been studied – notably by H. Phleps in his books on building among the east and west Teutons, and on German timber-framing. There are temporal as well as regional differences in the jointing of timbers: halving came first and tenoning followed later. The finest examples of halved timber-framing are found in Swabia, and Konrad Witz of Rottweil painted a specimen with obvious pleasure in his Nuremberg *Annunciation*. The town hall at Esslingen, which was built at this time (1430), and, even more spectacularly, the timber-yard at Geislingen, stand out – especially since in the Geislingen timber-yard the oblique timbers are halved and the edges are then chamfered. This gives the wall a plastic quality derived from the actual process of work, and accords pleasingly with the overhanging storeys. The use of halved (lap) joints to connect wall-plates and tie-beams in either normal or reversed assembly is thought of as a medieval practice in the north, too. Yet Konrad Witz himself noticed that joints were tenoned as well as halved. All the timbers were tenoned in the Town Hall of 1484 at Michelstadt. In northern Friesland during the seventeenth century it was the custom for brackets halved to the beams to be tenoned into the posts. Techniques did not change abruptly as fashions did. Both joints were

138a, b

181b

155

pegged with wooden nails which the builders did not trim off in the way that perfection-seeking restorers like to do, but left protruding an inch or two, to be driven home when the wood had dried. The protruding angular wooden pegs give the work a more lively air. Building techniques have evolved out of familiarity with the behaviour of wood. Thus in the Black Forest, in the Allgäu, Switzerland and the Tirol, the outstanding centres of wood building, builders used the *Schiebling* in floors and ceiling; this was a wedgelike plank which projected to the outside of the building and which was driven further and further in as the wood dried to keep the boards of floor and ceiling close-set.

Various theories have been put forward to account for the projection of the upper storeys that is a feature of every old timber-framed building. Some attribute it to cantilevering, whereby the projection of the joist beyond the sill enables the joist to support a heavier load inside the building; others see it as a consequence of the triangular formation which occurs in timber framing. The writer, who still builds timber-framed houses, would like to praise it also on the grounds of its efficiency: the jetty protects the ground sill from rain, secures the floor timbers better than if the joists merely protrude and, when the attic of the finished house is used for storage, loads can be hauled up without scraping against the wall. The jetty, which has obviously evolved out of a number of different causes, occurs everywhere and is everywhere declining in proportion to the lateness of the building.

Regional differences are clear-cut and if a feature which seems to be characteristic in one area occurs as an exception in others, we should remember that journeyman carpenters in particular were constantly wandering, and a master may have accepted some feature that was strange to him as an innovation. Old-fashioned features too may have survived longer in one region than in another. In Swabia, where halving (lap-jointing) is most often met with, the posts often extend to the stone footing of a house and there is a sill-beam interrupted by posts. Hermann Phleps interprets this practice as a survival of the original western Teutonic one of sinking the posts separately. We may assume from a regulation issued in Ulm in 1427 ordering the use of continuous sills that such construction was not yet taken for granted. The bailiff's farm of 1570 at Gutach in the Black Forest was still not framed on continuous sills.

But in north Germany too, as late as the seventeenth century, timber-framed farm buildings – such as for example a barn from Süderstapel in Schleswig, in which the ridge-piece is supported from the ground by ridge-posts, and a cottage from Alt-Duvenstedt (both in the Schleswig-Holstein open-air museum) – still have posts set on separate stones without continuous sills. In the first of these buildings there are interrupted sills, the purpose of which is not to secure the feet of the posts but simply to hold the studs and stiffen the interstices. Ancient practices are often long-lived.

The student who wishes to consider wood-building in its numerous regional variants will begin with an examination of the farmhouses; town architecture follows the same pattern. In peasant houses wooden architecture is seen at its best in the interiors, in the structure of the hall and store-room. By comparison with the

98c, d

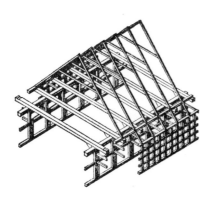

Framework of the Quatmann farm from Elsten, now in the open-air museum, Cloppenburg, 1805.

157

mighty hipped roofs covered with straw, rushes or shingle, the exterior walls are modest and may appear to be solid and built of brick without wooden posts and rails, although these are in fact wooden buildings. This is particularly apparent in the farmhouses of Friesland which are brick buildings on the outside but have a framework of posts inside, while their form is wholly determined by the wood. In town buildings the essential interior framework, the timber of the posts and beams, of the brackets and barge boards, plays a far smaller structural part. As far as the interior is concerned, the full potential of wood building is only exploited in the upper rooms within the great halls of north German town houses. Among farmhouses one finds the earliest buildings made entirely of wood: in the south the whole house complex and in the north the barns, which are usually aisled, are wooden. They represent a very long tradition going back to the Teutonic community. But we must discuss the variations and the great number of rural building methods.

The exterior wall of the 'Lower Saxon' farmhouse may be either solid or timber-framed, with wattle and daub or bricks for the infilling, but the interior is quite distinct from its neighbour the 'Frisian' *Gulfhaus* which also appears in the same area. The hall of the 'Saxon house' which runs the full depth of the house is flanked on both sides by heavy wooden posts. This range of posts is joined by an arcade-plate. Massive tie-beams, also acting as floor-joists, overhang the arcade-plate and combine with the posts opposite them to form a succession of bays. Resting on the ends of each tie-beam is a pair of rafters which supports the laths of the roof and which, by pressing on the ends of the ties, creates the tension enabling them to support the weight of the grain. Thus bay follows bay, forming a close-set file charged with energy. Between the posts and the low outer wall which stands at a distance from them is the *Kübbung* (the aisle of the farmhouse); its beams, supporting the roof, are tenoned or halved to the posts at some distance below the arcade-plate, and extension (or sprocket) rafters are laid from the plate of the outside wall to the mainspan rafters, so that the roof may cover the whole. These sprocket rafters lend flexibility to the roof. The whole is a clever construction; it creates the central empty space of the hall, a store-room for the grain over the tie-beams from which such grain as had to be threshed on the floor could be thrown down; and the hay for fodder could be stored on the beams of the adjoining aisles *(Kübbungen)* housing the cattle. There were several possible variations on this structure; the large door might be in the front or behind, the hall might be widened at the back, where the fire-place and the living-room were, by omitting a pair of posts and incorporating the windowed part of the aisles as *Luchten* (to lighten an otherwise dark hall), and the hearth might be in the middle of the hall or in a side kitchen. All these are of interest to the folklorist with a geographical bent, but are irrelevant to a short survey of the farmhouse as an example of the possibilities of building in wood.

The Frisian *Gulfhaus* is quite different. There is no free working space in the centre but store-rooms for corn – known as the *Barg* – from ground-level upwards. Like the old hay-shed out in the fields it is surrounded by four posts which carry the roof. They form the basic framework of the house in that each pair of tall posts becomes, by means of a tenoned tie-beam at the top, a square frame which supports the longitudinal beams, themselves secured by lap joints (i.e. halved over the tie-beams), on which the rafters of the roof rest. Tie-beams are laid on the overlapping ends of these beams to hold the rafters of the two other sides of the hipped roof; and the whole forms an economical construction of wide span. Rafters continue downwards from the high roof beams as far as the outside walls that surround the square at some distance from it; thus the granary is surrounded on four sides by deep rooms which are used as living quarters, threshing floor, stables and cow-stalls. This house, impressively strong both inside and out, has less of an air of close secrecy than the Saxon house and suggests greater activity; it was probably evolved in West Friesland, became known in Holland as the *stelp* house and attained its finest form in the *Haubarg* of the Eiderstedt region of North Friesland. The Roter Haubarg near Witzwort is so massive that a legend arose that Satan in person – outwitted though he afterwards was – had inspired such overweening arrogance. Here again wood building achieves monumentality, for the Frisian house is a wooden building by virtue of its inner core of vast posts, although the surrounding walls may be built of brick. In the older Eiderstedt *Haubargen,* such as the Roter Lau of *c.* 1600, now in the Danish open-air museum of Lyngby, beams are 'tenoned' through the brick wall to serve as anchor-beams.

When the dwelling and the farm buildings are no longer combined under one roof, as is the case most notably in the 'Franconian' farms, the house is built on the same principles as the town house. It often has many storeys, which overhang, and the walls – either solid or of jointed timber-framing – support the roof, which may possibly be reinforced by queen-post trusses. Side aisles or *Kübbungen* are sometimes added to the farm buildings, though this was commoner in the Middle Ages than it is today, if Dürer's drawings and watercolours of villages near Nuremberg can be accepted as records of medieval practice. A special decorative feature of Upper Hesse and Thuringia is the wooden gateway leading to the farm; these gateways have fine carved surrounds. Other Franconian farmhouses combine living space, stalls for cattle and granaries under the same roof. The walls of these houses too are built with principal posts.

The lay-out of the Swabian farmhouse is similar to that of the Franconian single-roofed house. Considerably more wood is used, however: thick logs may be used in place of timber-framing, in which case the lower part of the house is usually built of solid masonry and contains stalls. These houses are generally built of trimmed vertical planks or vertical squared timbers. As in the Bavarian farmhouse the great body of the Black Forest house is often surrounded by flat-roofed galleries. But whereas in Bavaria the roof is a saddle-back with a deep forward projection, often with vertical timber-work or lattice-work or even with a false gable on the front, in the Black Forest and in the north of Switzerland the roof is half-hipped; both are supported by a framed roof-truss but in the Black Forest the roof is covered with straw or pantiles and in Bavaria with shingles. The interior has many impressive aspects: a kitchen may rise through two storeys, or the hall, which is often long, may be vaulted; the external galleries are the most obvious feature. The balustrades are adorned with fretwork figures of the most varied shapes, boldly carved brackets

158

– which indeed are unsuitably named, for they resemble huge arches which divide the space under the projecting roof into sections. Like the Bavarian houses, those of the Black Forest are extrovert, they are more open to the space around them than the Austrian houses and so are intimately related to the landscape. In contrast the north German single-roofed houses are reserved and inward-looking.

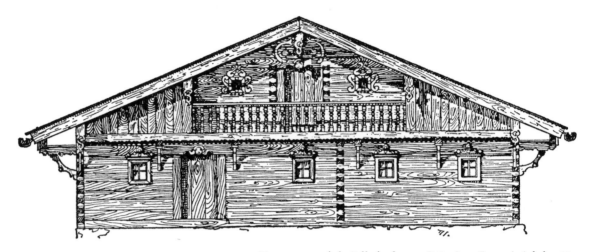

Upper storey of the Edhofer house, Brünning, Rupertiwinkel, 1682.

108a; 230d

The wooden houses of eastern Germany have a special significance. They have loggias and are built of logs, posts or timber-framing; they may be farmsteads consisting of several buildings, or living-space, cattle-pens and granaries may all be combined under one roof. The primary form must have been that which combines all functions under one roof and the origin was a single area with a loggia front. Venantius Fortunatus spoke of the carved loggias as early as the sixth century, after having visited the cities of the Rhine. Both the Norwegian stave-churches and the Silesian churches that were built of rough-sawn timbers *(Schrotholzkirchen)* have loggias. They have thus been known over the whole area of central, northern and eastern Europe. Greek temples were built of wood until the sixth century B.C. and a connection has been observed between the northern house with its loggia and the prostyle temple, which is taken as evidence of the northern origins of the Dorians. Thus the house with a loggia built of logs is of considerable antiquity and its individuality remains, though features of the Low German hall house may be observable in plank construction and particularly in timber-framing. The brackets of the loggia posts are magnificently carved and, particularly in the west Prussian houses, provide an easy and stylish transition from one archway to another. When the storey above the slightly projecting gable is timber-framed, the posts and studs are placed closer together at each successive storey and in the central field above the sill of the gable there is a motif of a diagonally crossed lozenge – absurdly called *Bauerntanz* (peasants' dance) by R. Virchow, who was better as a doctor than as a folklorist. The richness and elaboration is of a very unusual kind, and the urge to decorate is even more apparent than in the timber-framed houses of Hesse. For those who have been fortunate enough to see them, the beauty of the west Prussian loggiaed houses in the little open-air museum in Königsberg is unforgettable.

108a

There are plainer loggiaed houses in Mark Brandenburg (they are timber-framed), in the Spree Wald mountains, where they are log-built, in Silesia and, above all, in Bohemia. Among these is a type called the *Umgebindehaus* (a framed log-built house) which occurred most frequently in northern Bohemia. Here the range of supports which appears in loggiaed fronts surrounds the house on all sides but is a load-bearing framework standing close to, and removing the weight from, the log wall of the ground-floor behind. It supports the projecting upper storey. Posts, beams and balusters may be profusely embellished with axe, saw and knife; some of the decoration is natural to the material, some derived from prototypes in stone. These houses, whether undecorated or lavishly decorated, are everywhere of a very sturdy appearance, and despite the fact that the ground-floor is in two distinct planes, they have that close cohesion which is the mark of organic development.

In the town house timber-framing is even more common than in the farmhouse. We hardly ever find log-building as we saw it in Carinthia, Styria and Bohemia. But regional variants are no less apparent and areas of distribution may be even narrower and more strongly differentiated. Towns have their own rules.

The characteristic feature of Alemannic timber-framing, with which we will deal first, is the wide space between the posts. This was doubled, in order that the wall-plate above the posts should still be able to carry the weight of the upper floor. Interrupted or continuous sill, post and reinforced plate were jointed together by means of halved brackets. These, however, do not hide the broad panels between the posts. The effect of breadth is further emphasised when the panels enclosed by sill, post and plate are crossed by two rails, between which the windows, looking like little eyes in the surface, are placed. Oblique braces may combine with the posts to form figures of the '*Schwäbische Weible*' (Swabian wife) or the '*Wilder Mann*' (wild man). The whole surface is then covered with gaunt repetitive figurations. The several storeys project only slightly and sometimes rest on the floor joists above the wall-plate; the projecting ends of these joists are plain rectangles, so that the close-set heads under each storey look like a row of outsized dentils. Here we see the same severity as appears in the work of such Swabian painters as Herlin or Zeitblom and recognise that a combination of horizontal and vertical tension is the distinctive Alemannic feature.

In Alemannic Alsace, however, there is greater love of ornament: here, saltires made of curved and indented timbers and network patterns alternate in frieze-like rows. One is reminded of Late Gothic plant decoration and similar ornamental and naturalistic styles of the period of transition from the Middle Ages to modern times. The Maison Kammerzell of 1589 in the Place de la Cathédrale in Strasbourg is the most sumptuous timber-framed building of the south-west: it is almost overburdened with Renaissance decoration and yet remains sympathetic. In stone it would look like the work of a Mannerist amateur; as architecture in wood it retains a feeling of inner organic solidity.

Some have seen in the individual motifs of the timber-framed buildings of Alsace Franconian forms which have strayed into that region and which occur too in Baden. But the structure is more important than the decoration. The posts in the Franconian town house are more closely set than in the Alemannic and the brackets at head and foot are not halved but tenoned, so that the emphasis is on flexibility. Curved timbers

House, Marburg, 1320, demolished 1875

138a, b

137

Right: Market-place with the Old Stables, Miltenberg am Main, c. 1500. Page 162: Streets with timber-framed houses: (a) Colmar, Alsace; (b) 'La petite France', Strasbourg; (c) near St.-Maclou, Rouen; (d) Place de la Poissonnerie, Chartres.

162a, b

160

a

b

c

d

a

b

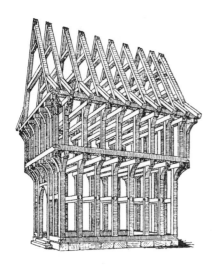

161; 164a; 181a; 238a, b

149a; 152; 166; 231a; 250b

165

are favoured and sloping braces are often set between sill and head rail. This gives a colourful appearance and greater movement. The jetties of the several storeys are less pronounced than in the Alemannic region and in the southern part of Lower Saxony. Between the wall-plate of the lower storey and the sill of the one above a fascia board was often laid to conceal the heads of the joists, and the rectangular squareness of the row of joists in the Alemannic house is replaced by moulded profiles. The oriels and balconies are, however, regarded as the outstanding features of Franconian timber-framing; there are, indeed, plenty of these in Hesse, but since the Romantic era the Franconian towns have been regarded as the incarnation of old Germany and they seem to be more at home in this region. The Lower German response to the same desire to look out into the street are the '*Utluchten*' or ground-floor bay windows.

In the Franconian timber-framed building the windows of each storey often lie between the rails of the sills and lintels, in which case they do not touch the head rail. This happens on the Central Rhine and on the Moselle because of the squatter overall proportions there. In other respects the timber-framed buildings of these regions are like an exaggerated form of the Franconian. The interlocked braces between the posts and rails look like elaborate lace-work and all sight of their structural purpose is lost. Compared with this love of playfulness, the original Franconian style is severe – severe as the Master of the Nuremberg Tucher Altar compared with Stephan Lochner. This frolicsome timber-framing can be seen to special advantage round the market-place at Bernkastel. Some of the earliest houses are monuments to Late Gothic freedom in wood; they have false gables with free-standing posts supporting the projection of the roofs. An early seventeenth century engraving shows that there were false gables in the market-place in Lübeck too, on either side of the town-hall.

Hildesheim and Brunswick were once high-watermarks of timber-framing. Only meagre fragments have survived the Second World War. The Knochenhaueramtshaus (Butchers' Guild House), considered by Viollet-le-Duc, the famous French restorer and architect, to have been the 'finest wooden house in the world' collapsed in ashes and rubble in March 1945. This house was claimed to be the most typical of Lower Saxon timber-framed houses. Yet the designation Lower Saxon seems too imprecise; timber-framing in the region of the Weser and the Lippe differs from that of the foothills of the Harz, and on the coast again there is at least one other individual idiom. The constant feature in all the variants is the strength of the timber frame.

The posts are set closer together than in the Alemannic house and the rails form regular, almost square, panels. Each storey usually has a sill, rail and wall-plate; the windows above the rails almost touch the plate. The tall panels favoured in Franconian timber-framing, where there is room for the timbers to be jointed in such a way that they form a 'man', are not usual here. The builders made do with angle braces at the foot of posts. In the Harz foothills these angle braces were often fully extended to form broad triangles which were fancifully carved, frequently including a motif of the sun above the horizon. The sill-beams too offer scope for the carver's knife. Scroll work friezes or *drôleries*, often of a robustly symbolic nature, find their place on the sill-beams.

In the Lower Saxon timber-framed houses each separate storey projects and the jetty is even deeper than that usually found in Franconia and Hesse. It differs from the Alemannic jetty in that each joist is supported by a post and there is no range of free-lying joists. The heads of the joists are frequently underpinned by brackets, in which case post, bracket and joist-head form a single element. Most of the timber-framed buildings in towns have masonry ground-floors so that the heads of the joists, now unattached, can be irritating – as is the case, for example, with the town-hall at Duderstadt. But there are posts on the upper storey to restore the rectangularity. The wall-plate is not doubled; between it and the sill above there is usually only a blocking-piece.

17d; 231a; 232a; 237a, d; 239c

The rule of the Lower Saxon timber-framed house that there is a post for every joist holds good even when the posts are covered in so completely as to be invisible. This often happens in the region of the Weser, where the whole space between sill and middle rail is panelled; the panels cover the framing and are decorated with rows of close-set sun motifs or strapwork friezes. In Hildesheim and Hanover this panelling has a stronger architectonic articulation than it has in more westerly regions. The lower part of the wall is divided into panels, each framed separately, and the framing timbers are flush with the posts. Long inscriptions may decorate the sills.

169, 237a

166; 167; 250b, c

169; 232a

The timber-framed buildings of the north are plainer. The houses have many storeys and rise steeply because sites are narrow; there is usually no ornament and only an occasional piece of carving. It is understandable that here and further up the lower Elbe the posts and rails should be weak, for there was little wood on the North Sea coast and it was expensive. In the buildings of the Holstein farmers, however, we find beams 12 inches square, and we should not regard such prosaic explanations as the only legitimate ones. There are many forests and much wood round Celle, whereas Lüneburg in the middle of the Heath is a predominantly stone city. Most of the buildings in the streets of Celle are of wood and the long ranges of timber-framed houses, fortunately preserved, are unusually well cared for by the citizens to the delight of the visitor. The situation was subject to change, fashion or other determining factors. The sixteenth century houses point to Brunswick and Hildesheim, but in the seventeenth century they were sober and much more sparing in the use of wood; and yet these later buildings are effective in their very plainness; they are shored like those of Hamburg, among which fire and clearance have played terrible havoc. The old city of Stade, a little further down the Elbe, escaped bombing during the War and gives an idea of what Hamburg – until 1842 still largely timber-framed – once looked like.

232a; 237c

180; 237a, d; 240a

The pinnacle of achievement among the timber-framed buildings of Lower Saxony was undoubtedly the Butchers' Guild House of 1529 in Hildesheim. Georg Dehio, author of the *Handbuch der deutschen Kunstdenkmäler*, whose judgments were always carefully weighed, had no hesitation in describing it as 'the most monumental of all the wooden buildings of Germany'. Since it was destroyed in 1945 we would do well to give it special consideration. It was greatly restored as early as 1852, after having been acquired by the city. The gable had to be renewed in 1884 after a fire; in 1911 the interior was entirely rebuilt. The Butchers' Guild House nevertheless

Plaque from a window-sill, Hildesheim.

166

Detail from a façade, Lower Saxony, c. 1600.

250 b

149 a; 152

remained Gothic in its towering structure and its steep proportions, and Renaissance in its rich ornamentation – in the German Renaissance style of 1529, in which emblems intimately related to daily life are surrounded by a wealth of leafy arabesques. But decoration in no way concealed the form of the house or the purpose for which it was built. The ground-floor was a hall into which opened the broad doorway in the centre of the decorative façade. On either side of the central passage lay the stands at which meat was sold, above cold cellars. No animals were slaughtered in the house. In the far corner of the lower hall there was an unobtrusive spiral staircase leading to a hall which occupied the whole of the principal floor. It was here that the butchers assembled and held their celebrations. The successive storeys became progressively lower and the top ones under the steep roof were used for storage. The market was surrounded by many four-storeyed timber-framed houses, each being restricted in the height of its floors. The houses on the east side, which adjoined the Butchers' Guild House, and linked it with the town-hall opposite, had taller roofs and lay parallel to the street. Yet because of its staggered jetties and because it faced the perpendicular stone front of the town hall, the Guild House dominated the market-place; neither the tall guild house of the woollen weavers nor the bakers' house made much impact beside it. This was not due to the sumptuousness of the carving and painting, for the Wedekind house of 1598 on the right was far richer in these respects and stood out much more boldly with its two great oriels. The Butchers' Guild gained its strength from the dynamism which lay in the combination of high building and discipline observed in all the parts. It resembled the mighty bows of a flagship and it was above all a demonstration of the peculiar potentialities of building in wood: possibilities constantly seized, initiated and developed, the vigorous projection of the brackets and the contrasting repose between sill and the line of the middle rail. Here, indeed, is monumentality, untroubled by the sculptor's pleasure in story-telling. Georg Dehio was fully justified in praising the building in terms appropriate only to great architecture.

The Wehlburg of 1750 near Quakenbrück has often been compared with the Butchers' Guild House of 1529 in Hildesheim: it seems to stem from the same origins. But the Guild House, rising steeply from a small base, is a town-building in its narrow proportions, compared with the Wehlburg, which is a broadly based, majestic farmhouse. Its yard is now surrounded by subsidiary buildings in keeping with it, and the four-stepped gable with its narrow bays pushes up out of this close huddle of buildings. The Baroque character of the bulbous brackets that support the deep jetties adds to the pervasive sense of solidity. Pure stylistic forms are not usual in farmhouses: if they occur here flawless, it is thanks to a high level of craftsmanship which has produced an artistic object when intending only a functional one. The Wehlburg is the most impressive 'Lower Saxon' farmhouse, just as the Butchers' Guild House was the most universally admired house in the world, both as a town timber-framed house and as a Hildesheim house.

We have now surveyed the great variety of wood building in central Europe and have seen that both construction and decoration vary from region to region: we have noted also that decoration is in no sense a mere extra but that constructional

167

elements are used decoratively, as befits wood which as a tree was both trunk and display of leaves. We must now turn to the question of wooden churches. As we have already seen, it is certain that most of the wooden churches were temporary buildings, the ultimate goal having been a permanent building in stone. The churches built in Silesia at the Peace of Westphalia (1648) were gracious concessions to the Protestant minorities immediately after the dismal end of the Thirty Years War; and of six large pilgrimage churches which the Evangelicals were able to extort from the Emperor fifty years later, three are wooden buildings and their exteriors are far from magnificent. This was a matter of sheer necessity. But the galleries give the interiors an artistic coherence. Otherwise, churches where the wood remains exposed, though quite widely distributed, are mere village churches and are not intended to cut any kind of figure. This applies to the timber-framed churches of north and central Germany as well as to the rough-sawn timber churches (*Schrotholzkirchen*) of eastern Germany.

There are numerous timber-framed churches round Hamburg. The most pleasing in this district is Curslack in the Vierlande, which dates from 1599; and Bergedorf, the tower of which was built in 1759 by Sonnin, architect of the church of St. Michael in Hamburg, dates from about the same period. Before it was burnt down and rebuilt at the beginning of the present century, St. Michael's tall tower, Hamburg's world-famous landmark, was a vast and unparalleled copper-sheathed structure of wood. Timber-framed churches are found also in the Harz, on the Rhön, in Hesse, Pomerania, Brandenburg and Saxony. Everywhere they are simple: posts, rails and braces at top and bottom are the Spartan elements of its structure. We seek in vain for elaborate interlacing or carved beams; sometimes the window with its horizontal lintel occupies the whole bay. The secular timber-framed building, the town house or the local town-hall has more imagination lavished upon it than has the country church. The interiors of these churches are a surprise, however; it is usually because of the way the space has been organised by means of galleries and because of the wealth of furnishing. This applies too to a church at Clausthal-Zellerfeld, a panelled frame-building put up between 1639 and 1642 in the market-place.

In east Prussia we find reed-thatched log-built churches with octagonal ground-plans. The logs are square-trimmed and, as in Scandinavian buildings, are interlocked

Wooden church at Lubom, Silesia, 1305.

58c

39

Right: Façade of the Willmann house, Osnabrück, 1586.
Page 170: Figures on brackets of timber-framed houses: (a) town-hall, Frankenberg, Hesse, 1509; (b) Canon's house, Hamelin, 1558; (c) 'Brusttuch', Goslar, 1526; (d) Wertheim, 16th century.
Page 171: (a) Figure on door-jamb of Paycocke's House, Coggeshall, Essex, c. 1500 (cf. 107 b, 150 b, 151 b); (b) detail of carving on the Guild Hall, Lavenham, Suffolk, c. 1500 (cf. 172 a); (c) carved doorway to a house, rue aux Fèvres, Lisieux, Calvados, c. 1500; (d) carved doorway, Haire Factory, Lavenham, Suffolk, c. 1500.
Page 172: Two-storey porches: (a) Guild Hall, Lavenham, Suffolk, c. 1500 (cf. 171b); (b) Warwick, c. 1600.

a

b

c

d

a

b

a

b

a

b

a

b

c

d

39

168

and crossed over one another at the ends; the three-sided lap-joint and the corresponding key produces a very solid appearance outside, and, inside, a striving after finish which barrel vaulting makes yet more uniform.

Space may be cramped but appropriate seats, pulpit and altar compensate for this. The rough-sawn wooden churches of Silesia (*Schrotholzkirchen*) are similar. These churches are log-built, the timbers are only roughly trimmed and their ends are sometimes crossed over and sometimes not; the chancel with its polygonal end is usually separate from the nave and forms the parish hall. The roofs often look as though they are sagging and are covered with shingles. In the interior the chancel is covered by an elliptical vault, while the wide nave has a flat roof.

A barely visible gap may be left in the beams outside and covered by a narrow shingle roof which surrounds the whole church like a flared hood-mould; this recalls the earlier wooden churches of Bohemia and Moravia and should perhaps be regarded as a retrogressive form, for in Czechoslovakia there is a roof at this level over a narrow open passage-way, which is one of the many forms of arcade we have encountered. In his book *Altslavische Kunst* Josef Strzygowski discussed these Bohemian and Moravian wooden churches; but he also said that they had been most ephemeral and that only a few such log churches were still standing in Slovakia. So all that remains for these squat Silesian churches, darkened with age and most at home in the depth of the forest, is the protection of a museum existence; this has been the lot too of a few old churches in the Soviet Union – far, indeed, from any forest, as for example in Novgorod and Suzdal.

Even when churches have stone exteriors, the built-in furnishings of their interiors may justify their being regarded as works of architecture in wood; it was in the interiors that artistic creation was first seen in western churches. We are not speaking of buildings where wood has been plastered and stuccoed to simulate stone or marble, as in the Baroque period, but of those interiors where wood has been used in a way which preserves its character, for posts and boarding, worked with axe and saw. Thus the medieval church of Ronshausen near Cassel was vaulted with a wooden barrel vault and, when in 1715 two-storeyed galleries were inserted round three sides of the church, it became a very rustic Baroque building. The wooden columns stand sturdily in the interior and the galleries suspended from them – the lower ones with closed parapets and the upper with open balustrades – closely circumscribe the space in front of the chancel, concentrate and model it. Octagonal at ground-floor level, becoming polygonal at the first floor gallery above an undulating core, this movement is finally carried up above into the elliptical vault; it works both horizontally and vertically and is fulfilled in a Baroque polyphony. This was achieved at Ronshausen five hundred years after the stone shell was built.

These highly individual spatial configurations produced by an internal wooden structure occur again and again; and when the interior has thereby become the dominant feature we must regard the result as a wooden building, regardless of the outer walls of stone. This applies particularly to churches built after the sixteenth century in northern German courts, towns and villages.

We might cite as one example the palace chapel at Gottorf (1590–1613); but

Page 173: (a) Town-hall, Saffron Walden, Essex, mid-19th century 'Tudor' style; (b) houses, nos. 115/117 High Street, Henley-in-Arden, Warwickshire, of 16th century origin but mostly 19th century.

Page 174: Façade of the Maison de la Duchesse Anne, Morlaix, Brittany, end of the 15th century (cf. 164b).

Page 175: Oriel of a house in Bishopsgate Without, London, Sir Paul Pindar, now in the Victoria and Albert Museum, London, c. 1600.

Left: (a) House at Neuleiningen, Palatinate; (b) house at Sommerhausen, Franconia.

two others merit special mention: the octagonal church of Rellingen near Hamburg, built between 1754 and 1756 by a Schleswig master-builder named Cay Dose, and that of Wesselburen. The Rellingen church is important as an accomplished brick building, the outer walls being raised in brick in an interlacing pattern. In the interior all is wood; there are eight massive columns; behind them run deep galleries, above which lies a massive system of beams supporting a wooden vault and a tall lantern of many lights. It is an extremely terse Baroque building on a central axis, of which the master-builder himself wrote that it 'achieves an uncommon beauty and excellence more inside than outside and has no equal in this country, but is found in Italy, France and England, also on a far larger scale and of a different character.' This is Baroque verbal exaggeration, and the invocation of England is inapposite. Even so, the architect is bold enough to see wood competing on equal terms with contemporary architecture of European reputation.

The other building is not a modern one; the ashlar-built tower and chancel of the Wesselburen church date from the twelfth century. In the fifteenth century a three-naved brick hall-church was built between them in place of the original aisleless parish hall, and this was burnt down in 1736, except for the outside walls. Johann Georg Schott, a Swabian carpenter, then built a broad Baroque interior inside the walls. Spaced wooden columns with galleries behind them support richly carved beams forming a cornice round the whole interior, including the old chancel; above it rises an immense mirror-vault, a broad floating surface the trough of which is broadened by contrast with the tunnel-vault of the chancel and an arch behind the organ. It is a uniquely powerful construction, cohesive and yet appearing to dissolve into space. Sophisticated calculation and much fixing and cutting have gone into suspending it from the roof-frame, so that the unseen background of the spatial freedom below is a forest of timbers. For this achievement Duke Karl Friedrich von Gottorp, son-in-law of Peter the Great, appointed Schott regional architect.

In addition to these churches built by carpenters away from the great cities, in which the spirit of current styles was reflected in an original way, there were others which show extremely remote connections and surprising adaptations. We may instance the village church of Brietzig in Pomerania. In 1697 a wooden vault with long pendants was added to the medieval building of square-hewn granite. English vaults were clearly the prototype here, though stone rather than wooden ones. In Protestant countries wood was no longer as makeshift as it had been in Silesia for the Protestant peace and pilgrimage churches, although there too there were impressively designed interiors, among which special mention may be made of the churches of Schweidnitz (1657–58) and Schmiedeberg (1743–45). The separation in time brought greater stylistic opportunities.

It should not be forgotten that many impressive tall spires of the great stone-built churches are of wood and are often technical masterpieces. This applies equally to the slender Gothic spires of Westphalian, Lübeck or Lüneburg churches and to the onion domes of the Frauenkirche in Munich with their beaten copper sheaths; it applies to numerous Baroque and Neoclassical towers, domes and *flèches*, including their galleries and arcades – as we have already seen in the case of St. Michael's in

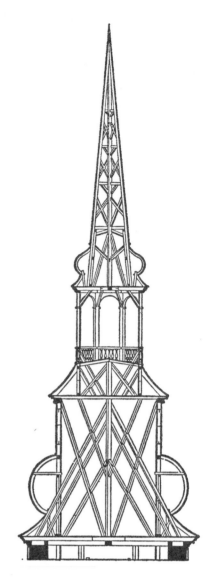

Framework of the tower of St. Cosmas, Stade, 1683 (section, cf. 54c).

54c; 178

178

Hamburg – and also to secular buildings such as palaces or town-halls. We may cite as an example the Baroque spire of 1683 on the church of St. Cosmas in Stade, the framework of which rests on the octagonal medieval brick crossing. Its type exemplifies the alternation, so popular in the north at this period, of onion-like bulges and a balustered gallery, the spire itself being a slender Gothic and quite un-Baroque structure. The finest two-storeyed church-spire of this type is undoubtedly that on the church of St. Katharine in Hamburg built by Peter Marquardt between 1657 and 1659 (replaced by a metal frame after the bombing of 1943). The church spire of Wilster is also worthy of note as a curiosity. When between 1775 and 1780 E. G. Sonnin replaced the medieval church by a new building, he retained the old tower, but, using specially constructed winches, turned the spire and raised it on supports by more than thirteen feet. This procedure demonstrates one of the special properties of wood, namely, the ease with which it can be moved.

After the last war and its destruction of irreplaceable art treasures, reconstruction began and new churches were to be built for communities displaced by evacuation. Otto Bartning – whose design in 1922 for a carved concrete church on a star-shaped plan, and whose uncompromising steel church in 1928 had shocked many conservatives – built a temporary wooden church. People liked and imitated it because its plainness and open construction expressed a new honesty. Steel churches have been built since, and concrete has become the universal material. But in the meantime imposing wooden churches have also been built in both Germany and France. They are more ambitious than Bartning's temporary church and spring from the new possibilities of spanning large spaces lightly with plywood, of articulating walls with laminated timbers and of achieving an elegance unknown to earlier builders in wood. These methods are now used for industrial, agricultural and cultural buildings too.

Wood building is thus by no means solely a historical phenomenon; it is still capable of solving great problems in its own right. When strong yet light buildings are needed, timber-framing may be considered. In modern churches where a solid tower is thought unsuitable, perhaps because the ground will not carry the weight, a wooden belfry is the right solution. There is much relevant tradition to point to, particularly on the coasts of Germany. The wooden towers found in this area are partly boarded and partly open and the style of carpentry mostly goes back to the Middle Ages. As examples of framing they are often masterpieces of the craftsman's imagination; they may not equal the English framing in which strong inward curving timbers or 'crucks' are used, nor achieve the tall stepped effect and distant visibility of the Swedish wooden towers; but they have the same logic, which often enables them to withstand the ravages of time better than a thick-walled stone tower. There has obviously been a continuous tradition here down to our own generation.

Where continuity has been unbroken regional traditions have been able to spread beyond their original borders. The wood building of Transylvania is derived from central Europe, and the farmsteads of Franconia shape the external image of settlements in Transylvanian Saxony. The settlers' first buildings were log-buildings, but when supplies of timber diminished and the method was replaced by the system of

179

68a, b

Wooden tent on timber-framed columns with steel cable stays, Bundesgarten Exhibition, Dortmund, architect: Behnisch, 1969.

179

posts and timber framing, methods of jointing and particularly of roof construction recall the building customs of their German home. Hermann Phleps has examined this question in a careful study entitled *Ost- und Westgermanische Baukunst unter besonderer Würdigung der ländlichen Baukunst Siebenbürgens* (Eastern and western Teutonic architecture with special reference to the rural architecture of Transylvania) and has pointed out that the forms of eastern Teutonic wood building occur in Yugoslavia. Timber-framed farmhouses in Wisconsin in the United States have been the subject of investigation, though the question has yet to be studied in greater depth. Large groups of emigrants from Pomerania settled there during the eighteenth century and built houses in their native tradition. There are plans for an open-air museum which will demonstrate these connections; it will display the similarities between the houses on both sides of the mouth of the Oder and the surviving original buildings of the colonists in North America; but it will also show that the settlers from Upper Franconia continued to build in the Franconian manner, while emigrants from Alsace in turn remained true to their style. All this would have been less apparent in solid-wall techniques.

We have yet to mention the Alpine log-buildings which differ from the timber-framed buildings prevalent elsewhere in central Europe in that they are not framed constructions but are built of horizontal logs or baulks. Farmhouses or town houses, from the Swiss chalet, the alpine house of the Tirol, the Allgäu, Upper Bavaria, Styria and Carinthia, with their balconies and broadly oversailing purlin roofs, to the similar buildings of the southern alpine valleys of the Grisons, all are of a common type, which may perhaps derive from an archetypal form of Celtic house. Whether, however, the distribution of central European timber-framing stems from the areas settled by the Teutons in the early Middle Ages is at least doubtful – considering that log-building is the prevalent technique in Teutonic northern Europe.

67; 73a, b; 75f; 76; 129b, d; 247a, b

Many questions still remain unsolved. German architectural historians have too long confined their studies to stone buildings; folklorists have been excessively fascinated by the singularities of particular instances. It is a good thing that the phenomenon of wood building is now being looked at in its totality. Research in this field will have much to gain.

House at Bäckerstrasse 3, Stade, 1590 (cf. 237a).

Right: Town-halls: (a) Bergstrasse, Heppenheim, 1557; (b) Michelstadt, Odenwald, 1485.
Page 182: (a) Restaurant de la Mère Pourcel, Dinan, Brittany, 16th century; (b) gabled cross-wing of a timber-framed hall house, Kersey, Suffolk, beginning of the 16th century; (c) the Red Hat, Tewkesbury, Gloucesterhire, 1664 (cf. 250d); (d) Gatehouse in kitchen range of Bishop's Palace, Hereford, early 16th century, with original trellis-framed doors.

180

a

b

a

b

c

d

a

b

c

d

a

b

c

d

VII Wood Building in Eastern and South-eastern Europe

Log-building in Villages, Towns, Churches, Mosques and Palaces

Wooden entrance gate, northern Russia, 17th century.

Page 183: (a) House in the Kuhgasse, Gelnhausen, Hesse, c. 1350; (b) carved façade, Gallardon, near Chartres, 16th century; (c) façade of a loggiaed barn, Botten, Norway, 1666; (d) façade of the Ancient House, Ipswich; the pargetting, with figures, is of the reign of Charles II.
Left: (a) Mol's Coffee House, Exeter, 1596, top storey added c. 1840; (b) timber-framed houses, Vannes, Brittany; (c) house in Place Henri IV, Vannes, 16th century, with saltire bracing; (d) monastery court, Trondheim, c. 1770.

In the year 1036, a bare generation after the baptism of the Grand Duke Vladimir, the walls of the five apses of a magnificent cathedral began to rise in Kiev, the centre of the kingdom of the Rus. Architects from Constantinople had drawn up the plan and were overseeing the work. The fifteen gilt domes which crown the great building proclaim the Byzantine character of the architectural ideas at work as clearly as the mosaics of the domes, where the faces of saints, gazing from eternity to eternity, proclaim the eastern mode of Christian piety that missionaries from the capital of the Greek empire had worked to implant on the banks of the Dnieper. And not only in Kiev and other south Russian cities, but also in Novgorod, that other centre far to the north on the highly important trade route 'from the Varangians to the Greeks', magnificent churches were being built. These were at first wholly Byzantine in spirit, but native master-builders were gradually learning to replace the Greeks and a specifically Russian type of church was evolving. During the following centuries this was to be embodied in a wealth of splendid churches both here and in Vladimir, Suzdal and Moscow, the new cultural centres which had emerged as a result of repeated shifts of power.

Yet these works of city architecture, monumental religious buildings of stone, should not blind us to Russia's great wealth of buildings, both religious and secular, in the plainer material of wood. Although the formal pretensions of these wooden buildings are usually more modest, their artistic expressiveness is often no slighter than that of the more ostentatious stone cathedrals.

Wood was *the* building material in the vast forest regions of north and north-east Europe which begin in Scandinavia and extend to Asia, almost to the Pacific Ocean. Not only the boundless coniferous forests of the Russian north with their almost immeasurable stands of fir, spruce, pine and larch but also the zone of deciduous trees with beech, aspen, alder, lime, maple and elm, and, at its southern fringe bordering the steppes, the rich oak forests, provide building material of great variety and in huge quantities. The same is true of the wooded Carpathians, much of which were likewise settled by the East Slavs. The number of words existing in Russian for 'forest' and for the various kinds of tree reflects this natural situation. In central Europe from a very early period the authorities had been obliged to issue all kinds of regulations to conserve the rapidly-diminishing supplies of wood for building; such cares, however, barely affected old Russia, and there was opposition to the restrictions on the feudal aristocracy's use of wood according to the rights of the common forest. Spruce and larch, and fir too for certain parts of houses, were the kinds of wood most used in the north; in the south aspen and especially oak were the favourites. But buildings of outstanding importance were built of oak even in the coniferous area – such as, for example, the first, wooden, church of St. Sophia in Novgorod (989) or the walls of the Moscow Kremlin (1339).

In contrast to the superabundance of building materials, the tools for working them were inadequate. It is difficult for us to believe that the only tools available to carpenters for erecting a wooden building, even a monumental one, were an axe and at most a primitive mallet and a few equally primitive wedges. The axe was used to fell the tree and to strip it of its bark; baulks were hewn with the axe and it performed the simple splitting by which boards were made; all decoration, whether on walls or columns, was carved with the axe. Leo N. Tolstoy was right when he once remarked that the Russian had for centuries been as skilled in building a house as in trimming a spoon with his axe. As proverb and popular idiom shows, the Russian has indeed an inner affinity, transcending mere expediency, with this tool which alone enabled him to survive in the rude forests of the north or in Siberia itself. The saw was, it is true, used occasionally in the advanced monastic establishments as early as the beginning of modern times; but the carpenters, to say nothing of the peasants, of the remote forest regions did not begin to use it until after the time of Peter the Great, and many of them not until the nineteenth century. We should remember this dependence not only upon wood as a building material but also upon the extremely simple tools available for its technical working if we are to understand the specific formal characteristics of Russian wood building and to appreciate the remarkable achievement of these modestly equipped carpenters.

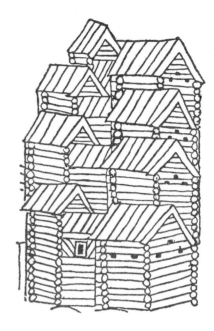

Northern Russian log-buildings, from a 17th century plan.

Wooden buildings are clearly much less stable than stone ones. By far the greater number of Russian farmhouses date from the last century and only in particularly favourable cases do some individual buildings date back to the seventeenth century. Of the surviving churches too only very few are slightly older. But if we consider that most of these buildings are in the north Russian territories – 'territory' being used here in the sense of an administrative unit (*oblast'*) corresponding to the pre-Revolutionary 'government' – or in the lonely villages of the Carpathians, that is in territories which are recognised cultural relics, we shall see that these surviving monuments are recent examples of archaic architectural forms; and from them it is possible, by critical examination of different literary and pictorial sources, to infer with some accuracy the form of earlier analagous buildings. The territories of Archangel'sk, Vologda and Olonec particularly, but also Vladimir, Yaroslavl', Novgorod and Tver', contain regions where the Russian Middle Ages had remained alive almost into the present century, where the richness of the early epics was still transmitted orally by *byliny* singers and where building methods and architectural forms of remote times, or at least traces of them, survived. The same is true of the territories of western Siberia which became incorporated into the Muscovite empire as early as the end of the sixteenth century thanks to the combined influence of the tsardom, the initiative of merchants and the thirst for adventure of Cossack groups. We have made the mistake of concentrating upon the history of Russia's rulers and battles to the exclusion of the colonisation – peaceful, despite much loss of life – of the forest wastes of the north, first from Novgorod, then from its rival Moscow and throughout supported in large part by the monasteries with their higher level of economic development. The economic and political circumstances of the period of colonisation

186

had a lasting influence on the development of the northern territories. These territories were divided into an eastern part, essentially under the influence of Moscow, and a western part which formed the hinterland of Novgorod. The eastern regions enjoyed their period of greatest prosperity before the reign of Peter the Great, especially after Archangel'sk had been founded to become Russia's only harbour; but they became impoverished when, in order to promote his new harbour at St. Petersburg, Peter put an end to trading via Archangel'sk; it was now the north-westerly areas which were opened up, both economically, through the setting up of early industrial enterprises, and to traffic, by means of roads and canals. Prosperity laid them open to the influence and taste of the city – and this also had its effect upon architecture in wood, whereas in the north-east the conditions of the period before Peter the Great, and with them all the archaic forms, were preserved unchanged for a hundred or a hundred and fifty years longer. This is where we may expect to find the old traditions surviving with the least disturbance, and the evidence of written sources confirms this premise.

186; 200 For prehistoric times these sources are the works of the writers of antiquity, for later periods the annals and chronicles of the eleventh and twelfth centuries, documentary records of, especially, the sixteenth and seventeenth centuries, land registers, the extremely informative contracts between owner-builders and the elders of the company of carpenters receiving the particular commission and, finally, accounts of foreign travellers, some of them illustrated; other sources include representations of churches and secular buildings on icons or on old plans of cities and monasteries, which used to show buildings as well. Popular writing naturally contains occasional descriptions of peasant houses or the interior of a Boyar palace, and nomenclature may provide important information.

In what follows, statements have been made about objects which are inherently not very durable, and which are at constant risk from fire: there is scarcely a settlement or town that has not either wholly or in part been more than once thus destroyed. But economic and technical conditions have remained largely unaltered for centuries; the use of wood determines the form of a building and basic methods of construction have hardly changed because of the unchanging character of the available tools. For all these reasons we may assume that the wooden churches and peasant houses of Russia have remained fairly constant in form. Yet we must be careful not to assume that folk culture in general and folk art in particular is unhistorical and totally static, as was believed until quite recently.

Are we justified in including the farmhouse, the Great Russian *izba* of the north and the Ukrainian *chata* of the south under the heading of folk art? Are these not purely utilitarian buildings, put up at best by a country carpenter, usually erected without artistry by the farmer himself, with nothing in mind but utility and without any aesthetic programme? The peasant settler's house must certainly have

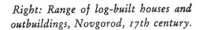
Right: Range of log-built houses and outbuildings, Novgorod, 17th century.

been primarily functional; it had to shelter him from the weather and protect him and his property from attack by enemies and wild beasts; it had to be adapted to the conditions of an agrarian economy – and it was. But this is exactly what in great part constitutes the essence of folk art: functionalism combining unreflectingly with decoration – clearly a basic human activity – to produce an object which is both practical and beautiful. It is not only the carved and painted decoration – probably a relatively late addition – which make these simple rural dwelling-houses and farm-buildings a delight to the eye, but first and foremost their proportions, the popular builder's astonishing feeling for correct dimensions. Their aesthetic theory – if the expression is at all permissible – was limited to a few rules of thumb – they worked with the basic ratio of lengths 1 : 1, 1 : 2, or perhaps they may also have used the diagonal of a rectangle as the unit of measurement. That they knew how to use a makeshift pair of compasses is demonstrated by the occurrence of six-pointed stars and whirling rosettes, motifs made with a pair of compasses which occur all over Europe; but they built without a ground-plan and without any fixed programme – and 'divined' the Golden Section with incredible accuracy. Professional carpenters, of course, had at their disposal a considerable body of experience; the first thing handed on from one generation of craftsmen to the next was knowledge of methods of construction, but this was later augmented by a body of knowledge of, for example, perspective effects and similar details.

Utilitarian form and artistic form created, as we have seen, an indissoluble unity in the peasant's wooden house. However, climatic conditions and economic demands remained the primary determinants. The two storeys of the *izba* spring from functional necessity and in turn necessitate the addition of an outside stairway leading to the upper, residential part of the house; if the ground-floor which houses the farm offices and the cattle stalls is buried in winter under deep snow, the upper storey remains light and free of snow and is always accessible by the outside stair-way. Another functional device is the division of the living area into summer and winter rooms; this division is characterised, according to the type of house and settlement, partly by the fact that they sometimes face in different directions, and certainly also by the different methods of heating used. This division, which is primarily the result of climatic considerations, has another quite different social func-tion; for the summer rooms, which lie on the gable side, are also incomparably better furnished. They are in fact the 'state' rooms, the rooms that are shown off, a func-tion which is underlined by the elaborate decoration of the staircase leading to this front part of the farmhouse, whereas the staircase which leads to the winter rooms, when it exists, is entirely undecorated, as befits the lesser standing of this part of the house. And a final result of functionalism is the tendency to roof over the whole of the farmstead, that is, as far as possible to place the living quarters and the farm offices under one roof, so that the cattle may be properly cared for even under the extreme climatic conditions of the northern winter. It is not surprising in these circumstances that the basic types of the *izba* are few, though they can, of course, be broken down into a large number of local variants. The centre of domestic life and work is the main living-room, for which the same word is used in Russian as for

Six-walled house, Volga territory.

Right: (a) Quayside warehouses, Sku-teviken, Bergen; (b) fishermen's huts, Smögen, Bohuslän, Sweden.
Page 190: Passage-way between ware-houses on Bryggen, Bergen, 18th cen-tury.
Page 191: (a) Side-wall of a church at Hingham, Massachusetts, 1742 (cf. 59); (b) stables, Canton, Massachusetts, 18th century.
Page 192: Timber-framed ground-floor on the Singel, Amsterdam, 17th cen-tury.

a

b

a

b

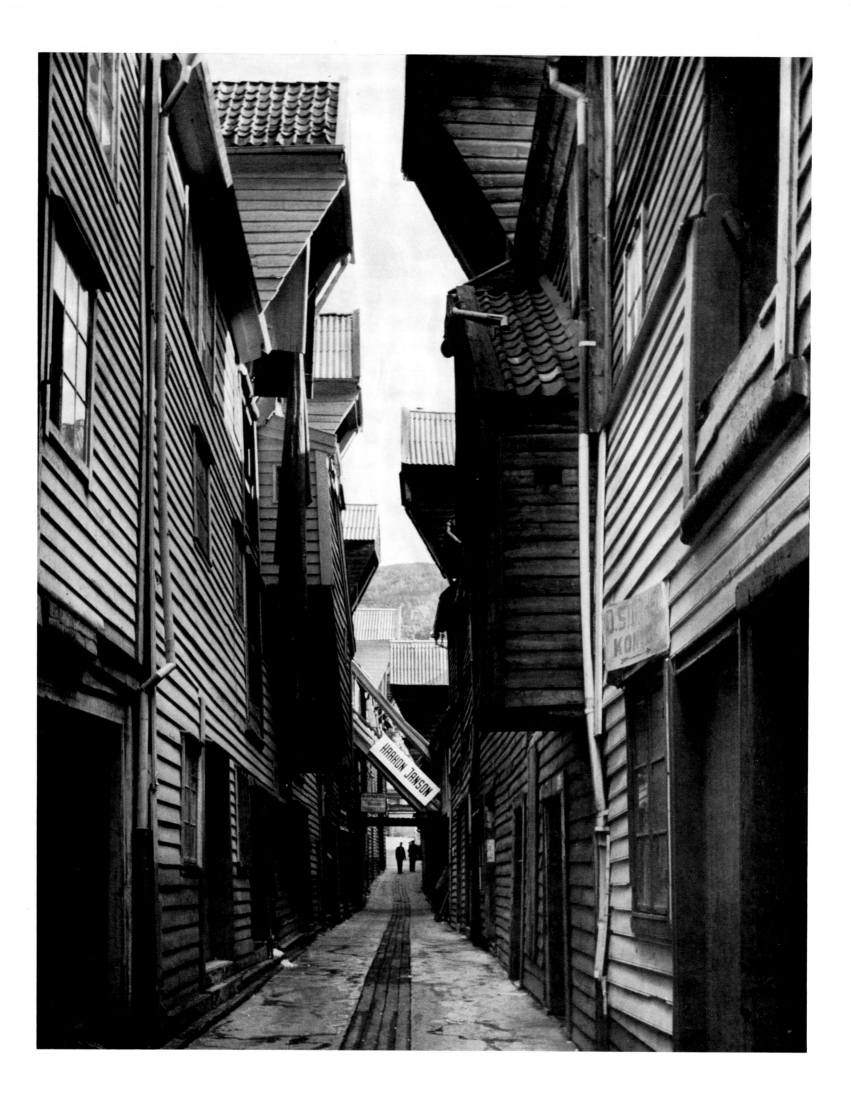

a

b

a

b

c

d

a

b

a

b

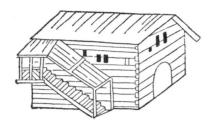

Dwelling-house in Novgorod, 17th century.

the whole house, *izba*, a fact that shows it is also genetically the original cell of the living quarters. The room is heated, for the baking-oven is here; whereas the winter *izba* is a 'black' or 'smoke' room, without a fireplace. Within the characteristic tripartite division of the northern Russian house, and among those larger, lighter and better furnished summer rooms of the 'front house' *(pered)* there is another room: it is the *gornica* or 'best' room, the room into which the visitor is taken, but which is otherwise used only for a few traditional occasions such as the celebration of annual feast-days or special occasions in the lives of the owners. Finally, the front of the house includes another or several other unheatable rooms. The central part *(seredka)* of the house, separated from the front and back parts by lobbies (here again a distinction is made between the 'summer' and the 'winter' lobby), includes the covered yard and the stalls; whereas the back house *(zad)* repeats the divisions of the front house, having its own *izba* and even its own *gornica,* albeit on a smaller and more modest scale. The difference in social degree between the summer and the winter rooms is expressed also in their furnishings, especially those of the *izba*; the furnishings of the front house are not infrequently decorated with painted ornament and the seats which run round all four walls have carved feet, while the winter *izba* seldom has such decoration. Furniture in the true sense of the word, that is, free-standing, movable domestic pieces, was anyway extremely modest in the old Russian peasant house and consisted only of a table and a low stool. Above the bench there was a shelf running right round the room at about shoulder height, and perhaps a small wall-cupboard, often carved or painted, or both.

75c

In the foregoing paragraphs we have examined the single-axis farmhouse of the territory of Archangel'sk and Vologda, and we should add that the main entrance to this type of house was seldom at the front but was usually on the southern long wall. A few other main types may be mentioned, for instance those of the more westerly territories, the ground-plans of which were rectangular, square or U-shaped. The interior divisions of the house vary accordingly, yet the basic number of rooms remains functionally determined.

78 c

The same goes for the separate components of the north Russian farmhouse, which, despite variations in the ground-plan, remain essentially unaltered. The basic constructional element is the *srub* (plural *sruby*). Four, often very thick, round tree-trunks are jointed at their ends by various methods to form a square and a number of such squares laid horizontally one on top of the other form the elementary four-walled constructional unit – that is, the *srub* – of the Russian wooden house. The surface area is naturally determined by the length of the trunks, which in simple building varies between fifteen and twenty feet, but may be as long as fifty feet and more. Obviously the diameter of the trunks (between ten and twenty inches, in special cases as much as thirty or thirty-five inches) also varies and with it the height of the individual squares.

This carpentered unit, usually comprising four walls, represents the real kernel of the building; then come the other constructional elements: the roof, openings for doors and windows, outside staircases, galleries and balconies, ranges of barns, floors and ceilings, elements which are entirely conditioned and defined by function but with regard to which the decorative urge too found expression at an early date. Even the distribution of the primitive window shutters, the only possible means of articulating the ponderous log-built walls, has an aesthetic effect derived from its deliberate asymmetry; also it makes the house warmer and more habitable, whereas the small windows in churches only add to the desired effect of monumentality. The outside staircase, too, transcends its purely functional purpose and becomes an important decorative adjunct, which in the dwelling-house again makes its effect through the symmetry of two staircases which lead up to the main entrance.

The numerous solutions of the problem of roof shape, especially in churches, can involve great artistry and we shall discuss them later. The Russian wooden churches were designed by master-builders, to produce their effect primarily by their size and their overall silhouette; while the farmhouse, being low, could be perceived in all its parts and was therefore a more suitable site for carving and painting. The surrounds

80; 199; 239d; 246d; 251b

of the doors and windows and the gable of the *izba* were the main features to be so decorated. Specific regional forms are identifiable, among which we may note as of particular interest the so-called ship-carving of the central territories (Gor'kiy, Ivanovo, Yaroslavl'). Here, on the upper reaches of the Volga, ship-building had been carried on since ancient times; and not only did the masters of this craft handle wood generally with sovereign skill, they were also distinguished masters of the art of using it decoratively. The carved decoration of the old Volga boats perpetuated all kinds of ancient animal and plant motifs. When in the course of the nineteenth century modern steam ships began to replace the old wooden boats, the shipbuilders lost their livelihood and had to seek new ways of earning a living; this they found in house-building. They now transferred their carvers' art from ships to houses, which they embellished with the old motifs. Within these territories, but nowhere else, the transfer – one of great interest to the social historian of art – resulted in a late flowering of wood-carving in the context of house-building; it began in the first third of the nineteenth century, reached its culmination in the 1870s and 1880s and declined swiftly around 1900. The motifs of these low reliefs vary from plant ornaments, among which the acanthus leaf is the commonest – an undoubted example of so-called 'sunken cultural treasure' – through purely geometric figures to figures of animals and mythical creatures, some of which should certainly be seen as typical of ship decoration. This applies particularly to the sirens found in these parts, though probably not so much to the lions above the entrance to a farmhouse barn in Opalicha (territory of Gor'kiy), whose striking similarity to stone reliefs of animals on the celebrated Dmitri Cathedral at Vladimir (1194–1197) – themselves partly Lombardic and partly Armenian in influence – must be mentioned, although it is not intended to claim direct dependance from them. In general the carved decoration of the *izba* in these territories at this period tends towards a certain excess and perhaps the formation of hybrid forms was one of the reasons why relief decoration on house and farmstead came to a sudden end – an occurrence for which there is more than one parallel in the history of folk art.

The decoration of the farmhouses in the northern territories (Archangel'sk and Vologda) is by comparison much plainer and more reserved, but not for this reason

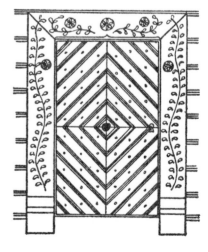

Surround of a door, Klubina, Slovakia.

198

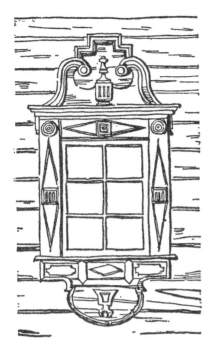

Surround of a window, Volga territory, c. 1800.

less pleasing. There are no figural motifs in the low reliefs, though in an area which can be fairly exactly defined geographically, the ends of the roof beams are often carved in the shape of fantastic birds or horses' heads, he-goats and stags. It is certainly a striking fact that these decorative forms occur only on *izba* and barn, in other words on secular buildings, and never on churches. If we add to this the fact that throughout the same territory numerous stylised figures of birds are found, set up on long poles near the dwelling-houses, we cannot exclude the possibility that all these are relics of pre-Christian beliefs and cult-forms, which may be causally connected with the animal style of Scythian-Sarmatic ornament. Recent folklore research, including that of the Russians themselves, has, however, repeatedly shown how problematic such assertions of continuity often are.

The varying forms of decoration that include painting, especially of flat surfaces such as the panels of doors, provide the basis on which to work out the local variants of the types of *izba* – the constructional principles of which, as we have seen, remain essentially unchanged. Even the farmhouse of western Siberia does not differ fundamentally from that of north Russia, only in a few regional peculiarities of the ground-plan and especially in the style of decoration. Particularly noteworthy are the rich carving and the lightness and colourful brightness of the painting on the facings of doors and windows and the walls and ceiling of the living-room.

The differences between the North Russian-Siberian farmhouse on the one hand and the Ukrainian on the other are, however, more important. The historical, political and, to some extent, religious development of the Ukraine has for long and decisive centuries taken a course different from that of the territories settled by Great Russia – and this despite the common origins of Russian history in the Kiev-Novgorod empire and the political reunion of the east Slav territories in recent times. It was impossible that the accession of the Ukraine and White Russia to the Lithuanian empire, as, later, that of the principalities of Halicz and Volhynia to Poland, should remain without cultural consequences, although the Ukrainian's profession of Orthodoxy, even after the union, counteracted too great a receptivity to western influence. Thus in their wood buildings, too, essential features of east Slav and Russian form persist, are overlaid by general Ukrainian stylistic characteristics and finally separate out into a series of local variants.

As is well known, the Ukrainians usually settled in steppe country, where trees were non-existent or scarce, and an entirely different method of building was called for; this involved the wattle and daub wall, a technique which does not interest us in the present context. The Volhynian house, for example, is, by contrast, a true wood structure, log-built like the north Russian but differing from it in that outside staircases are rare – because climatic conditions are more favourable – that its (hipped) roofs are thatched with straw and that its living quarters are surrounded by an earth wall which is supposed to deflect rainwater. The farm offices are separate from the living-quarters (another difference between this and the northern house) and are situated in the farm-yard according to no set plan.

A special form of the Galician house was evolved by the Huzulians who inhabit the hilly part of this area and have always been conspicuous for a rare gift for woodwork. It is not by chance that the axe is a kind of emblem for them; among their favourite carved objects are sticks with axe-shaped handles and many of their old folk-songs celebrate the tool which is so important to them. Their houses, in contrast to those of the rest of the Galicians, are not whitewashed; the roofs are covered not with straw but with boards. This means that wood as a building material produces a much greater effect than in the other Ukrainian dwelling-houses. The Huzulians are not farmers but shepherds and wood-cutters; the cheese-dairy occupies an important place among their farm offices, which are separate from the living-quarters. Because they were not farmers they were liberated early from the oppressions of serfdom, and carving as a home craft – a talent shared by other pastoral peoples – flourished among this small mountain people who preferred to live in isolated settlements. Carved icons and altar crosses, some dating from the seventeenth and eighteenth centuries, are effective in their archaic primitiveness; likewise parts of the house, tools and all kinds of utensils are covered with elaborate carved ornament and we shall find that the Huzulians were builders of remarkably original wooden churches.

White Russia has for its part evolved special local forms, some of which reflect the Great Russian, and some the Ukrainian-Galician. It is in keeping with the troubled history of this country, which has suffered repeatedly and seriously from enemy attacks and military campaigns of all kinds, that its churches are frequently fortified and therefore could often afford a last refuge to the ravaged population. The farmhouse – familiar to the peoples of western Europe from many paintings by Marc Chagall, who was born near Vitebsk – does not differ greatly from the types we have already discussed.

It was no arbitrary choice that led us to place the farmhouse at the head of our study of east European wood building. In its primal and primitive forms it represents the kernel of all Russian architecture in wood. The principles of construction involved in building it also form the basis of all other kinds of wooden building, be they defensive, religious or agricultural buildings; and the monumental church, as well as the sumptuous Boyar palace, are both constituted from the same basic constructional elements. The earliest religious buildings which we can infer or which have come down to us in more recent single monuments, already with differences, of course, differ from residential buildings only in the steeper pitch of their saddleback roofs. By this technique, steeper, and that means higher, roofs could be erected; all that was then needed was the addition of a small dome to distinguish the church from the surrounding secular buildings. It is characteristic even of this early form that the ground-plan is divided into three, a feature which was to remain a determining element in all other types of church. The Russian church consists of at least three *sruby*, of which the central, rectangular one, forming the actual 'church', considerably exceeds the others in height and size; a lower and also rectangular annexe for the altar is built on at the east end and at the west end there is a porch shut off from the central portion by a wall and a door, which is called a refectory. The dominant central portion is tall and tower-like and is surmounted by a small dome; the proportions of the lower extensions are always such that they fit most convincingly into the artistic composition of the whole. Most of the surviving church-

Monastic buildings in northern Russia, after a 17th century plan.

Right: (a) Jethro Coffin House, Nantucket, Massachusetts, 1686; (b) Van Nuyse (Ditmars) House, Brooklyn, New York, c. 1700; (c) Old Ship Meeting House, Hingham, Massachusetts, 1681; (d) Cupola House, Edenton, North Carolina, c. 1715; (e) Duke of Gloucester Street, Williamsburg, Virginia, beginning of the 18th century; (f) Parlange Plantation, Pointe Coupée, Louisiana, 1750.
Page 202: Jonathan Fairbanks House, Dedham, Massachusetts, 1636.

200

a

b

c

d

e

f

a

b

a

b

es of this type date from the seventeenth century; one may possibly go back to 1493. A special form, already complicated, is that in which there are four gables and the two pitch roofs intersect.

The desire to increase the walled-in area and so enable more of the faithful to tarry in the house of God was difficult to realise because the maximum length of the log-walls was limited by the natural length of the tree-trunks. The difficulty was overcome by creating an octagonal ground-plan in place of what had always previously been a square or at least a rectangular one. In this way the central part, already the most important part of the building, increased visibly in significance and this was further emphasised by raising it even higher above the two extensions and covering it with a tall pyramidal spire extending over the octagonal ground-plan. The dome remained insignificant in size and crowned the apex of the roof. This type represents by far the most popular form of the Russian wooden church and was built over and over again in new variants in all the territories of the north. A comparatively late example is the Uspensky church on the lake shore at Kondopoga, a town in Soviet Karelia. In this church – and this is a not unusual variant – the eight-sided block is set upon a large four-sided one, which gives variety to the silhouette of the building. The same end is served by making the topmost 'squares' of the four-sided block slightly wider and by doubling the breadth of the central and upper parts of the octagon; such a constructional procedure is characteristic of the churches of the territory round Lake Onezhskoye. The church of Kondopoga is 150 feet high, the breadth of the square about 23 feet, that of the upper octagon 28 feet. As the illustration clearly shows, there is no decoration, nor any carved ornament on either of the outside staircases which lead up to the church from north and south (because the west wall of the inconspicuous porch built out in front of the refectory stands right on the shore of the lake). The effect is produced solely by the severity of the round tree-trunks which form the log-walls, the monumentality of the central building – which at first sight may perhaps seem disproportionately massive, especially because its periphery increases towards the top, but this really only provides a termination and is not oppressive – and by the height of the pyramidal spire over the central *srub*. And finally, viewed from the east, there is the roof of the sanctuary with its convex curves meeting in a point at the apex and its obtuse inward angles at the base forming another, extremely effective, decorative feature. This form of onion-section gabled roof is extremely popular in Russia in both wooden and stone churches and there are many variations.

There is an extremely interesting relationship, of which many details have still not been fully explained, between wooden and stone churches in Russia. There is no doubt that artistic impulses have worked in both directions. Thus the wall arcades of stone architecture that originally served a structural purpose and were later used purely for decoration, the so-called *kokoshniki* (corbelled arches), were taken over and used for wooden churches, though in an altered form; in both contexts they represent a favourite decoration placed at the point of transition from the body of the building proper to the pyramid-spire of the 'tower'. The most powerful influence, however, was the Byzantine-Orthodox scheme which affected the wooden

58b

Windmill, northern Russia.

Page 203: (a) Town-hall, Sigtuna, Sweden, 18th century; (b) Tuinhuis (garden-house) of Ceres house, Krommenie, North Holland, end of the 18th century (cf. 195).
Left: (a) Entrance-gate, Uusikaupunki, Finland, c. 1860 (now demolished); (b) guest-house of a farmstead, Jämsä, Tavastland, Finland, C. L. Engel, c. 1830.

205

churches, by their very nature rooted in Russian soil, through the stone churches which were built mainly in the towns. The solutions of the ground-plans exemplified in these churches and well adapted to liturgical needs – the dome which crowned the building, and the later, canonically enjoined, form with five domes to match the high spirituality of the church – were all first embodied in stone and only subsequently in wood, and then, of course, in a manner suited to the more limited constructional possibilities of this material. Conversely, however, the stone church owes at least as much to religious architecture in wood, if not more. It has been claimed that the stone reliefs of the Dmitri cathedral at Vladimir and on other buildings of the same type were influenced by wood-carving. More important is the fact that in Moscow and its territory, by 1500 assuming the dominant role in political and therefore in cultural matters, not only did the old building traditions of Vladimir revive – together with a few Italian Renaissance elements introduced by such foreign masters as Ridolfo Fioraventi – but also the octagonal ground-plan of the 'tower' with the pyramidal spire was borrowed from native wooden architecture and long remained an active force. We may cite as the best-known example the cathedral of St. Basil in Moscow of 1555, and as the most characteristic the Church of the Ascension in Kolomenskoye of 1532. Anticipating events, we may suggest that the Ukrainian wooden churches of the seventeenth century in a later resurgence of Muscovite stone architecture (by way of that of the Ukraine) were to be the bearers of essential stylistic elements of the Baroque. But to return to the churches with pyramidal roofs and with octagonal or combined square and octagonal ground-plans for the central parts. So far we have examined only axially constructed buildings. The desire for more expansive and more spacious solutions inspired the architects of the wooden churches to add two extra wings, one at the north and one at the south. Thus there emerged a centralised building with a cruciform ground-plan which was appropriate to that characteristic feature of the Orthodox church, a nave culminating in a dome. This structure consisting of five *sruby* arranged on a cruciform plan is sometimes surmounted by five pyramid roofs of which the one that covers the central building is larger and taller than the others. The church of the Holy Trinity of 1727 in the cemetery at Nenoska in the territory of Archangel'sk is the purest example of this type.

Popular though the church with a pyramidal roof was with architects and the faithful, it found no favour with the ecclesiastical hierarchy. The purist movement of renewal reached its culmination in the seventeenth century under the Patriarch Nikon. His ecclesiastical reform of 1653 resulted in the *Raskol* or schism in the Russian Orthodox church; the Old Believers, cruelly persecuted by church and state, withdrew to the inaccessible regions of north Russia as the only place where they could continue to practise their traditional forms of worship. These people exercised an undoubted influence on the maintenance of the old style of church building in that part of Russia. Part of Nikon's reform was, in fact, a strict prohibition of the church with a pyramidal roof. Architects were charged with building churches 'according to the right and lawful disposition as required by ecclesiastic law and ordinance, with either a single dome or with three or five domes, but in no circumstance to erect

Wooden church in the territory of Vologda.

206

churches with pyramidal roofs.' In Moscow and in the nearer environs of the city the despised type disappeared fast, that is to say, no more churches of this type were built; but in those parts which were virtually beyond the reach of secular or spiritual authority – in the far north – they persisted for a long time, or else the prohibition was only half obeyed and the popular pyramid was made to resemble a dome. In this way a new type arose in which the central section, now usually square again, was surmounted by an onion-shaped tower which, however, finished in a point like the pyramid-spire.

It was not the first time that the population had resisted an innovation in the style of church building dictated by ecclesiastical authority. A chronicle for the year 1490 records incidents that occurred during the rebuilding, at the command of the Grand Duke, of the cathedral of Velikiy Ustyug, which had been burnt down. The metropolitan of Rostov sought to profit by the occasion and to enforce his intention of rebuilding from a new ground-plan that was more closely related to that of the Byzantine church; but the people of Ustyug 'did not like this' and staged a regular revolt; with the support of the Grand Duke, they carried their point that rebuilding should be 'in the old manner', which meant that it should be based upon indigenous forms. This attitude is undoubtedly in keeping with the temper of the 'people', that is always and everywhere traditionalist, yet it is certainly particularly characteristic of the conservative nature of Orthodox belief. Of course over the centuries churches did change their forms repeatedly and considerably; but they did it gradually, not radically overnight. We have given only cursory consideration to the pitch roof, the pyramidal roof, the onion-shaped tops to the 'tower' and the numerous variations and hybrid forms; we must underline the fact that in all these different types we are dealing basically only with interchangeable solutions of the roof elements, the external outlines. The ground-plan of the Russian Orthodox church was still restricted, and was to remain so, to the basic scheme of altar, area for the lay congregation, and refectory with or without porch; even when, in the cruciform ground-plan, there were the two additional wings at the north and south. This remains true also of the last two types to be discussed, the multi-levelled church and the church with many domes. The former is characterised by the complexity of its roof, in which a number of cubes or octagons, each smaller than the one below it, are set one on top of the other and are surmounted by one or several, usually small, onions. For the foreigner the most 'Russian' church is that with many domes, which is historically the most recent and structurally the most complicated. The two churches in the cemetery at Kizhi, one dating from 1714 and the other from 1764, are rightly celebrated. The earlier in particular, the Church of the Transfiguration, is a masterpiece of Russian folk architecture, singular in conception and execution. The anonymous architect has here achieved a consummation both technical and aesthetic of Russian skill in building in wood; almost all the constructional and decorative elements of earlier building are combined in a homogeneous formal idea: the central part is a tall octagon with log walls; there are besides four wings, one of which – the sanctuary – has five walls; there are gabled roofs of onion-section over two wings and over the projecting upper parts of the octagon; the second, smaller, octagon which is set on

Wooden church in Poltava.

207

top of the large one gives the dominant central part a stepped effect; there are also *kokoshniki* (corbelled arches); but the most outstanding feature is the number of onion-domes which decorate the building. There are twenty-two domes altogether, arranged in four stepped tiers on the east, west, north and south sides; in the penultimate tier the number is doubled by the addition of four more onion-domes set upon roofs built out from the octagon; there is an extra one over the sanctuary and all lead up to the single great, tall dome which crowns the centre of the whole building. It says much for the genius of the architect that despite the wealth of decorative accessories, his church does not look overweighted; the good proportions and rightness of the elements, both individually and in their relationship to the whole, are unsurpassed. It is surely not misplaced enthusiasm to count this church among the architectural masterpieces of the world.

36; 37; 45

No discussion of the east Slav wooden church would be complete which did not consider the west Ukrainian variants, some of which are very important. Here too the earliest surviving monuments date from the seventeenth century, but, as in the north, earlier buildings may be deduced from the sources. The Ukrainian churches are similar in many particulars to those of Great Russia, yet they also exhibit a number of singularities of outline. Among the common features are their division into three – sanctuary, church proper, porch – and their cruciform ground-plan; however, there is a special form, widely distributed in the south-west, which is a kind of three-aisled church; that is to say, three lots of three *sruby* may be placed side by side and each of them (this too is an individual feature by comparison with the north) may be built up like a tower and be roofed. Thus in addition to those churches which have three and five 'towers' – the latter when the ground-plan is cruciform – it is not unusual to find others with nine 'towers'. They are formed in the manner of the many-tiered church by a number of square or octagonal prisms which diminish in size as they ascend, and where they set back, a characteristic feature of Ukrainian Baroque, they are covered by curved roofs. The domes are often helmet shaped and roofed with wooden shingles. The churches of the Huzulians, usually built over a cruciform ground-plan (five *sruby*), are particularly archaic in appearance; here, indeed, as throughout the territory known as the Carpathian Ukraine, Catholic Magyar stylistic influences are apparent, whereas in Galicia and in the Ukraine proper Polish influences sometimes operate, although, of course, they are always adapted to the peculiarities of the Orthodox church. We cannot do more than mention the fact that during the Baroque period central European styles reached the cities of the Ukraine, such as Kiev, sometimes direct and sometimes by way of the wooden churches – churches with three and five towers, for example, stem from wooden architecture – and that these Ukrainian stone churches in their turn left their mark on the Baroque of Moscow.

The interiors of Orthodox churches in the north and in the south-west both form an extremely interesting chapter of eastern European folk art. Even in humble village churches some of the cult objects stem from more exalted spheres, in particular, of course, the icons, the making of which was for centuries governed by the strongest taboo, therefore to a large extent outside the province of the secular painter. Never-

Hay barn at Vysoka, Slovakia.

Right: The Rum Shop, Salem, Massachusetts, 1800.
Page 210: Redwood Library, Newport, Rhode Island, Peter Harrison, 1748–50; (b) Andalusia (house), Bucks County, Pennsylvania, Thomas U. Walter, 1833; (c) Ralph Small House, Macon, Georgia, attributed to Elias Carter, c. 1835; (d) Atheneum, Nantucket, Massachusetts, 1847; (e) Kingscote, Newport, Rhode Island, Richard Upjohn, 1841; (f) Stoughton House, Cambridge, Massachusetts, H. H. Richardson, 1882-83.

208

a

b

c

d

e

f

a

b

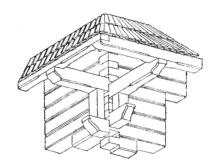

40

Corner of a house and eaves.

Page 211: Front entrance of a house at Hingham, Massachusetts, end of the 18th century.
Left: Interior of a Shaker house, Massachusetts, c. 1800: (a) built-in cupboards; (b) staircase.

theless, from several points of view the iconostasis is of interest even in our context, first because there are so many different ways of positioning it within the church, but especially because of the form of the so-called royal door, which was usually carved with extreme artistry and exhibited a variety of folk motifs. The same applies to the other church furniture, the pulpit, shrines, stools, standing and hanging candelabra and so on – all works of the popular master-carver and many of them painted too. Sometimes, though not always, the ceiling of the central part of the church, the 'heaven', carries a large painted icon modelled on the dome mosaics of the stone cathedrals. Another feature which is often noteworthy is the form of the wooden churches, whose ceiling is supported by two thick carved and painted beams, while along the interior wall – very much as in the farmers' *izba* – there runs a bench with carved feet. One cannot fail to notice the similarity of this part of the church to the farmer's living-room, and some scholars have chosen to see in it the survival of a pre-Christian cult room with a use similar to that of Christian times. At all events, it is certain that special care was usually lavished upon the building of the refectory.

Religious buildings in the wider sense include roadside crosses, chapels, which are often smaller-scale copies of churches, and bell-towers, which in Russia are detached from the complex of the church, as is the campanile in Italy. Though comparatively recent, historically, bell-towers are interesting as monuments, often of extremely archaic form, of the popular carpenter's art. The much-loved pyramidal roof was allowed to survive on bell-towers, for the pronouncement of the ecclesiastical authorities against it had been confined to the church proper; these roofs persist on bell-towers until far into the nineteenth century, indeed they appear to have been almost the only ones ever to have been considered for a carpentered belfry of this type.

Farmhouses and churches were not of course the only kinds of building where the carpenter's art had to satisfy the needs of medieval Russia. Two extremely important spheres where this branch of craftsmanship operated were the building of defences and the construction of towns, including the palaces of the prosperous and powerful citizens and boyars which had to be specially large and splendid. The wooden defensive systems have perished, it is true, except for a few watch-towers in western Siberia that are all that remain of the so-called *ostrog*, a simple fortification on the Siberian trade-routes in the seventeenth and eighteenth centuries. Pictorial sources and accounts in chronicles show that these palisades with their wooden watch-towers were, despite primitive tools, of a high technical standard. This is even more true of town houses and palaces. Although they do not differ fundamentally from the farmhouses, they are larger and have more rooms. The former palace of the Tsars at Kolomenskoye is famous; it stood beside Peter the Great's summer palace and consisted of a number of separate palaces, churches, fortresses and offices – all built of wood throughout. It was looked upon as the eighth wonder of the world. The reconstruction of Kolomenskoje, which, despite its magnificence, had certain rustic features, shows the singularity of the building. Most of the other wooden palaces have also perished and we can only deduce their appearance from secondary evidence.

Architecture in wood, both secular and ecclesiastical, stands nearer to the centre of the national culture in Russia than in the other cultural areas of Europe. In its character and history it belongs to the realm of folk art, but in its aesthetic intensity and its significance in the history of civilisation it belongs equally to high art, from which it received much impetus but which in turn it consistently helped to form. Influenced in details from outside – by Byzantium, by the culture of the Caucasus and other Asiatic cultures and by Poland – it remains thoroughly autochthonous, a completely indigenous art. The creative powers of the country have found in it what is perhaps their most powerful vehicle of expression. In its archaisms it is as great as the lapidary speech of the old Russian *byliny*. With all its love of monumentality it never falls into extravagance, even in its later hybrid forms.

The detail holds its own beside the whole, of which it is both an accessory and an integral part. The function of any individual building is always the first consideration; composition is secondary. But it is there; the will to form, to proportion, is always alive and ready to assert itself. Conditioned as they are by the nature of the material, the number of basic constructional processes, the principal solutions of the ground-plan, may be small; yet Russian wooden architecture is anything but uniform. Perhaps it is precisely this incomparable wealth of variation, its multiplicity in unity, that constitutes its most essential character.

Farmhouses in Poland are log-buildings, as in Russia. Apart from the mountainous country in the south (and the western part of the country, where timber-framing prevails) they embody a fairly homogeneous type, with, originally, only a few rooms on one floor. In the foothills of the Carpathians especially, the posts and gables, and the surrounds of doors and windows are often richly carved; here too we find a structure like an extra storey built out over the entrance to the house. Mention must also be made of the wooden synagogues of the eighteenth century with 215; 216 their high stepped roofs that are a special feature of Poland.

Log-buildings are in the majority in the country districts of the eastern Moravian Carpathians and in the Beskids too, while most of the houses in Bohemia are 75e timber-framed with dark, unpainted wood and whitewashed infillings. In the log- 213 buildings of Slovakia the timbers at the corners under the eaves intersect in such a way that the joints become a form of decoration; and the surrounds of doors and windows are usually much painted. The wooden houses of Walachia have white gables with polychrome painted eaves and inscriptions.

The rustic wooden houses of Hungary too often have finely carved details on gables, windows and doors; many of them have porticos, the carved columns of which often take the form of Neo-classical columns. The wooden churches of Bánffyhunyad, Körösfő and Magyarvalkó are impressive and seem to perpetuate a kind of popular Gothic. There are churches in northern Hungary which have coffered ceilings and fully panelled interiors with painted motifs in a popular Renaissance style.

In the villages of Romania, especially those of the mountain districts, wood has remained by far the commonest building material right up to the present day. Although there are few buildings left which are more than three hundred years old, ground-plans and carved decoration enable us to infer the nature of much older tra-

Farmhouse from the Don territory.

Wooden synagogue, Pograbyszcze, Poland, 18th century.

230a

ditions of Romanian wooden architecture. There is very often a porch, known as a *prispa*, which frequently serves as a living and working space. It is usually supported by posts and enclosed by balustrades, which may be masterpieces of artistic carving.

251d
246b

They are at their most distinctive in the northern part of the Moldova region, and in northern Oltland (Little Walachia); their ornamentation consists largely of geometric motifs, but plants and animals figure too. The same motifs mark the richly decorated wooden entrance-gates to the farmyards. Surrounds of windows and doors, ends of beams and the ridges of roofs are often carved. The most important of the Romanian wooden churches occur in Transylvania, northern Moldavia, Great Wala-

48b

chia and Oltland.

78a; 80d
131a
221; 131d
54d
260; 267b

Mosques were built either wholly or partly of wood; the one illustrated, in Montenegro, even has a wooden minaret. Most of the buildings in the wooded regions of Bosnia, Slovenia and Serbia are log-buildings. In the plains of Yugoslavia the houses are timber-framed and their façades are often white-washed, especially in the towns. Plovdiv in Bulgaria is one of the towns most worth seeing from this point of view with its old streets of timber-framed houses. Here too there are nineteenth century wooden rustic houses with terraces built up on columns and painted with obvious delight. The interiors of Bulgarian churches and monasteries are often painted in exuberant colour, and both form and decoration suggest traditions of an architecture in wood in which the presence of old Byzantine and Turkish features beside eastern and western European elements is unmistakable.

215

Wooden synagogue, Lutomiersk,
Poland, 18th century.

Right: Madewood Plantation, Louisiana, beginning of the 19th century.
Page 218: (a) Farmhouse from Kahi-
luoto, south-western Finland, now in
the open-air museum, Helsinki, c. 1780;
(b) house on the Alinenkatu, Uuskiau-
punki, Finland, c. 1860.
Page 219: (a) Country-house, Pennsylvania Farm Museum of Landis Valley,
Lancaster, Pennsylvania, 19th century;
(b) summer villa, island of Ruissalo,
near Turku, Finland, c. 1880.
Page 220: Wooden colonnades in the
Plaza, Albuquerque, New Mexico.

a

b

a

b

a

b

a

b

26b; 266d; 268b

Although less apparent than elsewhere, wood was always widely used for building in southern Europe until iron construction was introduced in the nineteenth century, though it was popular even after that. The relatively strong resistance of wood fibre to expansion and tension made it the only suitable material for beams, roofs, tie-beams on arches and vaults and wall-facings, as well as for certain tools and machines. A survey of historical buildings constructed entirely of wood in Italy or Spain, in contrast to the northern countries, would be bound to prove much slighter than one of stone-built monuments, and it must be remembered in this connection that such forests of the Mediterranean countries as were usable for building purposes, although less reduced than they are today, have always been of smaller extent and density than those of central Europe or of central Asia. However, some wooden architecture existed and it is not without interest. It is important to remember that architectural forms built basically in wood originated in Italy and in Greece. This tradition began with primitive buildings on piles or with prehistoric storehouses for wood and grapes of a type described by Vitruvius, which occurred throughout Europe.

The mature and complex structure of the Etruscan temple, which was built entirely of wood, dates back two and a half millennia, or at least to the sixth century B.C. It should nevertheless be noted that these temples are the earliest archaic evidence of a certain Italian dislike of a completely wooden building, for the appearance of the temple is not at all that of a wooden structure. It is rather a paraphrase or anticipation of the stone structure which was to become the classical Greek and Italic and, later, Roman building. It could perhaps be said that it is an unconsciously metaphorical architecture that simulates something other than itself. Yet the fact remains that its structural elements were made entirely of wood.

The brick walls of the Etruscan *cella*, too, were often reinforced, as they had been in archaic Greece, by embedded wooden posts. Planed tree-trunks were used for the columns of the inner portico and fragments of such columns were found in the arx of Misano at Marzabotto. Others, still made of wood, were found in the primitive temple dedicated to Tinia, Uni and Minerva on the Capitol and in temples in Florence, Orvieto, Veio, Civita Castellana, Civita Lavinia, Segni, Velletri, Satricum (Conca) and elsewhere. (To show how widely distributed the prototype of the column, the plain stripped tree-trunk, has been both in space and time, we need only cite the Plaza at Albuquerque in New Mexico.)

The frame of the roof was also, of course, made of wood; it was a two-sided pitched roof, covered with flat tiles, the eaves of which, like the ridge and the pediment, were surmounted by pinnacles of baked clay, the antefixae and acroteria. If we may assume the Etruscan paintings of Chiusi to be truthful, the Etruscan wooden

Page 221: Kojumdschiolu house, Plovdiv, Bulgaria, mid-19th century.
Page 222: (a) Pope-Leigh House Mount Vernon, Virginia, Frank Lloyd Wright, 1940; (b) summer house, Muurame, central Finland, Kirmo Mikkola and Juhani Pallesmaa, 1966.
Page 223: Wooden ceiling, Casa di Risparmio, Pisa, Pierluigi Spadolini, 1968.
Left: (a) Mount Vernon, Fairfax County, Virginia, 1784-87; (b) Congress Street, Cape May, New Jersey, c. 1870.

225

roof frame resembled the modern one, where the collar-beam takes the tensile strain in appearance only. The central brick column which here replaces the king-post suggests that in fact the weight of the roof is transmitted directly, that is, by the two rafters and by the tie-beam that would thus have to take vertical stress and not only horizontal stress, as is usually the case today. It was a primitive solution and was probably soon rejected, but for that reason serves to indicate the great antiquity of the system. The existence of these wooden buildings is confirmed not only by the paintings but by the fact that they have been in part reproduced in stone – for example, hewn out of tufa in certain tombs at Chiusi.

A Roman siege instrument (testudo).

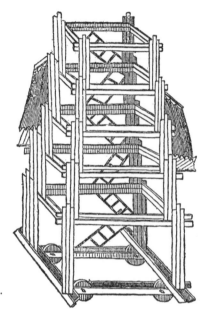

A Roman revolving siege tower.

As progress was made in the application of arches and vaults, and stone supports such as columns, pilasters and architraves became widely used, wood building fell increasingly into disuse, especially in Roman times. But it continued to be used for roof frames, balconies (for example, in houses at Ostia) and for building granaries; also for buildings and machines with technical and military purposes. There was wooden apparatus for lifting heavy weights with windlasses and pulleys; and innumerable wooden machines of war, such as the *tormentum*, a giant catapult, the battering-ram *(aries)* and the defensive *pluteus*, a half-cylindrical shelter made of hurdles spread with stretched hides and mounted on wheels, under cover of which soldiers stormed fortifications. There were also the *vinea* and the *testudo*, both wheeled shelters for the same purpose as the *pluteus*, and finally the *turris*, a revolving wooden tower which could be manoeuvred close to the walls of a fortress and could be raised automatically for the projectiles to make their full impact.

All these machines were described in about 400 A.D. by Flavius Renatus Vegetius and by earlier Roman military writers. With slight variations they dominated western military practice until the fifteenth century and were still frequently illustrated at this period – by Taccola, for example, and Valturio (1482), and in a more evolved form by Francesco di Giorgio and Leonardo, until finally, after gunpowder had come into use, the 'diabolical' invention of 'bombardment' revolutionised the

226

whole of military technique.

Roman field fortifications and siege-works were also wooden buildings in which timbers, trimmed roughly into squares, and earth were mostly used. The scheme is the classic *castra stativa* or permanent camp, to which innumerable European cities owe their origin. This Roman field camp, square at first but later often rectangular, with sides of between 2000 and 2500 feet in length, was surrounded by defences comprising a fosse and a rampart. It was reinforced by hurdles and long tree-trunks and branches. A palisade *(vallum)* was erected on top of the earth rampart. Within the fortifications wooden barracks lined rectangular streets.

Bridges, of which there are numerous records, were more elaborately carpentered. The one built by Caesar in 51 B.C. over the marshes at Breuil-le-Sec (Oise) and Trajan's bridge over the Danube were technically admirable. Caesar's bridge was in fact a special road built to enable the legionaries to cross the marshes with their equipment. The foundation was dried peat reinforced by hurdles and sticks; on this was laid a wooden flooring consisting of sheets in series measuring 10 by 11 feet; this made an even, stable basis which was then covered with broken stones and earth. Finally the separate sections of this long bridge were securely jointed to one another with wooden pegs. Trajan's wooden pontoon bridge over the Danube is accurately

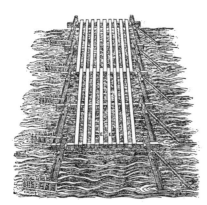

227

shown in one of the reliefs on Trajan's column in Rome and has for this reason remained famous until today. Caesar's own detailed description tells us about the construction of the bridge that he threw across the Rhine in 55 B.C. An exact reconstructional drawing was made by Palladio. The bridge was 13 feet in breadth and about 1300 feet long and consisted of two-legged trestles with piles rammed into the riverbed. Planks were laid on the trestles and boards on the planks. Stays on the downstream side reinforced the trestles against the pressure of the current; and on the up-stream side there were gratings to fend off any obstacles that the enemy might have thrown into the water from an up-stream position. This bridge is alleged to have been built in ten days. Another bridge which is famous because it appears in the bas-relief on Trajan's column was built over the Danube near Turnu Severin in Romania by Apollodorus of Damascus in 209–205 B.C. It was 1200 yards long, between 45 and 60 feet wide and consisted of twenty-one low wooden lattice-work arches resting on thick stone columns.

Caesar's excellent technical description was, as we have seen, not unknown to Palladio, and Palladio's bridge over the Brenta at Bassano – perhaps the most often described of any piece of architecture in wood in southern Europe – was in fact only a repetition of Caesar's principle. In 1569 Palladio replaced a roofed wooden bridge, which had already been famous since 1209, by the form in which it stands today, or rather in which it stands once more. For the bridge has been several times destroyed – in 1750, 1821 and 1948 – and has each time been rebuilt from the precise technical description in Book III of Palladio's *Dell' architettura*. His book also contains drawings of some other wooden bridges now destroyed.

Like Palladio, other Italian Renaissance architects drew upon ancient sources and it is a fact well known to art historians that their inspiration from the *quattrocento* onwards was derived not only from looking at the buildings that had survived

Caesar's bridge over the Rhine, reconstructed by Palladio.

140a

from antiquity but also from literary documents, especially Vitruvius. Most of these, it is true, relate to stone building, the dominant form, but they also discuss wooden bridges, roof frames, balconies, fortifications and technical equipment. As regards the last, special mention should be made of Domenico Fontana in the late Renaissance. In 1586 he contrived to erect the obelisk in the Piazza S. Pietro in Rome, a remarkable enterprise for which he used, in addition to eight hundred men and one hundred and forty horses, forty great windlasses on unusual wooden trestles which could be moved horizontally. Nicola Zabaglia, an inventor of genius, published in Rome in the year 1743 a book containing fine engravings of the imposing wood constructions of his mechanical inventions. In a work published in Venice in 1754 Memmo gives an account of Ferracina, another very active carpenter and mechanic. And finally Cavalieri di San Bartolo published in Mantua in 1831 a profusely illustrated survey of the whole Roman and Italian tradition of mechanical apparatus in wood.

There is an equally continuous tradition, dating from Roman times, of splendid temporary wooden buildings, most of them put up at short notice. It would be impossible to name all the gates of honour, triumphal arches, catafalques and wooden banqueting halls known to have been built since the *cinquecento*. They range from the wooden catafalque erected by Fontana in 1590 in S. Maria Maggiore in Rome for the body of Sixtus V and those created by Bernini for Paul V in 1621, Carlo Barberini in 1630, Muzio Mattei in 1668 and for the Duke of Beaufort one year later, to the wooden 'triumphal machine' built by Filippo Juvarra in 1701 in Messina for Philip V of Spain, and the triumphal arches erected in 1806 by Luigi Cagnola at the Porta Orientale in Milan on the occasion of the marriage of Eugène de Beauharnais to Amalie of Bavaria. It should be noted that in all these cases wooden constructions were used atypically, for these were buildings where wood was, so to speak, misused to simulate different, more costly, works in stone or brick, and there the structure was often masked by surface stucco and paint.

True wood constructions, however, those in which appropriate use was made of the material and which were not designed to simulate something else, were, apart from bridges, mechanical devices and the rustic alpine houses that we still have to discuss, limited by and large to great roof frames – which were often open – ceilings and wall panelling. We may at this point record an interesting structural detail, namely the gigantic wooden tie-beams designed to reduce the thrust of the vault that were put into certain Venetian churches towards the end of the fourteenth century, among them the Frari and SS. Giovanni e Paolo. The ceiling vaults of S. Fermo Maggiore and S. Zeno Maggiore in Verona, executed in about 1320, are also highly developed examples of the carpenter's art and splendidly effective from the aesthetic standpoint. These remarkable vaults are characteristic of the Veneto and must be related to the Venetian tradition of shipbuilding. The same tradition is the source of the marvellous architecture of the large wooden ceiling (90 by 260 feet) erected in 1306 by Fra Giovanni of the Eremiti over the so-called *salone* of the Palazzo della Ragione in Padua. Further examples of wooden roof frames, vaults and ceilings, often most lavishly painted and carved, are to be found in many Italian buildings.

Right: (a) Church and bell-tower at Kerimäki, Finland, E. Lohrmann, 1847 (cf. 65); (b) houses in the Gamle By, Aarhus, 16th and 17th centuries.
Page 230: (a) Front verandah of a house from Ceauru, Oltland, now in the open-air museum, Bucharest, 1875; (b) carved posts from the staircase of the Pokrowski church, Kizhi, Karelia, 1764; (c) arcades in the Place des Cordeliers, Dinan, c. 1500; (d) weavers' houses at Schömberg, Silesia, 18th century.

228

a

b

a

b

c

d

a

b

a

b

c

d

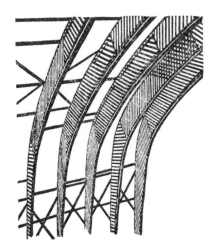

Wooden arch construction of an exhibition hall, Rome, Mario de Renzi, 1938.

As one example among many we may recall the wood-panelled Sala del Gran Consiglio in the Doge's Palace, on whose wooden ceiling there abound the most splendid carved and gilt garlands, between vast paintings by Veronese, Tintoretto and Palma il Giovane.

The most impressive building ever to have been built of wood in Italy is the Teatro Farnese which, until it was closed in 1732, was regarded throughout Europe as a miracle. Now restored after the destruction of the last war, it can be seen in the Palazzo della Pilotta in Parma, where Gianbattista Aleotti, called l'Argenta, built it in 1618 in the old armoury. Aleotti constructed a deep stage and a large *platea* or open stage, also an entirely wooden tiered auditorium and two rows of balconies or boxes on a horseshoe-shaped ground-plan. The theatre, which retains the classical form with an accent more Mannerist than Baroque, could seat an audience of four thousand five hundred, as was proved in 1628 on the marriage of Odoardo Farnese and Margherita de' Medici.

Except for some extremely noteworthy exhibition buildings, buildings made entirely of wood are seldom erected nowadays. Two of them are remarkable. One is Mario de Renzi's pavilion erected in Rome in 1938, a bizarre solution with parabolic timber-framed arches; the other is the ski-lift station built in 1948 by Carlo Mollino on Lago Nero. This consists of a pure, formally perfect, log-building on a raised platform of reinforced concrete. It is perhaps the only piece of modern architecture to remain true to the native and traditional rules of the Alps and it uses the material and technique of wood building without prejudice. It explicitly avoids the compromises found in other new buildings, not only in the Alps: structures of brick or concrete of which the exteriors are simply sheathed in wood. Thus Mollino's construction represents a new way of building in wood that contrasts with the Mediterranean techniques we have so far mentioned of building temples, fortifications, machines and palaces, all of which we must call rustic.

It is, in a sense, a 'timeless' art and embraces the native peasant architecture of all alpine valleys, not only those of Italy. It usually finds expression in log-buildings, from simple sheds and huts like the *masi* of Trento to the hybrid types. These include houses in which a wooden upper storey is built over a masonry ground-floor, or, especially in the Bergamask valleys, the plain of Lombardy and even in central Italy, houses which are walled on the south side and have at the back a light structure of wooden posts with surrounding galleries originally meant for drying the harvest. Most buildings made entirely of wood, however, are confined to the higher regions of the Alps. As a protection against rising damp and invading rats, they often stand on distinctive mushroom-shaped stones. All are log-buildings with horizontal trunks or beams that are jointed into one another at the corners in techniques which, though simple, are often extremely decorative. This method of log-building is found not only in all the alpine regions but also in Scandinavia, south-eastern Europe, Russia, Siberia and in the Far East. It may one day become possible to establish concrete historical, to say nothing of ethnic, connections between these buildings. Or it may be that similar needs and means produce similar results, although forms and anomalies of taste may vary endlessly – and certain details of structure and accessory such as shingle roofs

233

234

78d

245d

73b; 247b; 265c

46b

Page 231: (a) Timber-framed house on the Hinterer Brühl, Hildesheim, 16th-17th centuries; (b) street-front on Bryggen, Bergen, 18th century.
Left: (a) Brackets and carving on a timber-framed house at Celle, Lower Saxony, 17th century; (b) detail of the cornice of a country house in New England, mid-19th century; (c) consoles and carving on a house in Helsingör, 1577; (d) carving on Les Marmousets, a house at Ploermel, Brittany, 1585.

and walls, painted and carved window-frames, outside staircases and interior fittings are often very fine, if usually naive, works of art.

*Ski-lift station
at Lago Nero, Piedmont, Carlo Mollino,
1946–47.*

234

Imaginative building in wood is one of the great achievements of American architecture. From the early seventeenth century onwards and the first settlements on the North American continent, American architecture, whatever the material employed, was characterised by two distinct factors: a direct dependence upon and relation to current European architectural developments and the addition of typical American qualities of vigour of craftsmanship, inventiveness and adaptability of design, and eagerness to experiment with native materials. The combination of these two attitudes served to give it a clearly defined position in spite of the stylistic domination of the mother countries, mainly England, in the seventeenth and eighteenth centuries, and the subsequent emergence of a native style as a distinct entity in the nineteenth and twentieth centuries. In truth, American architecture has been a stylistic melting pot for over three centuries, a spirit which has sometimes been modified but never essentially altered.

Wood is the most abundant and plentiful building material on the North American continent. It is more abundant than in Europe, except for areas of Scandinavia, Germany, and Switzerland. Furthermore, the first settlers were familiar with its use, for timber-framed houses were the predominant construction for the artisan and agricultural classes in the villages of the south-eastern countries of England – Essex, Suffolk, Norfolk, Cambridgeshire, Hertfordshire, Kent, Sussex – the area from which most early colonists emigrated. Indeed, they could hardly build otherwise than in the comparable style and structure familiar to them from the frame buildings they had lived in just before leaving Old England for the shores of the North American continent. Striking similarities between the seventeenth and early eighteenth century homes of the New World and the Old reinforce this theory that the craft traditions of English architecture are the prime origins of the first Colonial buildings.

Any history of wood building in seventeenth century America must focus upon the New England states of Massachusetts, Connecticut, Rhode Island, New Hampshire, Vermont and Maine, as it is there that are preserved the greatest number of wooden buildings of any region in America. Nearly eighty frame houses survive – of the hundreds which are known to have been erected (mentioned in archives and documents of the period) – and are our greatest source of knowledge for the appearance of pre–1700 architecture.

The Jonathan Fairbanks House, Dedham, Massachusetts, *c.* 1636–1637, probably the oldest frame house extant in the United States, is characteristic of the Medieval, late Gothic character of New England style at that moment. It follows the mode of asymmetrical grouping of masses, of sharp contrasts of line and shape, and the dominance of the roof-line with its overhanging upper storey and bold projecting eaves. As in the central unit of the Fairbanks House, one might at this time find a

202

235

roof of extremely steep pitch, advantageous for shedding the heavy snows of the New England winter. Alternatively, one would have the 'gambrel' roof as seen in the two side wings or additions to the Fairbanks House. Gambrel roofs, which circumscribe a jagged outline because of the contrasting slopes – one, the lower, a long slope of markedly steep pitch and the other, a short upper slope of lower pitch – add to the asymmetrical and picturesque impression. The only predominant focal point was always the massive central chimney, the sole element, except for the stone foundations, not made of wood.

The construction of the Fairbanks House, as in all seventeenth century buildings, followed an English pattern. The substructure or skeleton walls of the building consisted of a timber frame of massive posts and beams, filled in with either wattle-and-daub (a combination of willow and plaster) or by brick masonry called 'nogging' inserted in the interstices of the frame. But a characteristic of the New England house was that the wall was not left exposed as was usually the case in England; the wooden skeleton frame has been moved in out of the weather and surfaced by clapboards, thin wedge-shaped boards about five inches wide and usually six feet long, laid horizontally over the walls.

All seventeenth century wooden American houses give an impression of singular strength because of the grouping of heavy, low masses of angular shape and the frequent, abrupt transitions from one element of the house to another. The period is also one of unrivalled simplicity; architectural ornament was confined to the carved pendants decorating the exterior overhangs, pendants whose upper, square section reveals the shape of the upper floor structural posts of which they are the logical continuation. Pendants had been a favourite decorative device in Tudor times when no less a personage than King Henry VIII had used them as terminations of the flatly moulded ribs of the Hall ceiling at Hampton Court Palace (1531–1536). But using the pendant as an exterior feature seems to be more common in America.

Another example of the clapboard-covered frame house of seventeenth century New England is the Jethro Coffin House, Nantucket Island, Massachusetts (c. 1686), significant because, in general form, it is the ancestor of a style of domestic architecture extremely popular for twentieth century middle class housing: the so-called Cape Cod House. Late Medieval still are the windows which are small in relation to the expanse of the walls, and the asymmetric placement of the main door-way. All of these elements, including the fact that the clapboards were customarily left unpainted to weather to a silvery grey in the salt wind (possible because of the proximity to the sea) and the low outline with the steeply pitched roof, are features which were to be carried on with little variation throughout the state of Massachusetts for almost three hundred years.

Early religious structures of the first century of wood building, sponsored by the Puritan community who did not have the heritage of the Gothic cathedral or parish church, took on many, if not all, the aspects of the private house; not the private house of seventeenth century Gothic New England, but rather that of the Restoration – the William and Mary style of the late seventeenth century English manor-house. Typical is the façade of the Old Ship Meeting House, Hingham,

86d

245b

201a

Right: (a) Carving on the house at Bäckerstrasse 3, Stade, 1590; (b) Vannes et sa femme, carving on a house in the Place des Lices, Vannes, Brittany; (c) doorway of a house at Celle, c. 1800; (d) figures on brackets in the Bäckerstrasse, Stade, c. 1500.
Page 238: Details of walls: (a) Monschau, Eifel, 17th century; (b) Wiesbaden-Frauenstein, Haus zur Linde, 17th century; (c) Warwick, end of the 16th century; (d) Zwiep, near Lochem, Gelderland, 1866.

201c

a

b

c

d

a

b

c

d

a

b

c

d

a

b

Massachusetts (1681); direct and honest in its strict five-bay symmetry, it denies the Gothic tradition of the established Anglican religion in favour of a secular concept wrought in the more modest guise of wood. Most traces of the Gothic seen in the Coffin and Fairbanks houses are gone. Windows have become larger, the façade balanced, and the roof hipped, and they form a comfortable, placid counterfoil to the expanse of the exterior elevations. The ground plan is four-square and symmetrical so that there is a sense of compact repose. The balustrade and belfry add a jaunty note to an otherwise academic concept. So secular does the Old Ship Meeting House appear that it might easily serve as an assembly hall for the business of the townspeople as well as a place of worship. Or, alternatively, if the building had been carried out on a larger scale and in a material such as brick or stone, it could easily have served as a prototype for the greater American classical mansions like the Governor's Palace, Williamsburg, Virginia, of a generation later. First and most important of all, is the extremely secular nature of all early American wooden architecture, most especially in New England; this is probably attributable to the fundamentalist, Protestant nature of seventeenth century American society, a community which emphasised domestic architecture at the expense of the ecclesiastical, and offering a sharp contrast to the building scene in Catholic Central and South America at the same moment.

It is a truism that the colonies of New England are loyal to English standards, and, as one moves down the Atlantic seaboard to the Middle Colonies of New York, New Jersey, Delaware, Pennsylvania, there is fidelity to the standards of other mother countries and to styles other than that of the late English Gothic. The Flemish, Dutch and Northern French were the first settlers of the Hudson River Valley. Of the two major regional building styles, the Dutch Colonial and Flemish Colonial, the 'Flemish' style was the first to evolve and was more eminently suited to building in wood. In the Jan Ditmars House, Flatlands, Brooklyn, New York, (c. 1700), the distinguishing features are wide clapboard sheathing, a prominent gambrel roof with exceptionally wide, flaring, projecting eaves, a deep front porch with spindle-like balusters which seem to, but do not, support the curve of the eaves. One might also be able to term this architecture 'functional' in that the flared eaves and gambrel roof provided for extra rooms on the two upper floors and also served the purpose of protecting walls of clay (before wooden sheathing was introduced) from adverse weather. Dependent as it was upon the heritage of Flanders and its vernacular architecture, the Flemish Colonial style of the Middle Colonies was to linger in this area until 1800 when it was displaced by the arrival of the Classic Revival in New York City.

Proceeding southwards, there are no surviving wooden buildings before 1700 in Virginia, North and South Carolina, and Georgia. But, by 1715, there is one distinctive house in Edenton, North Carolina: the Cupola House. This seems almost a transplantation of late seventeenth century Massachusetts style to the Southern Colonies and shows the persistence of the vernacular late Medieval into the earlier years of the eighteenth century. The walls are clapboarded, the upper storey has the identical overhang, the roof is of a steep pitch, while the cupola above is reminiscent

201b

Page 239: (a) Fabulous beast, carving on a post, stave-church of Hurum, Valdres, 12th century; (b) carving from the portal of the stave-church of Al, Hallingdal, now in the Universitets Oldsakssamling, Oslo, 12th century; (c) carved bracket, Steinkirchen, near Hamburg, c. 1600; (d) detail of carving, Abramov house, Nevyansk, Urals, mid-19th century.
Left: (a) Hahnentor, Stade 1658; (b) entrance gate, Niederaula, Hesse, c. 1600.

241

of the crowning belfry of the Old Ship Meeting House, Hingham, of thirty-five years 201c, d earlier. But, as yet, in none of the American Colonies, had anything approximating to an individual American architectural style been developed, and what structures survive are quite successful adaptations of European traditions, heavily Medieval, with only an occasional incursion of the strongly academic architecture to come later in the eighteenth century.

The persistence of a rural, farming community, especially in the rolling country-side of Pennsylvania west of Philadelphia, fostered the survival of this tradition, especially among the German settlers from the Renish Palatinate. They brought German standards and a highly trained heritage of craftsmanship, dependent again upon the Medieval – in these instances, those of the Rhine River Valley. Perhaps most Medieval and intensely German in flavour is the architecture of the Protestant, monastic communities near Lancaster, Pennsylvania. The members of these sects were celibate, practised numerous mystic religious services, and took vows of poverty, chastity and obedience. It was inevitable that their architecture should reflect this emphasis upon economy and traditional conservatism. The Society of the Solitary, 60b organized in 1735 near Lancaster, had erected their Saal (or meeting-house) at the Cloister at Ephrata, Pennsylvania, by 1740, and the Saron (Sister House for the female members of the order) and the Bethania (Brother House) soon after. Again, domestic architecture and not ecclesiastical or public buildings served as models, and the Saal has a rough-hewn appearance due to the split, oaken clapboard siding, the exceedingly steep roof of a German farmhouse and rows of dormer windows of the characteristic form called 'shed.' The small hood sheltering the entrance door is also Germanic in origin.

In complete contrast to the seventeenth century colonial style of the Atlantic seaboard where one might find wooden examples scattered throughout the country-side or in the small villages and towns, the so-called 'Georgian' style of the eighteenth century was confined to several main centres, metropolitan in character at that date even though several have shrivelled to little importance by now. Here, in the cities of Boston, Newport, Philadelphia and Williamsburg, architecture was rapidly entering a period of classically balanced composition and of finely executed Palladian detail. Taste and design alike were formed by the late seventeenth to early eighteenth century academicism of England, first that of Wren and his followers (masons, surveyors and carpenters associated with him on the Royal Works), and then by the Palladian revival fostered by Richard Boyle, Earl of Burlington. Not only were actual English buildings responsible for this change in design, but both the Wren and Lord Burlington styles were taken to the American Colonies via the medium of the printed pattern-book of architectural designs. Ground-plans, elevations and cross-sections appeared in the seventeenth century northern European editions of Serlio, Vitruvius, Vignola and the popular Dutch books depicting the houses designed by Philip Vingboons. In the eighteenth century, architecture fell almost completely under the domination of the rule of the Palladian revival sponsored by Lord Burlington with the help of Giacomo Leoni and William Kent. These men were responsible for the publication of fourteen editions of Palladian designs before 1738, as well as

William Kent's edition of *Designs of Inigo Jones*, 1727. In fact, Jones' work in the seventeenth century enjoyed an unparalleled popularity in the eighteenth as he was considered the English inheritor of Palladio's mantle. In addition to this flood of printed matter were the English carpenters' handbooks, so useful to the Colonial craftsman for details of carved woodwork, cornice lines, doorways and mantelpieces. Of

Log-huts in the North American West, 1865.

these, the editions most used were those by Batty Langley (*The City and Country Builder's and Workman's Treasury of Designs*, 1740, and *The Builder's Jewel*, 1741), and by William Salmon (*Palladio Londinensis*, 1734). Most Colonial libraries contained these volumes.

Without question, the Colonial capital of Virginia, Williamsburg, gave great impetus to the raising of academic, architectural standards. Its establishment as the capital in 1699 resulted in a building campaign and the almost immediate erection of its major government buildings: the College of William and Mary, the Capitol, the Governor's Palace, as well as the smaller houses and shops for the government officials and landed gentry who came in from nearby plantations to transact essential business or participate in the sophisticated social life of Williamsburg. The view along the major street, the Duke of Gloucester, shows that the balanced, academic quality of the major brick buildings of the town was reflected in the smaller, wooden houses and shops of white or cream painted clapboards. The whole effect is that of a late seventeenth century-early Georgian English town, Palladian in character, transplanted to American shores. Although the roofs are still steep and we see massive end chimneys (as in New England houses of nearly a century earlier), there is a repetition of the identical units of the dormer windows, a regularity of treatment, and the finely-executed detail of the cornice line with its richly carved dentils. Small and simple as the Brush-Everard House is, it still betrays incipient classicism.

The situation in Philadelphia differs from that of Williamsburg. William Penn's 'greene country towne' was built almost entirely of stone or brick, which was used for grand and humble houses, public buildings and churches alike. Elaborate carving in wood was confined to interior panelling or to the pretentious towers and steeples of the local Anglican churches, such as Christ Church, begun 1727 and steeple not completed until 1754, with construction directed by Robert Smith of the Carpenters' Company. The wooden spire of Christ Church rises to the great height of 196 feet and is a compilation of classical motifs – pediment, cornice line, and the octagonal lantern with its graceful arcading effect – all derived from imported English books or from the towers of Sir Christopher Wren's city churches. In fact, the uppermost motif of Christ Church's steeple is reminiscent of the final stage of Wren's famous tower on St. Bride, Fleet Street, London, (1702–1703), where one finds a motif almost like that of a Greek tempietto, an architectural form which, when placed at the focal point of a tower, gives an impression of even greater height. Other multi-staged English towers which might have served models for Philadelphia's Christ Church are Wren's St. Andrew-by-the-Wardrobe, London, or James Gibbs' St. Martin's-in-the-Fields, also in London, of 1721–1726.

In contrast to other eighteenth century cities where building was mostly in masonry, the influential centre of Newport, Rhode Island was a community of important wooden houses, churches and synagogues, and public buildings from its founding in the earlier part of the seventeenth century. One hundred years later, along with Boston and Philadelphia, it was one of the influential centres of fine architecture. By the 1730s, under the influence of Richard Munday's work at the Colony House, Newport, the houses of the city sported finely carved doorways as the focus of their symmetrical five or seven-bay façades. As in the Hunter House, the major door is surmounted by a pediment, broken, segmental, with scrolls, adorned by festoons or swags, flanking the realistically carved pineapple. Very linear pilasters support the crowning pediment. This type of segmental pediment had also appeared by 1730 on the river façade of one of the great plantation houses of Virginia: Westover, Charles City County. It is unlikely that one house was influenced by the other; both pediments are from an easily obtained source: the plates of William Salmon's *Palladio Londinensis,* a carpenter's guide containing many details for doorways, several of which must be the prototypes for both Westover and the Newport house. Typical of all these eighteenth century doorcases is the vigour and *brio* with which they are executed.

But without Peter Harrison, America's first professional architect (as distinguished from a carpenter-builder like Robert Smith at Philadelphia's Christ Church), Newport's architecture would not have been as significant. It is to Harrison's credit that he brought the Palladian taste and a greater sense of severity and monumentality to a Colonial city. In the Redwood Library, Newport (1748–1750) (p. 210), Harrison chose the design of a temple, thoroughly and rigorously Palladian, almost grave in its academic formality. Harrison was not only English born, but had travelled extensively in England during the 1730s and 1740s. There he began to acquire books for his architectural library and his choice of a temple design for the Redwood Library may be accounted for by the books he owned. The closest prototype for the façade may be found in his copy of Edward Hoppus's *Andrea Palladio's Architecture,* Book IV, 1736, while the ultimate prototype was the west front of Palladio's church of San Giorgio, Venice, engraved by William Kent (*Designs of Inigo Jones,* 1727, Volume I, plate 59). As both these volumes were owned by Harrison, he must have paid slavish

259a

Right: (a) Pendant, Preston Court, Gloucestershire, beginning of the 17th century (cf. 142b); (b) pendant, Turner House, Salem, Massachusetts, c. 1670; (c) detail of a granary in Canton Valais; (d) foundation of a traditional log building, Livigno, Upper Valtellina.
Page 246: Windows: (a) Berwang, Tirol, 18th century; (b) from Rapciuni, Bacău, now in the open-air museum, Bucharest; (c) Rouen, 16th century; (d) Vologda, Russia, mid-19th century.
Page 247: (a) Detail of the façade of the Rüedihaus, Kandersteg, Bernese Oberland; (b) shingle-covered wall of a house at Livigno, Upper Valtellina.
Page 248: Shop-fronts: (a) Helsingör, 17th century; (b) Hadleigh, Suffolk, 16th and 17th century; (c) Nieuwe Brugsteeg, Amsterdam, 17th century; (d) Cornhill, London, now in the Victoria and Albert Museum, end of the 18th century.

a

b

c

d

a

b

c

d

a

b

a

b

c

d

a

b

c

d

a

b

c

d

a

b

homage to the great Palladian folios of the era. His efforts to be Palladian (and, in his eyes, classical) are not only seen in the interlocking of the two great pediments, but also in his use of rusticated wooden siding to simulate the dressed stone masonry which would have been used in a more Grecian or Roman age. This imitation of stone in the less expensive material of wood was to continue to be popular in the American Colonies until after the Revolution at the end of the century.

Peter Harrison was also responsible for the designs for one of the most beautiful interiors in eighteenth century America, the Touro Synagogue, Newport (1759–1763). As he had been Palladian on the exterior of the Redwood Library and thus brought to America the classical temple front, so he now used his extensive knowledge of architectural pattern-books to create the rich, elaborately carved and unashamedly eclectic interior of the synagogue. There is little about its design that is reminiscent of a house of worship for Jewish services except for the rectangular ground-plan which resembles the Sephardic Synagogue of Amsterdam (familiar from engravings of the period). The graceful two-storeyed main hall is akin to the designs for a hall in Whitehall by John Webb, pupil of Inigo Jones, reproduced in William Kent's *Designs of Inigo Jones*, 1727, Volume I, plate 50, (as I have said, in Harrison's private library). Both have the two tiers of columns – Ionic below and Corinthian above with a finely turned balustrade at the gallery level. In the actual carving of the east end – the wall which houses the Ark of the Covenant – he has combined carving of unparalleled richness with a tightly-knit composition which serves as a focal point in an otherwise completely centralised building. For the upper portion he has cleverly utilised two designs for chimney pieces by William Kent (published by Isaac, Ware, *Designs of Inigo Jones and Others*, 1735, plate 48 and in Kent's own book, *Designs of Inigo Jones*, Volume I, plate 63). With this, for the lower section, he has fused a Tuscan altarpiece from Batty Langley's *A Treasury of Designs*, 1740, plate 108. This most bookish of architects in a period of American architecture noted for this quality, nevertheless, uses his sources with good taste, discernment and a strong sense of the elegant in architecture.

In contrast to the dependence on English style in the British Colonies of the Atlantic seaboard, there exist, in the area which was once the vast holdings of the French empire in the New World, a few remains of French Colonial building. The French character of the architecture is most pronounced in or near New Orleans, Louisiana, founded in 1718 early in the reign of Louis XV. The first houses erected in the bayou country of Louisiana were always of timber, heavy upright logs set several feet into the marshy ground only a few inches apart. The spaces between the posts were filled by *bouzillage,* a mixture of clay and Spanish moss. Commonly, the main living areas of the house were raised up one storey because of the danger of floods and the upper or main storey level opened on to an open *galerie* which served as a communicating passage from one living area to another. This pattern was modified but not essentially changed as the French owners of plantations could afford more spacious houses. Parlange, Pointe Coupée Parish, Louisiana, (c. 1750) is typical of the larger plantation houses in that it is a direct descendant of the first primitive cottage types of hewn timber posts. Parlange Plantation has a ground storey with its columns made

Page 249: Façade of the hotel 'Zur Krone', Trogen, Kanton Appenzell, Ausserrhoden, Switzerland, 1767.
Page 250: Detail of carving: (a) overmantel, Preston Court, beginning of the 17th century (cf. 142 b); (b) Wedekind house, Hildesheim, 1598 (destroyed 1945); (c) Frankenbergerstrasse 23, Goslar, c. 1600; (d) doorhead, The Red Hat. Tewkesbury, Gloucestershire, 1664 (cf. 182 c).
Page 251: (a) Front door, Korbach, Hesse, beginning of the 18th century; (b) front door, Gorkovsk, Russia; (c) church portal, island of Runö, Gulf of Riga; (d) wooden gate from Curtisoara, Oltland, now in the open-air museum, Bucharest.
Left: Doorways: (a) The White Hall, Long Itchington, Warwickshire, 16th century, altered 19th century; (b) church at Allna, Hesse, 1782.

201 f

of brick, but the remainder of the building is of wood, used imaginatively. The upper floor of the house is of cypress and *bouzillage,* the roof, now hipped, is of cypress wood too, and the *galerie* which now encircles the house on four sides has a light balustrade and gracefully attenuated colonnettes of wood. The beams above the *galerie* are left exposed which adds to the structural and aesthetic interest. Suitable for the excessive heat and humidity of the Southern bayou, this domestic, wooden style was to remain popular well into the nineteenth century.

But, meanwhile, during and immediately after the American War of Independence, led by two statesmen who were also informed and perceptive amateur architects, George Washington and Thomas Jefferson, the country was moving away from the Georgian pattern-book, Palladian revival style towards one of greater simplicity. No longer dependent on England and France, American architecture was entering its 'Federal' period of transition to the ideals of Neoclassicism and the Greek Revival of the half century before the outbreak of the Civil War of 1861–1865.

The James Semple House, Williamsburg, Virginia, (c. 1780), almost certainly attributed to Thomas Jefferson, shows the first evidence of taste progressing away from the late Georgian style towards the more scientific approach of the Classical Revival. The façade of the central, main unit of the house is treated like a temple portico; this feature is reinforced by the classical porch, a temple in miniature with two Doric columns supporting a full entablature above, and capped by a finely de-

Farmhouse, North America,
mid-19th century.

tailed triangular pediment. The delicate execution of the beading under the cornice line is another effect of the growing interest in Greek decorative motifs.

Perhaps the most interesting transitional wooden building in America is Mount Vernon, Fairfax County, Virginia, begun 1754, additions of 1773, and portico finished 1784–7. The first building period, controlled by the mind, if not the hand, of George Washington, brought the house into the Palladian style of the Burlington school. Even the dependencies linked by curved arcades to the main block of the house and the new walls of pine, bevelled in a way to resemble blocks of stone and then painted to heighten this illusion, were great contributions to Virginia architecture at this early date (1757). But the most significant innovation of all was the giant two-storey portico; as the first long giant portico to be erected at this date in America, it is, despite the fact that the columns are in reality square piers with simple panels (and probably inspired by a carpenters' guide such as Batty Langley's), a striking and

259b

224a

Country House, North America, mid-19th century.

influential feature. It is the ancestor of countless porticos, many with the dignity of that of Mount Vernon, during the next century of American architecture.

At the end of the American Revolution and the erection of Mount Vernon, the colonial attitude was dead, England was no longer a cultural and artistic inspiration and waves of new influences were breaking over American life and thought. The classical world, as a pure and better society, was idealised and imitated. Philadelphia, prominent in the seventeenth and eighteenth centuries, now became one of the leaders of the nineteenth century Greek Revival. The ideals of the newest architectural movement were propagated and perpetuated there under the leadership of some of the greatest American architects: Benjamin Henry Latrobe, Robert Mills, William Strickland and Thomas Ustick Walter. But never in the work of all these architects was there any sense of exact copying of ancient buildings. Rather, the architect was limited to Greek inspiration and was only archaeologically correct in details, such as the use of the orders upon some section of a building. He would try to design in the spirit of the Greek.

This movement was fostered, in the first instance, by an American published work: John Haviland's *The Builders' Assistant,* 1818–1821, the first book in which plates of the Greek orders were shown. To this publication was added the new consciousness of the United States as a political and cultural entity. And, in Philadelphia itself, there was the added, potent influence of its native son, Nicholas Biddle. Not only a banker, but also an informed dilettante in the best sense of the word, Biddle had travelled in Greece as early as 1806 – he was the first truly educated American to do so. In 1814, he published his findings in *The Port Folio,* establishing Greek forms as the most suitable expression for American architecture. His enthusiasm for the architecture of ancient Greece is embodied in his own house, Andalusia, where he commissioned Thomas U. Walter to surround the shell of the earlier house with a

Doric temple-type portico. At this point – 1833 – the Greek Revival was at its height, but it was still rare to use the plain temple model on domestic work. It was rather the favoured form for libraries, universities and civic buildings.

Unlike Andalusia near Philadelphia with its correct and complete temple portico, one has in other centres numerous houses which employ the orders but often with unparalleled freedom – born, no doubt, of a desire to personalize them in some manner. Such an architect is Russell Warren of Newport, Rhode Island, whose Levi Gale House, square and two-storeyed with a level cornice and recessed attic storey, employs the Corinthian order but without the correct capping pediment. Warren has achieved the flat surfaces appropriate to the Greek Revival by the use of siding instead of the common clapboards; indeed, the flat wood walls, with their horizontal scoring, almost seem to imitate stone. The façade is composed in overlapping planes, broken only by the single order of the giant pilasters and the small one-storey porch for entry. The recessed attic storey adds further spatial interest. Elsewhere in New England at this moment in American architectural history, there was great opportunity in the towns enjoying prosperity from the whaling industry for the new Greek style to prosper. The island of Nantucket, then at the peak of its financial and building boom, erected whole new streets of houses and public buildings in the dignity, restraint and power of the fashionable Greek style. By 1847, the Atheneum of Nantucket shows a richly detailed Ionic order, two columns set *in antis* in the deeply recessed porch. The triangular pediment set within the larger one of the same shape adds to the just repetition of shallow and overlapping planes.

Quite a different concept of the Greek Revival is seen when one looks at the Classical Revival houses of the South. In the first place, the best and most ambitious houses of the Southern states are relatively late in date (when compared to the rest of America); in the second place, they seem to have also been the heirs of the revolutionary influences of Washington's work at Mount Vernon and of Thomas Jefferson's feeling for romantic Classicism. It was always the two-storeyed colonnade, usually with Greek detail, which set the prevalent type in the small cities and rural areas of Georgia. The Ralph Small House, Macon, Georgia, of the 1840s, is the natural successor to the temple house initiated by Jefferson with the use of fine Greek moulding, but classically incorrect in that the pediment is not employed above the entablature. Relying less than Northern architects on the plates of the classical orders published by Asher Benjamin and other enterprising American designers, southern designers were bound to produce a generally confused, and even eclectic, version of a correct classical composition. The actual designers of all these Southern houses are generally anonymous and the houses' unique character results from their scale and monumentality, a palatial concept which did not survive the economic collapse of this region during the Civil War.

It is abundantly clear from these few examples that, following the death of the Colonial vernacular style, Greek Revival was *the* national architectural style in America through all the decades up to the American Civil War of 1861–5. Everyone built in much the same way and there was little development or change, except in the use of material which remained mainly white-painted wood for domestic architecture.

259b

210 d

Right: Wooden panelling and overmantel carved with Royal Arms from the Old Palace, Bromley-by-Bow, now in the Victoria and Albert Museum, London, c. 1606.
Page 258: Details of interiors: (a) Catharijnepad, house at Zaanse Schans, North Holland, beginning of the 18th century; (b) Jagerspad, house at Zaanse Schans, beginning of the 17th century (cf. 94 d, 193 c); (c) doorways into service rooms in a Wealden house, Harrietsham, Kent, end of the 15th century (cf. 94 a, 266 b)); (d) house at Oostzijde 322, Zaandam, North Holland, 17th century.

256

a

b

c

d

a

b

c

d

The popularity of the style is easily explained: it was simple and could easily be reproduced from handbooks. But, along with this *penchant* for the Greek Revival, there were other tendencies in American architecture. By the 1830s, the Gothic Revival had become a suitable alternative and, from this, the vogue for the Tudor cottage came into residential architecture. This 'Gothic or Tudor' Revival was essentially a romantic attitude and one of its foremost proponents was the architect Richard Upjohn. Kingscote, Newport, Rhode Island (1841), sums up the attitude of the period. Upjohn here follows the tenets of another architect, Andrew Jackson Downing, who, in his book of 1841, *Landscape Gardening*, said, 'Architectural beauty must be considered conjointly with beauty of landscape.' This love of land and nature is informal, opposed to the Greek Revival, and is expressed in a house like Kingscote. Here, the architect exploits the use of wood, uses it with a feeling for its structural expression and creates an asymmetrical composition of jagged outlines which is informal and picturesque in effect. The Tudor cottage mode is characterised by the lightness of scale and the breaking up of the mass and entity of the building. Structurally, it has always been considered a 'Stick Style' for it is based upon a skeleton of mortise and tenon, sheathed horizontally with wooden match boarding, usually painted a stony shade of grey.

A love for structural expression in wood was also characteristic of the architecture and handcrafts of a mystic, religious sect, whose membership was in the thousands in the first half of the nineteenth century: the Shakers, whose communities dotted the rural areas of northern New England and New York State, were celibate and their lives were dedicated to religious fervour and the making of fine, simple handcrafts and furniture. Their work was largely ignored at that period and it is only since the end of World War II that the fine proportion and the classic purity of their craftsmanship has been appreciated. The interior of the Round Shaker Barn, Hancock, Massachusetts, is a perfect example of striking, structural design, soaring patterns in light and shade, and all within a purely utilitarian building. Their furniture has the same simplicity which is the essence of its strength. The art of the Shakers, completely untutored, seems more twentieth-century in character than much of the modern design of the present day.

But the architecture of the Shaker Community was only a bypath in the history of American building and the latter part of the nineteenth century is marked by the development of more or less Gothic Revival modes, very popular in the domestic field where nearly all houses were built of wood. This almost careless attitude, the blending of many eclectic styles, is seen all over the United States and is very popular in the West. The interior of an opera house, Virginia City, Nevada, has woodwork and panelling in a variety of designs, careless in application, and even has a number of classical details in the baluster rails of the private boxes. Far more popular – indeed used so widely that it could be termed the 'veranda' or 'front porch' style — were the successors to Downing's veranda-version of the Tudor Cottage, the oft-termed 'Stick Style'. In the bathing resort town of Cape May, New Jersey, directly after the Civil War, houses and hotels were built to cater for the summer tourist. All built during the 1870s–1890s, the main square of Cape May is the picturesque Stick Style, *par*

210c

60a

56a, b; 88a

212a, b

Page 259: (a) Portal, Hunter House, Newport, Rhode Island, before 1746; (b) portal, James Semple House, Williamsburg, Virginia, attributed to Thomas Jefferson, 1782; (c) Levi Gale House, Newport, Rhode Island, Russell Warren, c. 1834; (d) Pink House, Cape May, New Jersey, c. 1870.
Left: Ceiling at the Monastery, Rila, Bulgaria.

269b

224b

excellence. The Pink House in Cape May is striking in its use of open, carved stick-work on the two-tiered veranda. The carpenter or designer in almost whimsical mood has adapted a picturesque style, probably descended from the 'Swiss Chalet' style, one of the popular revival movements; and in the charming virtuosity of the lacy arcades the very essence of wood in contrived gracefulness has been achieved.

259d

219a; 232b

But the more imaginative architects of the end of the century – such as Henry Hobson Richardson – were to react against the playfulness of the Cape May style. Richardson's high achievement in domestic wooden building was to be the M. F. Stoughton House, Cambridge, Massachusetts, commissioned in June 1882, still one of the most outstanding suburban houses in the United States. The Stoughton House seems almost the successor to the shingle-covered New England farmhouse of two centuries earlier for Richardson has returned to a sense of solidity and simplicity. As an architect, he designs and thinks in mass. The staircase on the inner corner rises in a tower-like projection, but, in spite of this, the roof-line is almost continuous and its shape merges with the rest of the building. Richardson had studied in France after Harvard University, but the Stoughton House shows none of the Romanesque Revival; instead, the architect concentrates on pulling all elements of the composition into a unified whole. He is the master of the wood shingled house.

210f

Another American architectural genius has also turned to wood as an expressive material for his private houses. As recently as 1940, Frank Lloyd Wright designed the Pope-Leighy House in Virginia, where he continues a style he had first established in an early house for C. S. Ross in Wisconsin in 1902. Both houses feature quite rough sheathing of board-and-batten, while in the later one slab roofs projecting towards the viewer are set at various levels and pierced through the wide projections in order to let light into the windows below. With this, Wright has coupled abstract and involved decorative patterns for the windows and the contrast is handsome and striking. The Pope-Leighy House may be considered not only as a dwelling but also as a powerful piece of sculpture in wood. In fact, a great part of Wright's creative powers and energies throughout his lengthy career were concentrated on imaginative treatment of the private house, very often in wood.

222a

During the past three centuries of American architecture building in wood has gone through a number of successive stages. In the seventeenth century, wood was used naturally, in an unabashed manner, and structural utility was the dominant consideration. During the eighteenth and nineteenth centuries, wood was considered the handmaiden of more academic form and it served the purposes of a number of revival styles. Wooden architecture has now come full circle and architects find that the usefulness of designing in wood is only surpassed by the sheer beauty of the resultant designs.

263   *Carpenter's workshop, North America,*
      19th century.

Editor's Note on Contributors and Acknowledgements

The chapters in this book are the work of the following different authors: 'Early Wood Building' (chapter I) is by the editor (citing works by Bühlmann, Haarnagel, Kähler and Ricke; see Bibliography); 'Wood Building in Northern Europe' (chapter II) by M.N.A.L. Berg, architect, of the Norsk Folkemuseum in Bygdöy (wood building in Norway), Toini-Inkeri Kaukonen, Superintendent of the Suomen Kansallismuseo in Helsinki (wood building in Finland) and the editor; 'Wood Building in the British Isles' (chapter III) by J. T. Smith of the Royal Commission on Historical Monuments in London, whose advice and assistance in the preparation of the English edition have been invaluable; 'Wood Building in the Netherlands' (chapter IV) by Herman Janse of the Rijksdienst voor de Monumentenzorg in Voorburg; 'Wood Building in France' (chapter V) by Emile Bonnel of the Centre de Recherche des Monuments Historiques in Paris; 'Wood Building in Central Europe' (chapter VI) by Professor Dr. Alfred Kamphausen, Director of the Schleswig-Holsteinisches Freilichtmuseum in Kiel-Rammsee; 'Wood Building in Eastern and South-eastern Europe' (chapter VII) by Dr. Georg R. Schroubek of the Seminar für deutsche und vergleichende Volkskunde at the University of Munich; 'Wood Building in Italy' (chapter VIII) by Agnoldomenico Pica, architect, Milan; and 'Wood Building in North America' (chapter IX) by Dr. Nancy Halverson Schless, President of the Society of Architectural Historians, Philadelphia, Pennsylvania.

Special thanks are due to Professor Alfred Kamphausen for reading through the whole manuscript before it went off to the printer. Professor Kamphausen is one of the greatest authorities on all aspects of the subject of European wood building, including historical research, personal knowledge of the buildings, practice of the craft and aesthetic judgement.

For ideas, pertinent information and other assistance the editor wishes to thank the following—in addition to the authors: Gösta Berg, Director of the Skansen Djurgården, Stockholm; Thomas M. Gehrig, architectural planner in Munich; Professor Dr. Gottfried Gruben, Director of the Institut für Baugeschichte at the Technische Hochschule in Munich; Dr. Tjaard W. R. de Haan, editor of the Nederlands Volkskundig Genootschap in Wassenaar; Professor Dr. Werner Haarnagel, Director of the Niedersächsischen Landesinstituts für Marschen- und Wurtenforschung, Wilhelmshaven; Frau Jondral, manageress of the tourist office of the city of Goslar; Dr. Roland Klemig of the Staatsbibliothek, Berlin; C. Th. Knokke of the Department of Documentation of the Rijksmuseum voor Volkskunde 'Het Nederlands Openluchtmuseum', Arnhem; Professor Dr. Friedrich Krauss, former director of the Institut für Baugeschichte at the Technische Hochschule, Munich; A. L. Miklashevski of the press department of the Russian Embassy in Cologne; Elisabeth Munksgaard, Inspector of the Nationalmuseet, Copenhagen; P. Nerrière, vice-president of the Syndicat d'Initiative, Chartres; Olaf Olsen, Inspector of the Nationalmuseet, Copenhagen; Dr. Helmut Ottenjann, Director of the Museum Village, Cloppenburg; Professor Sir Nikolaus Pevsner, C.B.E., Director of the Department of the History of Art in the University of London; Herr Schneeweiss of the press office of the city of Hildesheim; David Sellin, Professor of the History of Art at Colgate University, U.S.A.; Professor J. J. Terwen, Director of the Afdeling der Bouwkunde of the Technische Hogeschool, Delft; J. Rhys Thomas, Preston Court, Gloucestershire; Fartein Valen-Sendestad, Director of De Sandvigske Samlinger Maihaugen, Lillehammer, Norway; H. Winter, head of the information and press department of the Pro Helvetia Foundation, Zürich; and Wolfgang Wurster of the Institut für Baugeschichte at the Technische Hochschule, Munich.

The present translation has been made from the German versions of the authors' articles, with the exception of the chapters by J. T. Smith and Dr. Nancy Halverson Schless which appear in their original form.

Right: (a) Portal of a wooden house, Sweden, end of the 18th century; (b) inner courtyard, Lille Strandstraede, Copenhagen, 18th century; (c) farmhouse, Lillaz-Cogne, Val d'Aosta; (d) front door, Cranz, near Hamburg, 1653.

Page 266: (a) Original staircase with solid treads in a Wealden house, Harrietsham, Kent, end of the 15th century (cf.); (b) Palazzo Davanzati, Florence; (c) house from Curtisoara, Oltland, now in the open-air museum, Bucharest; (d) loggiaed barn from Bergkarlas in Mora, now in the open-air museum, Skansen, near Stockholm, 1574.

Page 267: (a) Capital, stave-church at Urnes, Sogn, end of the 11th century; (b) capital, Church of the Holy Trinity, Bansko, Bulgaria; (c) wooden staircase from a house in Morlaix, Brittany, now in the Victoria and Albert Museum, London, beginning of the 16th century; (d) arcaded gallery surrounding the stave-church at Borgund, Sogn, c. 1150.

Page 268: (a) Hall of Allegiance, town-hall, Goslar, end of the 15th century; (b) Sala del Gran Consiglio, Doge's Palace, Venice, 16th century.

a

b

c

d

a

b

c

d

a

b

c

d

a

b

a

b

a

b

a

b

GENERAL

Hoffmann, Kurt, and Griese, Helga: *Bauen mit Holz*. Stuttgart 1966.

Horn, Walter: 'On the Origins of the Medieval Bay System'. *Journal of the Society of Architectural Historians*, XVII, 1958, 2–24.

Liebold, B.: *Die mittelalterliche Holzarchitektur*. Halle 1875.

Mumford, Lewis: *Sticks and Stones*. New York 1924.

Ostendorf, F.: *Die Geschichte des Dachwerks*. Leipzig 1908.

Smith, J. T.: 'Cruck Construction: a Survey of the Problems'. *Medieval Archaeology*, 8, 1964, 119–151.

CHAPTER I

Bibby, Geoffrey: *The Testimony of the Spade*. New York 1957.

Bühlmann, M.: 'Vorstufen dorischer Architektur'. *Münchner Jahrbuch der bildenden Kunst*, XII, 3. Munich 1922.

Durm, Josef: *Die Baukunst der Griechen*. Leipzig 1900.

Haarnagel, Werner: 'Wirtschaftsform und Arbeitsleben in der frühgeschichtlichen Siedlung Feddersen-Wierde'. *Arbeit und Volksleben*. Marburg 1966.

Haarnagel, Werner: 'Vorläufiger Bericht über das Ergebnis der Wurtengrabung auf Feddersen-Wierde bei Bremerhaven im Jahre 1956'. *Germania*, 35 (1957), 275–317.

Jankuhn, H.: *Haithabu. Eine germanische Stadt der Frühzeit*. Neumünster i. H., 1937; 3rd ed. 1956.

Kähler, Heinz: *Das griechische Metopenbild*. Munich 1949.

Maiuri, Amedeo: *Pompei, Ercolano e Stabia*. Novara 1960.

Martin, Roland: *Monde grec*. Fribourg 1966.

Orlandos, A.: *Les Matériaux de Construction et la Technique Architecturale des Anciens Grecs*. Part 1. Paris 1966.

Overbeck, J.: *Pompeii in seinen Gebäuden, Altertümern und Kunstwerken*. Leipzig 1866.

Ricke, Herbert: 'Bemerkungen zur Ägyptischen Baukunst des Alten Reiches'. *Beiträge zur Bauforschung und Altertumskunde*. Zürich 1944.

Riska, Tove: *Suomen kirkot — Finlands Kyrkor*, 1–5. Helsinki 1959–1968.

Rudolph, Martin V.: *Germanischer Holzbau der Wikingerzeit*. Neumünster 1942.

Sackur, W.: *Vitruv*. Berlin 1925.

CHAPTER II

Bjerknes, Kristian: *Era hov til stavkirke*. Bergen 1948.

Bugge, Anders: *Norwegian Stave Churches* (translated by R. Christopherson). Oslo 1954.

Dietrichson, L.: *De norske stavkirker*. Christiania (Oslo) 1892.

Gardberg, C. J.: 'Den nyantika stadsbyggnadskonsten i Åbo 1800–1880'. *Skrifter utgivna av Historiska Samfundet i Åbo*, III. Åbo 1952.

Hämäläinen, Albert: 'Keski-Suomen kansanrakennukset'. *Suomolaisen Kirjallisuuden Seuran toimituksia*, 186. Helsinki 1930.

Hauglid, Roar, and Grodecki, Louis: *Norwegen, Bilder aus den Stabkirchen*. Munich 1955.

Heimala, Aarne (ed.): *Rakennusmuistomerkkimme ja nüden suojelu*. Helsinki 1964.

Jutikkala, Eino, and Nikander, Gabriel: *Suomen kartanot ja suurtilat*, 1–3. Helsinki 1939, 1941, 1945.

Lilius, Henrik: 'Die Steinarchitektur und die Bretterverkleidung von Holzbauten'. *Suomen Museo*, LXXII, 1965. Helsinki 1965.

Lilius, Henrik: *Der Pekkatori in Raahe, Studien über einen eckverschlossenen Platz und seine Gebäudetypen*. Helsinki 1967.

Lindberg, Carolus: *Suomen kirkot*. Helsinki 1934.

Lindholm, Dan: *Stave Churches in Norway* (translated from the original German). London 1969.

Marstrand, Vilhelm: *Arsenalet i Piraeus og Oldtidens Byggeregker*. Copenhagen 1922.

Nikander, Gabriel: *Byar och gårdar i Helsinge från 1750 till 1865*. Helsinki 1916.

Olsen, Olaf: 'Die Häuser der Wikinger'. *Dänische Rundschau*, 33. Copenhagen 1968.

Pettersson, Lars: 'Die Problematik der Doppelkreuzkirchen von Hamina'. *Die Sitzungsberichte der Finnischen Akademie der Wissenschaften*. 1959. Helsinki 1960.

Pettersson, Lars: 'Türöffnungen mit Dreikleemotiv in finnischen Holzkirchen'. *Suomen Museo*. 1954. Helsinki 1954.

Rácz, István, and Cleve, Nils: *Suomen rokokoon ja uusklassisismin taideaarteita*. Helsinki 1969.

Stigum, Hilmar: 'Husene og tunet'. Kristofer Visted and Hilmar Stigum, *Vår gamle bondekultur*, I–II. Oslo 1951–1952.

Strzygowski, Josef: *Early Church Art in Northern Europe*. London 1928.

Suolahti, Gunnar: *Suomen pappilat 1700-luvulla*. Porvoo 1925.

Valonen, Niilo: 'Zur Geschichte der finnischen Wohnstuben'. *Mémoires de la société finno-ougrienne*, 133. Helsinki 1963.

Page 269: (a) Coffered ceiling in the Palazzo Davanzati, Florence, 15th century; (b) interior of the Opera House, Virginia City, Nevada, mid-19th century.

Page 270: (a) Interior of the Uspensky Church, Kondopoga, Karelia, 1774; (b) living-room of a peasant house from Hyrynsalmi, northern Finland, now in the open-air museum in Helsinki, beginning of the 19th century.

Page 271: (a), (b) Ceiling beams at the château of Blois, 16th century.

Left: Baronial hall, Schloss Heiligenberg, Baden, 16th century.

Vikstedt, J.: *Suomen kaupunkien vanhaa raken-nustaidetta*. Helsinki 1926.

Vilkuna, Kustaa: 'Varsinais-Suomen kansanraken-nukset'. *Varsinais-Suomen historia*, II. Porvoo 1938.

Vreim, Halvor: *Norsk trearkitektur*. Oslo 1947.

Vuorela, Toivo: *Etalä-Pohjanmaan kansanraken-nukset*. Helsinki 1949.

Wiegand: *La Glyptothèque Ny Carlsberg*. Munich 1896–1912.

CHAPTER III

Ambler, L.: *Old Halls and Manor Houses of York-shire*. London 1913.

Briggs, Martin Shaw: *The Homes of the Pilgrim Fathers in England and America*. London 1932.

Charles, F. W. B.: *Medieval Cruck-Building and its Derivatives*. London 1967.

Crossley, Fred. H.: *Timber Building in England*. London 1951.

Davie, W. G., and Dawber, Guy: *Old Cottages in Kent and Sussex*. London 1900.

Davie, W. G., and Curtis-Green, W.: *Old Cottages and Farmhouses in Surrey*. London 1908.

Fiedler, Wilhelm: *Das Fachwerkhaus in Deutsch-land, Frankreich und England*. Berlin 1903.

Forrest, H. E.: *The Old Houses of Shrewsbury*. 4th ed. Shrewsbury 1935.

Forrester, H.: *The Timber Framed Houses of Essex*. Hertford 1959.

Fox, Sir Cyril, and Raglan, Lord: *Monmouthshire Houses* (3 vols.). Cardiff 1951–4.

Gotch, A.: *Architecture of the Renaissance in Eng-land*. London 1894.

Hewett, Cecil A.: 'Jettying and Floor Framing in Medieval Essex'. *Medieval Archaeology*, X. London 1966.

Horn, Walter, and Born, Ernest: *The Barns of the Abbey of Beaulieu at . . . Great Coxwell and Beaulieu St. Leonards*. Berkeley and Los An-geles 1965.

Macdonald, R. W., and Atkinson, F.: 'Aisled Houses in the Halifax Area'. *Antiquaries Journal*, XLVII. 1967, 77–94.

Mason, R. T.: *Framed Buildings of the Weald*. Handcross (Sussex), 1964.

Nash, J.: *The Mansions of England in the Olden Time*. London 1839–49.

Nevill, R.: *Old Cottage and Domestic Architecture in South-west Surrey*. Guildford 1889.

Oliver, Basil: *Old Houses and Village Buildings in East Anglia*. London 1912.

Parkinson, J., and Ould, E. A.: *Old Cottages, Farm-houses and Other Half-Timbered Buildings in Shropshire, Herefordshire and Cheshire*. Lon-don 1904.

Smith, J. T.: 'Medieval Aisled Halls'. *Archaeologi-cal Journal*, CXII. 1955. 76–94.

Smith, J. T.: 'Timber-Framed Building in England'. *Archaeological Journal*, CXXII. 1965. 131–158.

Smith, J. T., and Stell, C. F.: 'Baguley Hall. The survival of pre-Conquest Building Tradition in the 14th Century'. *Antiquaries Journal*, XL. 1960. 131–151.

Taylor, Henry: *Old Halls in Lancashire and Che-shire*. Manchester 1884.

Wallace, Carew: *Paycocke's*. London 1964.

Walton, James: *Early Timbered Buildings of the Huddersfield District*. Huddersfield 1955.

CHAPTER IV

Agt, J. J. F. W. van: *De Nederlandse Monumenten van geschiedenis en kunst*, VIII, I, *Waterland en omgeving*. The Hague 1953.

Bernet Kempers, A. J.: *Vijftig jaar Nederlands Openluchtmuseum*. Arnhem 1962.

Bernet Kempers, A. J.: *Toen Marken nog 'het Eiland' was*. Arnhem 1965.

Hekker, R. C.: 'Fachwerkbau in Südlimburg'. *Ar-beitskreis für deutsche Hausforschung, Tagungs-bericht*. 1961, 49–74.

Hekker, R. C., and van der Poel, J. G. M.: *De Ne-derlandse boerderij in het begin der 19e eeuw*. Arnhem 1967.

Husslage, G.: *Windmolens*. Amsterdam 1965.

Janse, H.: 'De overkapping van de Oude kerk te Amsterdam', *Bulletin van de Koninklijke Ne-derlandse Oudheidkundige Bond (K.N.O.B.)*. 1958, 141–178.

Janse, H.: 'Bouwbedrijfen houtgebruik in het ver-leden'. *Houtvoorlichting*. October 1960.

Janse, H.: 'Middeleeuwse houten tongewelven in Nederland'. *Bulletin K.N.O.B.* 1961, 181–194.

Janse, H.: 'De abdijschuur van Ter Doest'. *Bulletin K.N.O.B.* 1964, 189–202.

Janse, H.: 'Constructie, ondersteuning en versiering van balken en houten vloeren tot omstreeks 1650'. *Bulletin K.N.O.B.* 1967, 303–328.

Janse, H.: 'De Zaanse Schans'. *Spiegel der Historie*. 1968, 26–32.

Janse, H.: 'Gordingenkappen in Nederland'. *Bulle-tin K.N.O.B.* 1969, 1–10.

Janse, H., and Devliegher, L.: 'Middeleeuwse be-kappingen in het vroegere Graafschap Vlaan-deren'. *Bulletin Kon. Comm. voor Monumen-ten en Landschappen*, XIII, 299–380. Brussels 1962.

Niemeijer, J. W., and Janse, H.: 'Het huis van Cor-nelis Schoon te Broek in Waterland'. *Spiegel der Historie*. 1967, 263–269.

Stokhuyzen, F.: *The Dutch Windmill* (translated from the Dutch by C. Dikshoorn). London, Bussum 1962.

Trefois, C.: *Ontwikkelingsgeschiedenis van onze landelijke architectuur*. Antwerp 1950.

Weyns, Jozef: 'Het Kempische boerenhuis'. *Kunst-historische verkenningen in de Kempen 1*. Oisterwijk 1960, 43–103.

Weyns, Jozef: *De stoffelijke volkskultuur in Bel-gisch-Limburg en haar uitbeelding in het Open-luchtmuseum te Bokrijk*. Bokrijk 1964.

Weyns, Jozef: 'Het Vlaamse Openluchtmuseum te Bokrijk in Belgisch-Limburg'. *Bulletin K.N.O.B.* 1969.

Zantkuyl, H. J.: 'De houten huizen van Holysloot'. *Bulletin K.N.O.B.* 1968, 11–26.

CHAPTER V

Blondel, J. F.: *Cours d'architecture ou traité de la décoration, distribution et construction des bâtiments*. Paris 1772–1777.

274

D'Albaret: *Différents projets relatifs au climat et à la manière la plus convenable de bâtir dans les pays chauds et plus particulièrement dans les Indes Occidentales.* Paris 1776.

Fiedler, Wilhelm: *Das Fachwerkhaus in Deutschland, Frankreich und England.* Berlin 1903.

Fourneau, N.: *L'art du trait de charpente.* Paris 1770–1802.

Gauthier, J. S.: *Les maisons paysannes des vieilles provinces de France.* New ed. Paris 1951.

Horn, Walter, and Born, Ernest: 'Les Halles de Questembert'. *Bulletin de la Société Polymathique du Morbihan* 1963, 3–16.

Horn, Walter, and Born, Ernest: 'Les Halles de Crémieu'. *Évocations* 17, 1961, 66–90.

Jousse, M.: *L'art de charpenterie.* Paris 1651.

Laprade, Albert: *Croquis: Région de l'Ouest.* Paris 1969.

Le Muet, P.: *Manière de bastir pour toutes sortes de personnes.* Paris 1623.
The art of fair building . . .published in English by R. Pricke . . . London 1670.

Quennedey, Commandant Raymond: *L'habitation rouennaise.* Rouen 1926.

Quennedey, Commandant Raymond: *La Normandie, Architecture civile de l'époque médiévale au XVIII siècle.* 1926.

Robert, Jean: *La maison rurale permanente dans les Alpes françaises du Nord.* 1939.

Rondelet: *Traité théorique et pratique de l'art de bâtir.* Paris 1804.

Tillet, J.: 'Les églises de bois en Champagne'. *Congrès archéologique* 1911. Vol. II, 362–375.

Winter, Heinrich: 'Das Wandgefüge im Umkreis des französischen Zentral massives'. *Arbeitskreis für deutsche Hausforschung.* 1959, 55–98.

CHAPTER VI

Baumgarten, Karl: *Zimmermannswerk in Mecklenburg. Die Scheune.* Berlin 1961.

Bilderatlas zur Geschichte der Holzbaukunst. Leipzig 1883.

Burghein, Alfred: *Der Kirchenbau des 18. Jahrhunderts in Nordelbingen.* Hamburg 1915.

Clasen, Carl-Wilhelm; Kiecker, Oskar; Kiesow, Gottfried; Wirtgen, Bernhard; and Wohltmann, Hans: *Die Kunstdenkmale der Stadt Stade.* Munich 1960.

Dehio, Georg: *Geschichte der Deutschen Kunst* (3 vols.). Berlin and Leipzig. 1919–1921.

Das Deutsche Bürgerhaus (series)
Helm, Rudolf: *Das Bürgerhaus in Nordhessen.* Tübingen 1967.
Ossenberg, Horst: *Das Bürgerhaus im Bergischen Land.* Tübingen 1963.
Winter, Heinrich: *Das Bürgerhaus zwischen Rhein, Main und Neckar.* Tübingen 1961.
Winter, Heinrich: *Das Bürgerhaus in Oberhessen.* Tübingen 1965.

Eitzen, Gerhard: 'Die älteren Hallenhausgefüge in Niedersachsen'. *Zeitschrift für Volkskunde* 51. 1954, 37–76.

Eitzen, Gerhard: 'Zur Geschichte des Südwestdeutschen Hausbaues im 15. und 16. Jahrhundert'. *Ibid* 59. 1963, 1–38.

Fiedler, Wilhelm: *Das Fachwerkhaus in Deutschland, Frankreich und England.* Berlin 1903.

Franke, Heinrich: *Ostgermanische Holzbaukultur.* Breslau 1936.

Grundmann, Günther: *Schlesische Barockkirchen und Klöster.* Lindau 1958.

Haupt, Albrecht: *Die älteste Kunst, insbesondere die Baukunst der Germanen.* Berlin 1923.

Haus und Hof Deutscher Bauern (series)
Vol. 1 Wolf, Gustav: *Schleswig-Holstein.* Berlin 1940.
Vol. 2 Schepers, Josef: *Westfalen-Lippe.* Münster/Westf. 1960.
Vol. 3 Folkers, J.-U.: *Mecklenburg.* Münster/Westf. 1961.
Vol. 4 Schilli, Hermann: *Das Schwarzwaldhaus.* Stuttgart 1953.
Vol. 5 Götzger, H., and Prechter, H.: *Das Bauernhaus in Bayrisch-Schwaben.* Munich 1960.
Vol. 6 Gruber, Otto: *Bauernhäuser am Bodensee.* Konstanz and Lindau 1961.

Kamphausen, Alfred: *Das Schleswig-Holsteinische Freilichtmuseum. Häuser und Hausgeschichten.* Neumünster 1965.

Kletzl, Otto: 'Holzkirchen der Tschechoslowakei'. *Mitteilungen des Vereins für Geschichte der Deutschen in Böhmen.* 1928.

Lachner, Carl: *Geschichte der Holzbaukunst in Deutschland.* Leipzig 1887.

Liebold, B.: *Die mittelalterliche Holzarchitektur.* Halle 1875.

Maximov, P. N.: 'Die Holzbaukunst im 17. Jahrhundert'. *Geschichte der Russischen Kunst.* Vol. IV. Dresden 1965.

Ottenjann, Helmut: *Freilichtmuseum Cloppenburg* (guide). 4th ed. Oldenburg 1966.

Pfister, Rudolf, Erhard, Wilhelm and Volbehr, Heinrich: *Alte bayerische Zimmermannskunst am Bauernhaus des Ruperti-Winkels.* Munich 1926.

Phleps, Hermann: *Ost- und Westgermanische Baukultur.* Berlin 1934.

Phleps, Hermann: *Deutsche Fachwerkbauten.* Königstein im Taunus 1951.

Phleps, Hermann (ed. Mix, Ernst): *Alemannische Holzbaukunst.* 1967

Schäfer, Karl: *Die Holzarchitektur Deutschlands vom 14. bis 18. Jahrhundert.* Berlin 1889.

Scharfe, Siegfried: *Deutsche Dorfkirchen.* Königstein im Taunus 1934.

Schilli, Hermann: *Vogtsbauernhof in Gutach im Schwarzwald.* Freiburg im Breisgau 1968.

Stoob, Heinz: *Hamburgs Hohe Türme.* Hamburg 1958.

Stüdtje, Johannes: *Mühlen in Schleswig-Holstein.* Heide 1968.

Thiede, Klaus: *Das Erbe germanischer Baukunst.* Hamburg 1936.

Walbe, Heinrich: *Das hessisch-fränkische Fachwerk.* 2nd ed. Giessen 1954.

Zippelius, A.: *Das Bauernhaus am Unteren Deutschen Niederrhein.* Wuppertal 1957.

CHAPTER VII

Afanasev, K. N.: *Postroenie architekturnoy formy drevnerusskimi zodochimi.* Moscow 1961.

Ashchepkov, E.: *Russkoe narodnoe zodchestvo v zapadnoy Sibiri.* 1950.

Bednarik, Rudolf: *L'udove stavitel'stvo na kysuciach*. Bratislava 1967.

Bezsonov, S. V.: *Architektura zapadnoi Ukrainui*. Moscow 1945.

Cross, S. H. (ed. Conant, S. J.): *Mediaeval Russian Churches*. Cambridge, Mass. 1949.

Eliasberg, A.: *Russische Baukunst*. Munich 1922.

Ivanov, V. N.; Maksimov, P. N.; and Toropov, S. A.: *Sokrovishcha russkoj architektury*. Moscow 1950.

Kletzl, Otto: 'Holzkirchen der Tschechoslowakei'. *Mitteilungen des Vereins für Geschichte der Deutschen in Böhmen*. 1928.

Krasovskij, M.: *Kurs istorii russkoe architektury I. Derevyannoe zodvestvo*. Petrograd (Leningrad) 1916.

Makovetsky, I. V.: *Pamyatniki narodnogo zodchestva verchnego Povolzhja*. Moscow 1952.

Makovetsky, I. V.: *Pamyatniki narodnogo zodchestva srednego Povolzhja*. Moscow 1954.

Makovetsky, I. V.: *Pamyatniki narodnogo zodchestva russkogo Severa*. Moscow 1955.

Makovetsky, I. V.: *Architektura russkogo narodnogo zhilshcha. Sever a verchnee Povolzhe*. Moscow 1962.

Makovsky, S. K.: *Lidové umeni Podkarpadské Rusi*. Prague 1925.

Strzygowski, Josef: *Die Altslavische Kunst*. Augsburg 1929.

Strzygowski, Josef: *Early Church Art in Northern Europe*. London 1928.

Voronin, N. N.: *Zodchestvo severo-vostochnoy Rusi*, XII, XV. 2 vols. Moscow 1961.

Zabello, S. Ivanov, and Maksimov, P.: *Russkoe derevyannoe zodchestvo*. Moscow 1942.

Zderciuc, Boris; Petrescu, Paul; and Banateanu, Tancred: *Folk Art in Rumania*. Bucharest 1964.

CHAPTER VIII

Memmo: *Vita e macchine di Bartolomeo Ferracina*. Venice 1754.

Palladio, Andrea: *I quattro libri dell'architettura*. Venice 1570.

Pica, Agnoldomenico: *Recent Italian Architecture*. Milan 1959.

San Bartolo, Nicola Cavaliere di: *Istituzioni di architettura statica e idraulica*. Mantua 1831.

Vitruvius Pollio, M.: *De Architectura* (Rome c. 1486). Ed. A. Rose. Leipzig 1867.

Vitruvius: the Ten Books on Architecture. Translated by M. H. Morgan. Cambridge, Mass. 1914.

Zabaglia, Nicola: *Ponti e Castelli*. Rome 1743.

CHAPTER IX

Bridenbaugh, Carl: *Peter Harrison, First American Architect*. Chapel Hill, North Carolina 1949.

Briggs, Martin Shaw: *The Homes of the Pilgrim Fathers in England and America*. London 1932.

Condit, Carl W.: *American Building: Materials and Techniques from the First Colonial Settlements to the Present*. Chicago 1968.

Donnell, Edna: *A. J. Davis and the Gothic Revival*. New York 1936.

Downing, Antoinette F., and Scully, Vincent J., Jr.: *The Architectural Heritage of Newport, Rhode Island*. Cambridge, Mass. 1952.

Fitch, James Marston: *American Building: The Forces that Shape It*. Boston 1948.

Hamlin, Talbot F.: *Greek Revival Architecture in America*. New York 1944.

Hitchcock, Henry Russell: *In the Nature of Materials: The Buildings of Frank Lloyd Wright, 1887–1941*. New York 1942.

Hitchcock, Henry Russell: *Architecture, Nineteenth and Twentieth Centuries*. Harmondsworth 1958. Baltimore, Maryland 1963.

Hitchcock, Henry Russell: *The Architecture of H. H. Richardson and His Times*. New York 1936. Hamden, Connecticut 1961.

Hornung, Clarence P.: *Handbook of Early American Advertising Art*. New York 1947. 2nd ed. (2 vols.) 1953.

Kimball, S. Fiske: *American Architecture*. Indianapolis 1928.

Kimball, S. Fiske: *Domestic Architecture of the American Colonies and of the Early Republic*. New York 1922.

Morrison, Hugh: *Early American Architecture*. New York 1952.

Schwartz, Martin D.: *The Martense Schenck House. Brooklyn*. New York 1964.

Scully, Vincent J., Jr.: *The Shingle Style*. New Haven 1952.

Waterman, Thomas T.: *The Dwellings of Colonial America*. Chapel Hill, North Carolina 1950.

Zantkuyl, H. J.: 'Het Jan Martense Schenkhuis te Brooklyn'. *Bulletin K.N.O.B.* 1964, 57–80.

Acknowledgements for Illustrations

The editor wishes to thank the following persons and institutions for photographs and other originals from which the reproductions have been made (where the sources are books or articles, these are cited within parentheses and are further recorded in the bibliography): Marianne Adelmann, Zürich (58 d, 59, 86 c, d, 191 a, b, 209, 211, 245 b); Hördur Agustsson, Reykjavik (86 b, 132 d); Franco Albini, Milan (18 d); Edizione Alinari, Florence (140 a); Rudolf Bednárik (L'udové stavitel'stvo na ky-suchiach — 198, 208, 213); Arne Berg, Oslo (23, 24, 29, 30, 32, 41, 43, 44, 49); (Bilderatlas zur Geschichte der Baukunst — 83 a, b, 91, 118 left); Geoffrey Bibby (The Testimony of the Spade — 22 bottom); Federico Borromeo, Milan (131 a, 265 a); British Travel Association, London (139 a); Fred H. Crossley (Timber Building in England — 110 a); Photo Ellebé, Rouen (144 d, 196 b, 246 c); Elsevier, Amsterdam (118 right); Etnografski Muzej, Belgrade (80 d); Wilhelm Fiedler (Das Fachwerkhaus in Deutschland, Frankreich und England — 70, 89, 90, 102, 127, 135); Photo Giraudon, Paris (87 a, 99 c, 131 c, 140 b, 141 d, 164 b, 271 a); Sam Gray (259 c); Werner Haarnagel (Wirtschaftsform und Arbeitsleben in der frühgeschichtlichen Siedlung Feddersen-Wierde — 12, 13, 22 top); Hans Jürgen Hansen, Gräfelfing vor München (57 a, b, 84 a, b, 106 a, 131 b, 232 a, c, 237 a, c, d, 240 a, b, 246 a, 248 a, 265 b); Cecil A. Hewett (Jettying and Floor-Framing — 103); Historia-Photo, Bad Sachsa (74 b); Historic American Buildings Survey, Washington (201 a–f, 202, 210 a–d, f, 222 a); Clarence P. Hornung (Handbook of Early Advertising Art — 254, 255, 263); Herman Janse, Amsterdam (26 a, 34 b, 64, 87 c, d, 94 d, 97 a, 113 c, 121, 123 c, 124 a, b, 193 a, c, d, 238 d, 258 b); Josef Jeiter, Hadamar (39, 68 c, 73 a, 149 a, b, 162 a, c, 163, 170 a, b, 174, 176 a, 182 a, 250 b, 251 a); Editions d'Art Jos, Châteaulin (141 b, 184 b, d, 230 c, 237 b); M. Krasovskiy (Kurs istorii russkoye architektury — 206, 207, 214); Ilse Krohn, Rumohr (94 c, 95, 98 c, 99 b); Carl Lachner (Geschichte der Holzbaukunst in Deutschland — 160, 165, 166, 167, 168); Albert Laprade (Croquis — 148); H. Lehmeyer, Herford (249); Walter Lüden, Wyk auf Föhr (54 c, 58 c, 93, 98 d, 100, 113 b, 129 b, c, 150 a, 170 d, 228 b, 239 c, 264 d); Mährisches Museum, Brünn (74 c, 80 a); I. V. Makovetsky (Pamyatniki narodnogo zodchestva — 188, 199, 205); Photo Marburg (28, 55 a, b, 114 b, 137, 141 c, 162 d, 171 c, 251 c, 252 b, 271 b); Paolo Monti, Milan (73 b, 245 d, 274 b); Museum of Finnish Architecture, Helsinki (34 c, 222 b); Nationalmuseet, Copenhagen (75 a); National Museum of Finland (34 d, 47 a, b, 68 d, 74 a, 75 c, 86 f, 114 a, 132 a, 218 a, b, 219 b, 270 b); New York Historical Society, New York (86 e); Novosti Press Agency, Moscow (37, 40, 45, 58 a, b, 75 d, 78 b, c, 80 c, 123 d, 230 b, 239 d, 246 d, 251 b, 270 a); Olaf Olsen (Die Häuser der Wikinger — 63); A. Orlandos (Les matériaux de construction — 14, 15, 18); Helmut Ottenjann (Museumsdorf Cloppenburg — 155, 157); J. Overbeck (Pompeji in seinen Gebäuden — 21); Pennsylvania Farm Museum of Landis Valley, Lancaster, Pennsylvania (219 a); Ursula Pfistermeister, Artelshofen (9, 10, 19, 25, 46 b, 54 d, 77 a, 79, 86 a, 87 e, 99 d, 113 d, 129 a, d, 130 a, 131 d, 138 a, b, 164 a, 176 b, 181 a, b, 189 a, 221, 238 b, 239 a, b, 260, 267 a, b, d); Preiss & Co., München-Ismaning (27, 46 a, 54 b, 77 b, 80 b, 87 b, f, 88 b, 94 a, b, 96 a, b, 97 b, d, 99 a, 104, 106 b, 107 a, b, 108 b, 130 b, 139 b, c, d, 141 a, 142 a, b, 143, 144 a, b, c, e, f, 150 b, 151 a, b, 171 a, b, d, 172 a, b, 173 a, b, 175, 182 b, c, d, 183 d, 192, 193 b, 283 c, 245 a, 248 b, c, d, 250 a, d, 252 a, 257, 258 c, 266 b, 267 c); Gualterio B. di Puccio, Lucca (223); Rijksdienst voor de Monumentenzorg, Voorburg (34 a, 38 a, b, 54 a, 119, 194 a, b, 195, 258 a, d); Rijksmuseum voor Volkskunde 'Het Nederlands Openluchtmuseum', Arnhem (66); Photo Rochus, Goslar (170 c); Royal Commission on Historical Monuments, London (98 a, b); Scala, Florence (26 b, 266 d, 268 b, 269 a); Nancy Halverson Schless, Philadelphia, Pennsylvania (210 a, e, 259 a–d); Toni Schneiders, Lindau (20, 97 c, 113 a, 161, 169, 189 b, 190, 231 a, b, 238 a, 272); Schweizerische Verkehrszentrale, Zürich (67, 75 f, 76, 108 d, 245 c, 247 a); H. Schumacher, Goslar (268 a); David Sellin, New Orleans, Louisiana (53, 56 a, b, 60 a, b, 87 a, 196 a, 212 a, b, 217, 220, 224 a, b, 232 b, 269 b); Staatsbibliothek Berlin, Picture Archive (8, 36, 152, 162 b, 215, 216, 243); Staatliche Graphische Sammlung, Munich (2); Syndicat d'Initiative, Chartres (33, 123 a, 183 b); Thaning og Appel, Copenhagen (132 c); Ullstein Bilderdienst, Berlin (132 b); N. N. Voronin (Zodchestvo severo-vostochnoy Rusi — 185, 186, 187, 197, 200); Kurt Wagner, Kulmbach (48 a, b, 65, 68 a, b, 78 a, 183 c, 184 a, d, 228 a, 264 c); Editor's archive (75 b, e, 108 a, c, 116, 122 b, 147, 179, 183 a, 226, 227, 230 a, d, 234, 246 b, 251 d, 266 a, c).

form of, 15; on origin of classical frieze, 16; on **Trojan union of timber-framing and dried bricks,** 14

Builders' lodge, itinerant, postulated for Norwegian stave-church builders, 42

Byliny singers of Russia, 186, 214

Byzantine influences: on Finnish and Russian dwellings, 61; on Russian churches, 185, 205, **207**

Canons' library, of Noyon cathedral, 1507, 145

Canopy of halls (over dais, high seat), 92

Cantherii, of early Roman temple, 18

'Cape Cod house' described, 236

Capitals, of English medieval halls (example of wood following masonry style), 70, 71

'Caroline Baroque', Finland, 61

Carpenters, carpentry: British Isles' distinct regional traditions, 101; Europe (North), early Christian era, 21; France, 125; high quality, in Netherlands, 117, 122; regional conditions affecting evolution of wood architecture, 70; old Russian, 186; Teutonic early trade guild, 153

Casa a Graticco, house at Herculaneum, 18

Castra stativa, Roman, as origin of European cities, 227

Catafalques, Italian wooden, 228

Ceiling supports, wooden, of Greek temple, 15

Cella, Etruscan, 18; brick and wood elements of, 225

Celtic wood building traditions, 21

Charnel-houses, France, 136, 145

Chata, S. Russian farmhouse, 187

Chimney, types of: America (North), massive central stone, on wooden house, 236; Bresse *sarrazines,* 146; common stack for range of identical houses, 110; massive 'end', Williamsburg, 243; Savoyard chalet, 146–7; Scandinavian, on roof, Middle Ages, 44 (after 1600, over open fireplace, after 1600, 49); of terra-cotta or brick, 104; *see* Internal chimney

Churches: Bulgarian, 215; carpenters' additions to granite, brick, etc., 177–8; concrete and steel, 179; East Prussian, 168; European tradition of wooden, 32; European (Central) early Christian, stone replacing wood 153–4; Finnish early and special type of cruciform, 51; French relatively few wooden, 133–4; German (North) 16th c., 177–8; German, some outstanding interiors, 168; Great Britain, 70; Hungarian, 214; new possibilities (e.g., large areas spanned by plywood), 179; Netherlands, Holland's early Christian, 117; 17th c. state-protected Reformed, 120; Romanian, 215; Ronshausen and others, wood and stone elements in individual spatial configurations, 177; Russian: few survivals of wooden, 186; general considerations, 188, 198; of Huzulians and the Carpathian Ukraine, 208; many domed and multi-levelled, 207–8; of three or more *sruby,* 200, 205; octagonal with spire, 205; old Russian stone (also first, wooden, S. Sophia, Novgorod), 185–6; relation between wood and stone, 205; West Ukraine variants, 208; White Russian fortified, 200; Silesian, 154, 168; Silesian rough-sawn, 177; Silesian, with loggias, 159; Soviet Union, protected by 'museum existence', 177; stave, *see*

Stave-church; Venice, late 14th c., gigantic wooden tie-beams, 228

Cladding: dependence on saw-mills, 49; horizontal boarding, Russian, used in Finland, 61; of log-built Swedish church, 1730, 50; Netherlands methods, 119; of prosperous French dwellings, 133

Clamping beams, function of, 41; *see* Stave-churches; modifications (with wider chancel openings, etc.), 41–2

Clapboard sheathing, North America, 235–6; of Flemish colonial style houses, 241

Classic revivals, *see* Neoclassicism; in New York City, replacing Flemish colonial, 241–2

Clay: as traditional building material, 11, 14; late use of fired, 14; pinnacles of baked, on pitched roofs of temples, 225

Close studding, 103

'Closed farmstead' of Finland, 61

Collar purlin, *see* Roof

Columen in early Roman temple architecture, 18

Columns: based on plain stripped tree trunk, 225; Doric, development of, 14–15; Doric and Mycenaean, absence of base explained, 15; downward-tapering wooden, 15–16; introduction of stone, 14; Ionic, of timber, in two-storey market halls, 115; Mycenaean transition of wood to stone, 15–16; of temple in Thermon (proportions of wood, stone and brick), 16; use of, in North American classical revival, 254 *seqq.*

Concrete churches, 179

Continuous sills, function of, 156

Corbels, a particular role of (three-quarter house), 112

Corner-post, enriched, of range of jettied houses (in early speculative building), 110

Cornices: early (Old Kingdom, Egypt), 14; applied, as distinct from dividing rail in timber-framing, 103

Corona, 17

Cretan column capitals, 16; rectangular stone columns, 14

Cross-vaults, wooden, on stone prototypes, of Finland, 18th c., 51

Crown-post roofs, variations on, 72

Cruciform church: Finnish form with huge central dome, 52

Crucks, 179; lingering, in Welsh marches, for large open halls, 103; *see* Roof

Cusp: defined, 92; trefoil and quatrefoil, shaping structural members (Wales), 72; for lightening appearance of heavy main trusses, 72

Décharges couplées, 128; *see* Braces, paired

Dehio, on the Butchers' Guild House, Hildesheim, 1529, 166–7

Domes, 207–8; wood-sheathed 'onion', 178–9

Doors: decorated, portal-shaped of *lofte,* etc., 44; of farmsteads, Netherlands, white surrounds of, 120; finely-carved doorways, Newport, Rhode Island, city wooden houses, 244; Palladian doorcases, North America, 244

Doric forms, *see* Columns; Doric stone buildings, forms of wooden buildings traceable in, 17

Double cruciform church (early Finnish), 51

Drawbridge, Dutch, as individual form, 121

Dutch colonial style, North America, 241

Dwelling-houses, *see* Alpine rustic building, Farmhouses, *also* names of regions; of British Isles

285

287

DATE DUE			
			PRINTED IN U.S.A